T0168284

TRACTATÜUS
PHILOSOPHIKÁ-
POETICÜUS

AMIR PARSA

TRACTATÜÜS PHILOSOPHIKÁ-POETICÜUS

Afterword by
Gregg M. Horowitz

 www.upsetpress.org

P.O. Box 200340
Brooklyn, NY 11220
www.upsetpress.org

Copyright © 2015 by Amir Parsa
First Published in English by Editions Caractères, Paris, in 2000

All rights reserved. No part of this book may be reproduced, stored in a retrieval system, or transmitted in any form or by any means without the prior written permission of both the copyright owner and the above publisher of this book, except in the case of brief quotations embodied in critical articles or reviews.

Established in 2000, UpSet Press is an independent press based in Brooklyn. The original impetus of the press was to upset the status quo through literature. UpSet Press has expanded its mission to promote new work by new authors; the first works, or complete works, of established authors—placing a special emphasis on restoring to print new editions of exceptional texts; and first-time translations of works into English. Overall, UpSet Press endeavors to advance authors' innovative visions, and works that engender new directions in literature.

Book design by Wendy Lee / wendyleedesign.com

Library of Congress Control Number: 2014950582

ISBN 9781937357924
Printed in the United States of America

— A Book for the Wicked
A Book for the Merry
A Song for Wanderers
A Book for the Weary

Once

upon a time it was, once upon a time it was not, on a tightrope strung above the city from a midnight hand of the clocktower to the spire of the cathedral, dangling atop with my beam, trembling, saved from the fall...

With that mask of the acrobat, gentle reader, the whiteface and the colored nose, hair spiked devil-like, checkered waistcoat of the jester adorning my frame, wicked gaze of a magician upon my brow: without wings yet hovering on secret-teller toes, one step, one more, in my plaid pantaloons hiding a key, high above on tightrope holding beam, across a forlorn bridge, above the city's domes, across the city's dawns, once upon a time,

> *Toot, toot, toot, where do you go*
> *What's your name, how do you know*

I whistled into the haze, into the deserted road, at last...

Quite to my heart's content, I must admit, and to the partial resurrection of my selfhood. For I was once again made captive of my own dereliction, partisan, at once, of the bewitching pull of Reason, tinctured all the same with the wild gallops of Imagination: a sauntered citizen of many a land, awake and aware at the oddest Hour, dozing into dreamlands at the most inopportune of times, a visitor, almost, in the slovenly quarters of Superstition.

With a price to pay of course, how it goes: senseless delirium, primitive deprivations, basic decrepitude, and the poor twisted tongue itself warning—incessantly—of its (imminent!) rebellion. How it goes when at untamed curiosities are directed the wraths of perched progenitors of truths; when order and its fervent keepers on scaffolds stifle laughingly fanciful hypnotists—worse: gouge out their eyes; when prolongers of agonies, prolongers of pleasures, whisk away fellow dreamers or drunken souls; when Eblis himself, roaming excitedly in the city, among them not of them, calls again for a companion, wanderer at night, by day an onlooker from bowers afar, yet in our midst, so close…

There I stood then: like a valiant vagrant enamored by the endless quivers, guided by the perverse oath to the Possible, playful in torment, playful with: there, unmoving, amid laments a chronicler of muted cries, the unrepentant eyes of other worlds, the riddle of the towncrier, weep again, scream again, say: the treatise then, the ecstatic chant in hidden alley, the stages—prismatic—on the path, epic in shards, rhapsody in I minor—story, after all?—will, in this manner, ladies and gentlemen, be fully singular, One: this twist it is then, this it will be, this tongue, the once upon a time I wandered into a deserted street at last, whistling:

Gna, gna, gna, can't get away
Sing the trouble, slay the foe!

Deserted street with landscape, that is, which fit, quite easily, the traveler's expectations.

A wide expanse of cobblestones paved the main throughway, bordered by your usual sidewalks, the lone street-lamps and the illuminating rays of storefronts now in recess. Along the road, houses built in rows, distinguished merely by color and the extent of decay on their frames, appeared fully occupied: light flickered through windows, a silhouette swerved on a kitchen floor, a child's bicycle lay, on its side, on the lawn. Stifled barking of dogs could be heard, and the rattling of machines, and the remnants of sinful conversations in various sanctuaries. The writings remained, above the awnings, across the small bricks, the white plaster, in the narrow lanes, on abandoned banners, on the ground, on the walls.

It was these very signs that were troubling however, for it was in the midst of what invited the impression of heightened activity that I was noticing the sinister blend of a timid, melancholy, stillness. I had yet to see a single creature that I could, with some degree of certitude, recognize as unmistakably alive. I had yet to hear a veritable exchange, a friendly chat, a scolding even, a pleading, a request. No wayward glances, no one watching, no sitters or walkers, no one: ghost town I was seeing, and without the ghosts at that! Had I truly stumbled upon an improbable land, I wondered, or merely a most honored guest, I, at unspecified time, in a corner all too common? What had become of me, I posed in quite unfettered language, where had I been, and how did I find myself, here, now, in this most precarious of locales?

These and other interrogations crept upon me unwillingly, unnecessarily, perhaps, for there was no purpose, in effect and in truth, of these musings at such hours holding supremacy over my thoughts. As to the village itself, although it seemed, by many sensations, that I had, in the least, passed through, and perhaps even spent a fortnight or two, I remained, with a considerable degree of annoyance, unable to identify: I felt foreign, that is, genuinely foreign, to the entire place, unrecognizing of the most dominant element, as well as the most precious singularity.

Before resorting to a hasty retreat though, I concluded that I had not occupied my current position long enough, and that, ultimately, a wide array of explanations might be proffered. I surmised also that my stationary occupation of the scene

13

would not generate the desired contact and decided to engage in the grand opportunity of a prolonged stroll, undeterred by the possibility of hostile run-ins, feeling unending passion, in fact, for such delectable meandering. Besides, I had already let out the required calls, asking if anyone was there, if anyone could hear: each had generated its own echo, none the one I craved. Without further ado, humored by a most prurient predicament, I began to walk down a deserted street, in a deserted town: in the manner of many a heroic personage of the lore of many a folk, burning to save the day, burning to tell the tale...

I was carrying little and had, in my name, quite a negligible amount of material goods that I could safely call possessions. I also brought it upon myself to commit full concentration to a perpetual observation of the environs, to detecting and distinguishing all movements and irregularities, as well as the most intimate details. Nothing will escape my tyrannical gaze, I promised. The required alchemy of things, I mused, each blending into another. I will bypass nothing, I thought, I told, imposed and repeated: not the most seemingly insignificant blink, not the simplest raising of the brow, not the most extraneous of banalities. I had previously believed these obsessions to have spelled my downfall, but now, unable to forsake such driftings—credulities as they may be, scarcely visible and O how better left ignored and branded insignificant—unable to shake the hold and the awful habit, quite incapacitated, in addition, in the domain of beliefs, of even that most venerable of conducts, the expression of an opinion, I acquiesced to my own primary subservience: the detection, that is, of the minutiae: the scowl of an old man at a common curb, the frown of an angry bum, the slow bending of a child: all to me was wonder! O doomed and damned chum, I thundered within, I laughed at this appointed Hour, a world is yours to make!

———■———

And so it was—on what I presumed to be a glorious day entrusted with guile and games, with blandness and bewitchments all, drowned in my own helpless swings from remembrance to reproach—that I proclaim, I submit, I exclaim, I say, I saw, slowly strolling up the road, same road that I was currently occupying, town without frontiers, another coming up the road, another sharing my predicament, coming up the road, in the direction opposite to my own, sharing my predicament.

As I cautiously took each of the next steps that brought us ever closer (for his rhythm was in synchrony with mine), and although I had yet to pass by others, I fancied that this encounter would prove to be only the first among many, and sensed, therefore, no urgency in addressing my counterpart, whose uncommon convulsions, it must be said, subdued momentarily yet exploding the next—as if The Burden he carried helplessly on his back!—showed a deeply wounded individual. What is more, his entire countenance seemed familiar in unseemly ways: the attire (the loose pants, the wide top, the hat, etc.), the physical attributes, the cadence, the bags: the gait even—and the gaze: all bore an uncanny resemblance to my own! And to such improbable degrees that I could not help but believe this first vision to be merely a mirage (I must add: the road and the sun—and my own hallucinatory disposition—did not rule this out), only to look again more attentively, and see the same!

I did flinch, I vacillated, it is true: and as I glanced his way, so the glance was met with a stare uncommonly mirroring its hues: silence around us without even the soothing hum of the breeze: from afar wishing to enjoin, uncertain about the mer-

15

its, fearful, perhaps overly so, of the tangles. As we approached, I did not dare utter the slightest word, nor did I instigate any move that would bring us together. And when he had finally passed, I confirmed that he was indeed weeping, and quite profusely at that. (Had I acted poorly again, I thought. Had it not been my duty to generate an exchange? Up to me to ease the load? Am I to be blamed? Was it not my domain, difficult as it was to deny, to console, to comfort? Don't be so hard on yourself, I mumbled in more familiar terms, this is not so easy either, don't take it so hard…)

I continued along nevertheless, disgruntled and ever so distraught, knowing that I had so far failed at formulating the most tenuous of answers even, or the least acceptable of alternatives. And in these less than congruous circumstances, I admit, it was not without a creeping fright that, unprotected, cautious yet vulnerable, easy-target and all, unrecognizing of the old, brave, self, I carried on like many a lonesome figure: senses at high awareness, proud fellow, peeking left and right, accelerating on occasion, slower at other times, back, forth, back…

After a protracted period, I reluctantly dismissed the likelihood of other encounters, the first now proving to be nothing less than a genuine Miracle. Where to turn, then, what to tell—I could not resist, I had no choice, I had to ask! I did have one place to entrust my faith, however, and that was in my own record. Record, that is, in generosity and goodness, confident that the gods would provide me with the appropriate guidance. Allow me then this: not a confession, not an advertisement for a beleaguered mortal, merely the recitation of the record, an honest-to-goodness recitation, in case the deeds do not speak for themselves. Here it is then: I have not, I swear, to my knowledge, wronged a single being. I have never stolen or cheated. I have lied, it is true, but only for the honorable end of saving embarrassment or delaying profound agony. I have conferred assistance when the call for help has risen, and although prone to fits of disappearance, I have fulfilled my obligations in a respectable manner. The force be with me, I have been good! And as I repeated it then to comfort my harried heart, I do so once more, this time as a warning that I emit selflessly, a summary, if you will, a statement of fact: for indeed, I wish no suspicion on this most crucial of matters: that I am not, nor have ever been, maledictions be heaped upon my soul if I am being disingenuous, an embellisher of events, am not an exaggerator of happenings, am no spicer of truths, I. I lay claim to honesty, to absolute, untainted sincerity, in order to propose, insist even, that true to my vocation, to my duties and my habits, true to my innermost workings, I did not, repeat, did not, invent what will follow, did not spin a strange fable, did not contrive a charmed fiction. No, there is no imaginary plot, no introduction of surprises, not a grain of fantasy, not a morsel of reverie, not a single twist of fortune. Nothing of the sort. What then, I am asked? Then this: there I was, on the deserted street in a deserted town expecting naught, tired of the playfulness of the rising dust on the roads, that, unbeknownst, in a manner so swift, so rapid that after many attempts at reconstruction, I have remained incapable of recalling the actual development of the apparition, stood, before me, suddenly, incredibly, an old man, rigid, unblinking. Extremely thin, short and bald, he did not emit a single sound. Coldly, he stared beyond me, heels to his side, unflinching, and, strangely, expectant.

Proud disciple of discretion, I let out no visible signs of alarm. I decided, instantly, that the best reaction would consist of the furling of some quotidian parlance, took the appropriate measures, and softly let out the familiar salutations. He did not move, did not respond, not even a single gesture. I repeated, ever obliging, with utmost amiability. No smile, no frown, no answer. Perhaps I will be like him, I thought, I will be as removed and uncaring. And since I knew, somehow, that the absence of reaction was not connected to the admittedly folksy form of my greetings, I abided, without shame or guilt, to my latest resolve.

He was joined, and quickly so, by a legion of other characters: a child holding the mother's hand, a tall gentleman in a hat, the shirt and the frock, a young peasant in overalls: an entire throng, in fact, progressively expanding around and behind him, while he stood, steady, in the middle, in the front.

Wherefore these sudden appearances, I tried, in vain, to comprehend. Could with a mere whisper the landscape transform so? With a mere wink the expansion of the crowd? For was it not with each closing and reopening of my eyes that I detected the additions in the masses? (Yes indeed, I thought, indeed yes!) Impossible to cease, I fathomed, unless I went blind immediately! Whence my pleading: to allow the oft-quoted exclamation—I promise I will no longer utter such impertinent irrelevancies—for I could not help but holler, inwardly of course—and how the suffering is grander thus!—to holler, and holler again, and to repeat incessantly as if an awkward, inner echo, where am I, where am I...

And then, before I knew it, before I could even have guessed what had come upon me, the words: they delivered themselves, without invitation, without incitation. Entire phrases without restraint. Flowing, restless, unchained. Rivers and falls. And no sooner had they reverberated that the houses along the borders began to separate, the streets expanded (wider and wider), open fields appeared near and far, and a tower in the distance slowly swerved from the ground (how imperfectly it grew, all twisted in the sand). Neon signs illuminated the city, a litany of fountains sprouted, ancient statues and scaffolds were raised, and, all around me, around us, the space of our gathering rapidly mutated into a public square, along with its own stage (at present unoccupied), stairs that led to the vaunted podium, and the poles, the high poles...

And the scenery, yes, the scenery: the young boy rolling forward a rock, and the stray cat skipping about; two robed clergymen slowly making their way, and a maiden on the terrace, leaning against the golden railings, watching from above; men and women, boys and girls (and everyone in between), standing against the pillars and the walls of the surrounding homes, and two young friends peering ahead, side by side, one with a wheelbarrow stationed in front, the other with a barrel by his side; rooftops and facades freckled with tiny windows, chimneys rusty and gray, blowing smoke, thick, swirling rings of smoke, all black and puffy; barking of dogs (always, everywhere), painted murals and faint sounds of unreal carnivals, landscape bathed in shameless fancy: a thief in the distance robbing absentminded listeners, a liar in overcoat and top hat scurrying across; the murmur of sinful scribes, the growls of a miser, and a beleaguered mime who cries of a travesty unknown; a towering man, standing in the rubble and the ruin, amidst the mud and the soil of future graves, standing in the burial places of taletellers without voice: beyond the bridge unseen, among the shattered castles, resting saddened watching the horizon, a fortuneteller feigning doubt: when I appear in the tight quarters of the poet who daily strolls on these morbid grounds, where he has begged me to go, the mask I will wear in the company of the eternal prey: before a quivering man, hungered, staggering from an alleyway to another, a solitary shadow when he sees his assassin: stillness of air in panic, the turn and the run,

19

the long, hysteric strides, noiseless, stumbling awkward his swerving,

the pursuit, beast-like, through the alley overturning cans, the debris, the litter, the burnt paper, around the ruins of cities: a poet saunters on these grounds,

daily he peers into the empty cavern he stands by the tombs, he peers from afar at the kneeling men, dotting the hills in black:

he had never approached me, he had never addressed me: he walked by me not so long ago, he summoned me, held my hand, asked me to show: at given hour, on given day, for another would be christened,

with the blood of his toil—:

a trickster at the corner, the instant of his wink, his whisper to the world, before the revolution:

with this stutter I summon thee lord of suffering and scorn, with this gaze the agony of the limbless and the lost, with the wave of a hand, the furrowing of my brow, one command, this fiendish nod of the head, I summon thee,

O chants O cries O woes and writings on the walls, O withering morrows, I summon thee, furtive glances, dances of the dead: with this wink I enjoin thee, I am a tale for the revolution, a friend of the forlorn, a trembling teller without tongues! O tricksters all: in the annals of our book, in the secret caverns of our world, they cannot tell the story without this Cry:

after the revolution this maze: the riddles and the warning: fear me, foes of the unconvinced!

And, within, the sullen murmurs: am I the one who vanished, am I the expected… I am not a preacher, I thundered— and they knew. I am not a god, I thundered—and they knew. I am not a saint, not a seeker, no guide: and I heard the ridicule of an unsuspecting crowd that already knew.

Now fully inculcated into the affair, a full participant in the drama that was to unfold, helpless as to the direction (or?—), I was, lo and behold, unable to situate myself: to recognize my own: voice or transforming visage: a mask or I, I wondered, and I knew no more.

I did not hesitate another instant: I let down my guard and abandoned myself to my functions. I raised my arm and fixed my hat. I brought to my lips the bugle I had strapped to my shoulder, angled it ever so slightly to the sky, closed my eyes and sounded the call to the confluence. I then bent down, laid by my feet a case carrying my belongings, placed the bugle next to the case, raised the sling to which a drum was attached from my left shoulder and swung it around my neck, so that the drum was before me, conveniently resting against my chest. With the drumsticks I had already withdrawn from a pocket on the side, I began, at first slowly, and subsequently faster, to do a drum roll, and to holler the dutiful hear ye. I relented soon and peered at the assembly. I raised my head, brought out a long sheath of paper, held it before my eyes. I let out again the thunder of the drum, rhythmic and increasing at first, soon ceased and unrolled the long sheet.

I told of the returning one, all eyes set upon him, all songs for him, all: the bitter shouts of the fleeing, the hollow whimper of exiles, last words of the blindfolded on scaffolds on rooftops. I told of the shots in the square—and the fire, and the howls: I told of the streets and the writings on the walls: flames and burning, darker nights above graveyards among ghosts under the bombs, the face in the moon. And so I told of the conference of shadows in secret hideaways, and the congregation of spirits, their anguish, their lust. And I told of the mothers by the red desert sand by the sea. I told of the father kneeling, his face buried in his hands, grieving, by

21

the grave of a murdered son. And I told of the tombs, and I told of the gardens, and I told of the verses on the tombs: angels descended, across the desert surrounding us, the sea surrounding us, across the land. And then I ceased, before me the flock, quiet and obedient. Their silence I answered with a gaze: my gaze answered with silence.

Shall I tell, thundered I then with decadent laughter and without dread, of the fool, the clown, the walker in the night?

At ease now, I raised my head slowly and addressed, for the first time, all those presently gathered: I will tell of the massacre at B__, I clamored—and I told of the massacre at B__. I will tell of the master puppeteer, I said—and I told of the puppeteer. I will tell of the poet who lived by the sand— and I told of the poet who lived by the sand. I will tell of the disgruntled in distant dunes, of tales and of myths, of the books. And I told of the infamous doctor, of the confessions in the bloodied carousel, of the fanciful flights. I thundered at the onlookers, this tale after the bombs, this riddle under the bombs, how to go on if to go on: I asked the watchers before me: I asked the figurines before me: I asked the tremulous before me: how to.

No response, of course: the masses about, bewildered. I rolled back the paper, paused and placed it in the case from which I had previously retrieved it. I slowly packed my equipment and readied to leave. Perhaps unreasonably, I had assumed that the swift formation of the crowd and the subsequent transforma- tions at my arrival would disintegrate when I prepared to part, when I had said my last words. And perhaps my own delusions were entrapping me, but I insist that all those on whom my eyes rested, however fleetingly, and perhaps at the very precise moment that I chanced upon them, remained, or turned, fully motionless, as if suspended in time. And, on closer inspection,

22

I did indeed confirm the general, unobstructed, inertia. Had my illusory urges extended beyond the acceptable limit? Had my senses failed to function, at least minimally, in accord with a savory notion of reality? Was I at fault again, did I do this, where did I go wrong? I was troubled and weary, yes—but I was also done. There was nothing else to say, little to do, no remedy in sight. I seemed to be the only one willing and able to leave, and did just that. I flung my bags on my shoulders, picked up the case, swung the drum behind and headed back the way I had come.

———■———

I soon noticed, confirmed, rather, that the city, the roads, the houses, all had kept the arrangement they had acquired upon my first utterances—they had not, that is, reverted back: where I had seen for example, on my initial passage, a bicycle and a forsaken room illuminated by a shaft of light, now I saw the house with worn-out walls and untended lawns. Traces of a different kind, indeed. Before my passage and after, I mused: one world, then another! So be it, I said, I had come, I had told, I was gone. And expected to, perhaps, but I will never know.

I carried along then, humming a happy tune to heighten the spirits, when I remarked, in the distance, once more, another coming towards me. I checked again (always guarding against delusions!) and concluded that there was, in fact, not so far away, a silhouette moving much as I pictured myself to be thus engaged: walking (in my direction, he) at, unmistakably, my pace, with very much my gestures, my mannerisms, my mien. I inferred that it was the same fellow I had passed a while back and deemed myself fortunate to cross his path again, having failed to initiate any contact on the first occasion. I pledged

23

that I would not, this time, let the chance slip me by. This time I will not be a dupe, I thought, this time I know better. Besides (I was now fully conversing with myself), he might have a few answers to some unresolved questions! I will be helped! Assisted! Perhaps he knows... And in my excitement, I quickened the pace, and noticed that he did the same, at the precise moment as I!

Although the demeanor of this passerby was quite similar to that of the first, I picked out, upon further examination and as we moved closer to one another, certain peculiarities that, I thought, clearly distinguished the two. The first, for example, walked with the neck bent slightly downwards, whereas this one peered perpetually ahead, a confident swagger about him, very seldom even moving the shoulders. Also, whereas one could safely deduce that the first had been continuously weeping, this present fellow obviously had not, although there was a profound despondency that seemed to be engulfed within, an unavoidable anguish, as if he were a designated Porter of Misery! He did, also, as the last of my judgments made clear, walk with a clear and definite limp— whereas the first, I am certain, did not. It was at the final stages that I validated the impressions: I was now certain that my fellow wayfarers, so to say, bore an uncanny resemblance to one another, and, as I have insinuated, but perhaps not insisted well enough, a singular likeness to yours truly! So be it, I thought, odder things have occurred. Besides, I was not—I had made a pact with myself—about to let the encounter flounder again, under any pretext. For indeed, the *boiteux* appeared quite aloof, much like myself on the initial trip, and so I set out, this time without reservation, a slayer of timidity, to do the accosting: at the crossing, finally: as politely as I knew, steady, smooth, sincere:

'Where to, friend?' I started, to which my counterpart, slowly coming out of his daze, responded only with a reluctant nod.

'You're going to the village?' I asked again, with more resolve, too stubborn, at this point, to allow the opportunity to flutter away.

'The village, yes,' came the reply, intoned as if being asked, yet an answer, to my query.

Decidedly, he was only now beginning to come out of his very private universe: he became more aware, acquired a fresher look, slowly shed the previous state of suspension:

'Yes, yes, the village,' he added. 'I think they're waiting for me. Or should be, anyway.'

I was taken aback with the last words, for, with all of the uncanny similarities that I previously noted, he harbored definite expectations, whereas I had been quite lost, fully unaware in fact, of how and why I had found myself in such a spot. What is more, he knew of the presence of a lingering horde—or, did he, really?

As I was mulling over the significance of this unintentional admission, I was further confounded by the desire of the previously distant chap to actually continue our chat. Not only that, but he managed to propound more shivers with his latest: 'You did see,' he began, question-like, only to pause, nod the head, raise the brows, demur, as if I should have known whom he meant—'didn't you?'

Outwardly settled, revealing not the trepidation that was creeping up inside, facing one whom I had greeted out of civility (and boredom), but whose deportment and insinuations resembled, increasingly, the playful coquetries of a seducer of sorts, I merely looked at him and attempted to calm my senses. But I remained, to say the least, quite unnerved by the implications. How did he know of my first encounter? How was it

25

that, although I had ignored the path all along, the character standing now before me spoke as if the affair might have been planned and predestined? And if the matter were, after all, of a serious nature, how was it that I, keenly uninformed of my inquisitor's identity or importance, had actually accosted him and further instigated the dialogue? What, I simply marveled, if I had not? What if I had simply carried on, cowardly, in the programmed direction? For it seemed now, all extravagances and exaggerations aside, it seemed, from his ever-graver countenance, from the general feel of the exchanges, that the very fate of *this* world rested somehow on, yes, *our* shoulders! The fate of this world on my questions, then?! How could this be? Staring silently at him, I sensed a heightening unease, yet felt, also, that the preoccupations, urgent and consequential, demanded unequivocal attention.

Shedding all trivialities, bypassing polite poses, I confronted him: 'What if I had not asked?' I said. 'What if I had not asked the first question?'

The retort surprised me, not out of suspiciousness but out of sheer banality: 'Well then,' came the reply, 'then *I* would have!'

And a mischievous grin broadened, the graveness vanished, the stiff composure was fully erased.

Now, since he seemed to know that another encounter had taken place, seemed to propose, in fact, that it had been inevitable, I also gave hints of curiosity about the provenance and the destination of the first fellow. Although he remained reticent—not even the coincidences were enough to evince a commentary!—I was not deterred, for I could not withstand the uncertainty, most especially the circumstances under which the three of us had come to meet. Barely could I contain the escalating anxiousness, the torrent of emotional bursts. Queries galore! Had my present interlocutor ever ad-

26

dressed the first passerby? Or was it somehow communicated that such an encounter would take place and that all must be aware? A script being followed? Or a genuine adventure? I told also of the occurrences upon my arrival: the apparition of the old man, the expansion of the crowd, the physical transmutations. That nothing had changed once I had left, save for the complete suspension of all movement, of all speech. Had all remained same, as I spoke? And had everyone traveled that far? I received, again, only clever dismissals. But I was not to be deceived, not to be derailed, could not lose this one, would insist, push, and insist again.

'You limp,' I jumped, perhaps at the height of both curiosity and irritation, 'and the first did not! He was weeping, and you are not!'

He paid little heed but entreated nevertheless, as if a bit weary of my apocalyptic manners: and in a tone that was both paralyzing and comforting, he stopped me from expounding.

'Listen,' he said, 'this, the whole scene... the landscape, the sounds, you, I, none of this is unexpected, none of it unusual. I don't mean to be difficult, but that's how it is: the weight, the chosen life...'

'And always on call!' he went on after a brief pause, growing increasingly tense. 'The barter, cannot stop now must go on, and what that means! Am I ready for this, is it me, the tears, the shrieks, the news: why I'm here, and not there: it will never end never end: instant of repose and lightness: carry on why must carry on why: nothing to say, once upon, silence before, toot toot, where do you, sharks in the sand, gna gna, devil on the potty: nothing to add, never wither, nothing never, will not, carry on why must carry on why, must!'

He turned suddenly to the side, and back again, grave still but more composed. 'It's amazing how a lifetime can make an expert out of you!' (A remark made in passing, as if a private sigh to which I had been invited by dint of circumstance.)

He relaxed a bit, finally, and, looking me straight in the eye, said: 'You know what I mean. I think you know, exactly, what I mean.'

Then, ever so quickly, his countenance changed again, as if he were floating back to his first state of detachment.

'You wouldn't happen to have a cigarette, would you?' he asked.

I checked, one left, uttered the same, 'One left'—and extended the prize: protected by all fingers, of one hand, like a bouquet.

The departure was swift: a wave on my part, a quick salute from the other, without much ceremony: for although the earlier moments had provided quite a number of benign exchanges, the latter portion of our meeting had been subsumed by a strangeness and heaviness that bore the marks of watchful Fate. What exactly did he mean? What was he referring to?! Was I now expected to wait, expected to abide by his edict? I was not ordered to, this was true—but he *had* proposed. To stay if I wished, to listen. But he had warned also, not to turn, not to flee, I among them and you so far...

The tone alone smacked of a *défi*: the mere suggestion, that air about him: not to turn, not to flee...

Let it be, I thought to myself, it is so and not such, there is a day and there is not, let it stand: faster than I had anticipated and too swift to be wise perhaps, I had decided to not abandon the post, to mill about, listen, watch, and see what I could muster, what I would discover, what would be imposed: see what it was, in short, that the good fellow had to offer. So I chided myself, I goaded and pushed (Contemplate/Meditate/Make a home/While I wait), not cognizant of what lay ahead, or the duration even, of the experience. Was I, once more, attempting to convince a fragile self when I had, in fact, conceded defeat in advance? Should I abide by the prompting of a minion I meet on the road? No matter what the inclinations and the insights? Shall I blindly follow the commendation of the master dodger of questions, one whose artistry at conceit and concealment had been amply demonstrated? Or shall I excuse myself, take the road back, pretend nothing had occurred? Settle down and forget, decline and desist, say good-bye and thanks? I was engaged in such calculations when I heard, in the distance, unbeknownst, the first rumblings...

Led, no mistaking it, I could conclude, led by none other than the same fellow, designated martyr so to say, standing before an assembly, the very assembly I had left (the only logical option). It was indeed he who generated the sounds: with inordinate potency, with god-like power, he who incited the roars, the jeers, and the screams: rising and screeching, acquiring a frightening pitch, a truly mesmerizing level. True to his Duty, he'd proclaimed—and there!

I still had no inkling to conduct myself in the terms against which I had been warned (to turn, that is), but I noticed, also, that the chorus soon ceased, that the multitude was now enjoined, and that all was, amazingly, emanating from one source, from one only. But a source whose power had, in essence, enveloped each and every one of the individual screams—losing nothing of the volume of each—and assembled them into a magnanimous echo across the land. From one only, and none other than my reluctant interlocutor: the same intonation, the same traits, the same dreaded timbre, now thundering throughout.

I attempted to avoid a senseless, potentially tragic reaction, but it was becoming increasingly more difficult to stand unprotected. In quite a short while in fact, my eyes began to

29

bulge, the face was contorting, the body flailing and gesticu-
lating like a wounded animal's. Head moving to the right and
left, back and forth, in no certain pattern, I shielded my ears
with both hands and crumbled to the ground, hands pressed
pathetically against the temples. (Not to turn, not to flee: a
worthy request perhaps, but not a prerogative. No need to fol-
low, after all: unknowing, I could chance upon ruin or upon
joy—one way or another, upon despair, or upon wonder...)

On my knees, drifting, suspicious of the designs of even the
kindest trickster, I still heard the scream, the same scream that
had preceded, generated, actually, my floundering, the same,
screeching, reverberating—Cry: a scream emanating from afar,
the same scream, of dunes, of seas, of deserts: a scream em-
anating from afar, across the land, a wailing cry, rising, not
among us with us, how I sit by windowpane watching, hunger
a moment and the next in ecstasy, lightness overcoming, one
day perhaps on scaffolds afar begging or brave, another stum-
bling in darkened alley ravaged and lost, drifting, how I must,
restless among shadows among souls, in stranger outposts, by
strangers' glances.

I stood, again, and freed my hands. I flung the bag around
my shoulder and stared ahead: once upon, toot toot, silence
before, with the wizard with the king: now I knew, now I knew
indeed, the faces, the fellow comrades: the weeper yes, and
the teller—and the scream: one towncrier, and another, and
another: what had been the fate, where I had been, what I'd be-
come: the riddle of: the story, the game: and the mystery, and
the puzzle—and the myth! Yes I knew, I, the voice, the mask,
myself or another like, among, how to tell, the echo, across the
land: once upon, toot toot, silence before, silence during, with
the wizard with the king, will you play, and play fair, truth or
dare, truth or dare, truth, or, dare:

Although

it is true that my initial encounter with the citizens of Q__ abad did not come about in a manner wholly unforeseen, still I insist that I would not judge myself untruthful if I told of an utter lack of preparation in conducting affairs as I wished. I would stumble accidentally upon the happenings, I mused, in the midst of an excited crowd eagerly awaiting one caller or another, captivated by distinct and peculiar premonitions...

According to legend, Q__abad owed its existence to the perspicacity of its citizens, a group, that is, of former thieves, minor crooks and convicts of all stripes, pimps among them and hustlers, who had taken it upon themselves, once upon a time, through an intricate network of plans, meetings and congresses of various proportions in undisclosed locales, to convert the ruins atop the hill, long-standing ruins of much fame, into a flourishing polis.

Long-standing ruins indeed—longer than any citizen or living member of the town below or of nearby villages could remember, almost sacred ruins, one might say, which did also have their worshippers and their shrines, if not of the usual type. Many recounted the pilgrimage of those most averse to all followings, those who, according to repute, recognized no hallowed sanctuaries, knew no higher deity or any other figure worthy of devotion: they, oddly enough, constituted the secret wayfarers of Q__abad, and had thus masterminded, in the most brilliant fashion, the conspiracy to launch the settlement. Not even after extensive searches and seizures, after extensive torture of innocent bystanders, it was said, had the authorities succeeded in tracking the hideaways of the organizers. Both the physical and the philosophical foundations of Q__abad had thus taken root in this style of swift engagement and sudden abandonment: traceless wandering, erasing the very contours of personhood: with me sail away, with me vanish, the signs of light…

As for my own intervention (and the wide array of grotesque deformations and frivolous inventions that would constitute the gist of my contribution), it had been unduly delayed, and, I assume, irreversibly altered, by my involvement in a fledgling enterprise. A project I had undertaken with quite a bit of trepidation in fact, in which I had, mistakenly I know now, put a great deal of trust, and which had unceremoniously disintegrated right before my eyes. The mounting disagreements among factions, the inconceivable pressure exercised from every direction, the entanglements whose relevance was often in question (in my humble opinion anyway), the debatable nature of the foundations, and the further necessity of forging ahead unencumbered, all in addition to the highly suspect motivation and the more dubious ends envisioned, contributed to the slow—and painful—demise of the venture, not to mention the blinding of most practitioners concerned. Even though the initiative had not progressed as I would have wished however, and even though the prospects did not resemble (in the least!) the expectations I had drawn—for, I often mused, if anyone here is occupying a universe to which they are alien, it is none other than myself—still I felt awkwardly relieved by the dismantling of the entire machinery, which I sensed I had, somehow, duly and purposely, provoked.

I was not in the least disturbed then, nor did I count my losses as the sign of a tragic downfall that would carry over to future endeavors. Not only untroubled, but perhaps even gratified, in a most primitive way: I sensed that I had managed to avoid entrapment, to avoid and elude (to put it politely!) the disputable, fragile, local, pillars upon which even the grandest of the previous monuments had been erected: the vapid constructions, the elaborate transpositions, and the lifelong admiration of the disciples. I quickly returned (had I not always been there!) to a mode of circulation to which I was more accustomed, to a pace and a conduct better suited to my instincts, to the exploration and the infinite elaboration (complication?) of designs I had, always, secretly, cultivated. Thus, in a leisurely mode, I made my way about, purchased the necessary material, and began to make preparations for the adventure. I contacted confidants and loved ones, informed them of recent developments, expounded on my plans. I made a few final adjustments, arranged my dwelling as it would stand for the duration of the operation, and took the last measures to ensure the precautionary well-being of the most precious accessories. Without any more thought, or any further complications, I set forth.

———■———

Since the tale of Q__abad had always preoccupied me, I managed to inquire about the town as often as possible. In hostel after hostel along the road, with beggars and drifters on dusty trails, among the mountaineers and the solitary fishermen, from the ablest of storytellers to those most aloof, I never failed to provoke a discussion of the topic. And I had even noticed, both to my quiet satisfaction and my slight unease, that when *I* ceased to be the culprit, inevitably my presence would incite a resurgence of the question of Q__abad, or rather, of the tale.

And so it went, that on a brief respite in a small tavern, with friends, acquaintances and a few others I knew little about, who looked a bit conspicuous in fact—and in quite an un-

33

usual manner: a bit mechanical in their movements, very stiff, they nevertheless had an aura of singular ambiguity emanating from their pores: friends of the friends, I presumed, although no one knew, for indeed, it dawned upon me only a while later, after I had politely left the company of these worthy folk, that these creatures, strangers to myself, may well have been strangers also to my acquaintances, each one of us assuming in turn that the others were familiar with another among us, each silently convinced of this, none daring to ask, none aware, alas, how it was that the party had attached itself to our own (happenstance, a mere marriage of tables uniting the lot of us, and our respective orbs? I could not deny the possibility!): trick of the comedian, you may say, or just plain dull: perhaps, but the truth would be revealed only after our separation, when it had become irrelevant: but it was so, and not thus—that one among these fellows once more evoked Q__abad, then cautiously went on to speak of the town, transfixing the lot of us in his very seductive style: that indeed, since we had all heard the inklings of the 'legend' (his word), that since now we were all familiar with the first grains of the fable, it was his duty to carry on the task: and tell the story of Q__abad: not only, he began, had the group expanded, not only had they succeeded in recruiting countless devotees, but in the end, they had all conquered their fears and ascended to the mythical province high in the hills, meeting little resistance.

'They managed to slowly rebuild, occupy the new town, bring along family and friends,' he continued, 'to the point where the ruins were transformed into a thriving, expanding, vibrant collectivity—quite a legitimate society, if you will, with all of what is expected of such a place. And yet,' he smiled, 'and yet, conspicuous by only one thing of course, the absolute absence of any type of criminal activity! A miracle, surely, if you consider the very nature and disposition of the inhabitants!' He laughed, awkward fidgeting from all sides accompanied the hushed stillness he had provoked, then resumed.

'The legitimacy of the town reached such proportions that all agreed, barring an eternal isolation—there was, I might add, a contingency that campaigned, unsuccessfully, for such a status—that the new, vigorous community needed, quite simply, a name: in their rush and excitement, and despite the work that had gone into its creation, the progenitors had forgotten this first basic task. No sooner had the problem been exposed, however, that the solution was offered: in haste, one could say, and without consultation, the name was given. Now,' and here he paused again, slowly sipped from his cup, 'now it is again a matter of debate as to whether this was the cause of what followed: for as we all know—I did not—on the fortnight after the naming of Q__abad, in the early hours past midnight, the citizens were awakened by sudden shrieks and tempestuous screams. Houses ablaze, destruction and burning, wailing of women and children, unprecedented hullabaloo. Soldiers invaded from all directions, on foot, on horseback, in an assortment of vehicles, and proceeded to their historic looting and devastation. Nothing was spared, no one escaped without at least a glimpse of the horror. Beatings and rapes went on throughout the night, a cataract of pleadings, Q__abad enveloped in absolute chaos. Quite a fantastic episode indeed! And I am even willing to gamble that most of you know, exactly I mean, what I am referring to: for, did not the scene depict, enliven in fact, bring to *life*, almost in every detail, in an uncanny pose of portraiture, the very scene of carnage in one most celebrated of such paintings!

'The ignominy lasted through the night until a swift meeting by leaders resolved that, for their own safety and that of

35

their families, the citizens were to abandon their homes, however reluctantly, and seek refuge in surrounding towns. When the night had passed, all of Q__abad had been razed to the ground. No trail of the ancient, and nothing of the new, stood. Not even Ruin, in fact, was spared: there was to be no trace of Q__abad, not even a semblance of a trace. Mercifully, everyone had managed to escape, and it was assumed that most had found shelter. But the demolition had proven overwhelming and total, the resistance minimal. And no one dared, after the affair, challenge the wisdom of the swift abandonment. Come what may, Q__abad existed no more.

'Still, the intentions and the identities of the authorities who had ordered the destruction remained blurry. Some speculated foul play, or even secret collaboration of Q__abadians with unknown enemies. Nor could it be ascertained whether the invasion was an elaborate plan or merely the ensuing result of a feast gone awry. A mere coincidence, or was it all in the Name: had calamity been wrought upon Q__abad by some mysterious decree, by the sudden urge of the mighty, or through the pertinacious wrath of masked riders at the naming—*any* naming—of the New? Mortal foes or in fact allies of stranger stripes, the citizens of Q__abad and their suspected looters? The outcome sealed forever, or endless battles of the duels? This encounter, the carnage, the last of ruin even, the dance, the march, the mask: I ask you, all gathered: folly, or fate? Which?'

The teller ceased here, left everyone in suspense. His was quite a provocation: riddle and myth, question and not, accentuated all by the tone and the glare in his eyes! He remained silent, of course, seemingly content with his effort, giving no indication that any attempt at elaboration would ensue. Speechless and eager, others at the table peered shyly about, uncertain as to whether the fellow would carry on: uncertain also, as to where it all might end. Several in the company, citing their obligations, politely excused themselves, paid their portion of the expenses, shook hands (after extending them of course), and were on their way. I remained, along with two others, and the one who had initiated the tale. He sat quietly now, his hands resting, his eyes cast downward. The disappointment of those present was obvious: we anticipated the rest, and his reluctance to continue managed only to raise the collective ire. He did not, finally, fail to surprise.

'I'm not going to go on,' he blurted out, sensing the rising expectations, when the table had cleared and his three loyal listeners had settled. 'Someone else now, it's up to someone else.'

Nothing to be done, that was it for this fellow. It was only a short while before I also excused myself, saluted the company and headed towards the entrance. I turned once more to see the three, all inert around the table I had just occupied, the entire house haunted by an impossible stillness. I turned again, exited and marched into the cold.

———■———

It is with abundant clarity that I recall the previous episode, for several elements had succeeded in etching the experience in my mind: the queer, devilish gaze of the teller, his subsequent refusal to go on, the utter absence of even the slightest noise in the entire tavern—was everyone listening so intently?—the shifting lights that seemed to accompany the vagaries of the account, and my last glance of course, at the three, seated around so lifelessly, when I was about to leave. By nature a creature of curiosity (and often reluctantly so, for have I not, yes indeed, bore the inclemency of the Content), still I had not been overly enamored by the story of Q__abad. Significant it seemed, this much I concede, and all the more unforgettable, but I sensed no urgency, as I have at other junctures, to pursue the matter any further. I was quite at ease with allowing Q__abad to slowly unveil itself through the tales of my fellow wanderers, weaved, alas, with the knots of my own driftings...

After my exit of the dreary establishment (there was a quaint aroma emanating throughout, a magnificent yet troubling blend of wines, the quiet trickling of raindrops outside in the city at dusk in a solitary lane), I walked along for quite some time and finally entered the bazaar, situated in a remote area, and accessible only with much patience.

Now most among the gentle readers are cognizant that the bazaars I speak of, those rendered immortal in tales of far-aways and bygone eras, are, often, if not always, found in the most bustling neighborhoods, in the midst of cluttered cir-culation, noise and pollution, chatter and yells. This one in particular, however, although characterized in its interior by all that makes the traditional bazaar—the young boy cruelly bent carrying loads on his back, merchants in small groups chattering, twisting methodically their *tasbihs*—was surround-ed not by the usual cacophony, but by what intimated a very tranquil nature, the very peace and pristine essence commonly associated with mythical gardens. From the tavern, one was led through a maze of streets, through a steady slope, and finally to the peak, from which a view of the hills proved quite entic-ing. But the most peculiar aspect was that not a single creature was ever seen in the area, on the hills, at the ridges, in the hollows or the sheltered nooks. Not even on the roads, or the dustier passes that gave way to the entrances! No: no one was ever seen entering or exiting, no one ever seen hovering in the proximity: no messengers or pilgrims, no visitors, no princes or knights outside the magical world of this bazaar. And yet, several steps more along these same trails and the traveler was soon among the porters and the yellers, nudged to one side or another, tempted and seduced, courted and cursed. No one, it seemed, had ever told of the Bazaar in the midst of the hills. Not even Legend, I surmised, was aware—or dared to tell!

On this the latest installation of my own entries, as on all previous occasions and all future possibilities, I stood bewildered, awed, in fact, by the absolute disorder in which I admittedly took perverse pleasure, only to be snapped out of the reveries, brutally, I might add, by a harried thug pulling a large number of rugs on a heavy trolley. And although on this day like all others, I immediately entered a private universe of delectable musings through the labyrinthine alleys, still I was genuinely troubled by the fear? the fancy? the frolics? of the fellow in the tavern, and his refusal to carry on with the tale. He did not seem, after all, so terribly overcome by the details of his intervention, as are those whose emotional dispositions simply do not endure the recounting of matters overly intimate. Surely, I reasoned, he could have continued! Not even the anticipation or the annoyances of the others—none of which, granted, were expressed—had generated any reconsideration. A swift fable, a swift floundering: the inexplicable nature of the unfolding troubled me, it is true, but it seemed, furthermore, that his version simply did not stand up to scrutiny.

It was, he construed, immediately after the naming, and, he insinuated, because of it, that the destruction had been wrought upon Q__abad. But as he himself related the episode, the devastation had been a disciplined, rigorous, methodical affair. Had it been initiated by the citizens in Q__abad themselves, it seems, there would not have been time enough for such swift and sure preparation before the naming. If indeed the tragic outcome had been generated by the new measures,

39

it could have occurred only with a more extended temporal lapse: between the heresy, that is, and the hell that ensued. If the culprits were Q__abadians themselves then, the naming could not have been the instigator. And, frankly, it would have been quite unimaginable for such a force, with such an arsenal at its disposition, to have sprouted from within without a significant portion of the population gaining suspicion or alarm. A conspiracy from within, one could safely conclude, was highly unlikely! Now, it was true, and I knew this myself previous to the elaborations in the tavern, that, prior to the full blossoming of Q__abad, neighboring villages and the higher authorities of the region enveloping the still unpopulated parcel, had all expressed their concerns at the increasing occupation, going so far as to propound creative obstacles in order to undermine any progress. It was not clear who, though, if anyone, had jurisdiction over the unused land, or who in particular could have sufficient motivation to derail the development, and with such enormous vigor. It was said, after all, that the bandits had ascended to the unnamed ruins without much resistance, and with little intention of troubling any existing worlds. Who then, the question remained, would have taken it upon themselves to demolish the fable in the making? The theory of a night of festivities or of debauchery extending to such cataclysmic actions was still more farfetched than the propositions of methodical collaboration or external intrusion. There was, after all, no record of any such festivities occurring anywhere near Q__abad on the fateful night, nor is it likely that travelers from a distant orgy would loot with such precision and finality. No: not only had the fellow not answered, as I have already expressed, his provocative queries, but the very options he had presented seemed dubious, a clever trick directed at the unsuspecting to derail personal options! A yes or no, a this or a that, with or without apologies: none of these would do. All of which prompted *me*, anyway, to doubt the general outlines of his account, his sincerity, at least his accuracy. One must harbor, however, that to the legend of Q__abad was now attached an Enigma—relating, what is more, to a Calamity, and to its Name! Sure recipe, I mused, for inclusion in the immortal catalogue of lands and cities, of fable and of myth!

———■———

I was drowned in these mental calculations, taking little notice of the swarm of color, clothes, lights, and people through which my limbs were automatically guiding me, becoming slowly more cognizant of my surroundings, yet still preoccupied with my own private and certainly irrelevant thoughts, when I was interrupted, in a manner of speaking, by a fellow known in these quarters, and in very uncomplimentary fashion, as the 'pained painter' of the bazaar. It was in a small corridor, less populated than the others but still as chaotic as most, that I chanced upon him. A boy with a lamp and pointed shoes walked swiftly by, as did a pirate and his boat. As per usual, the painter bore the grave features of an Undesirable, a genial eccentricity emanating from his being. What was further known about him, and cruelly joked about in various circles, was that this painter had never uttered as much as a single word. I, like all those in whose presence he had been mentioned, had never heard him speak either, so intent did he seem—in his prodigious folly!—on imposing only his *own* vision, his *own* universe, through the daily sketches he patiently construed. Thus it was that the painter of the bazaar was known also as a deaf-mute, and, for this most common of frailties, likened to a crippled mind, whose strokes of genius were attributed to those very sources, to those very workings within that had also

41

deprived him of speech and hearing: to the intrusion, that is, of the devil in his soul. No matter: although I was taken aback by the encounter itself, the actual shock of hearing a very distinct voice, unusually soft and sensuous, quite articulate and uncommonly gentle, struck me as I would never have fathomed.

'But you see,' he had begun, with an entirely delicate carriage, in a tone that contradicted fully his physical appearance, 'I only suggested, you understand, merely *a suggestion*. I did not in fact impose anything! You do understand, do you not, what I mean. Do you not?'

I was, at this point, in such disbelief that I scarcely knew how to react, although in quite a crude, unbecoming manner, a response it was that sputtered from my lips: 'I must be on my way,' I intoned. 'Your sketches are quite extraordinary today,' I followed. 'I'm certainly glad I made the effort of strolling this way,' I ended: monotonous, insincere, hurried.

But before I could be away, 'Wait!' he implored, skipping hurriedly towards me on his hands, dragging his legless limbs behind. 'Wait, I must tell you the rest, I must tell you the rest.'

I had already started away from him that his tone reached an urgency I would not have expected: 'I tell you I imposed nothing!' he said. 'I was asked, *told*, rather, I was told, *draw*, and that I did! The looting, the drunkenness, the orgy and the rapes, the fires! I did not mean it to! I should never have done so…'

His pleading became more distant as I continued my way, for indeed, I had not, despite the panic I had detected in his voice, turned back or slowed down: and although he was swift, his dragging torso and skillful fingers were no match for my regular, footed, pace.

I had, needless to say, left him behind and was soon attending to my own excursion: untroubled, I admit, not only by a gnarled man in dire need of help and compassion, but by what seemed, after all, to be quite a fantastic occurrence. I paid no heed—not to the event itself, not to the intonations, not to my own creeping skepticism.

I carried on in the bazaar, a bit more attuned to my surroundings, halting on several occasions to inspect curious objects. It was not long before, at the end of a small corridor, I ran into a confidant busily judging fabrics spread out in front of the store, who was known throughout as the 'anonymous' poet. He was wiping his mouth with the sleeve of his right forearm, after what resembled a hearty sampling of djigars, when he extended his neck, placed two fingers, tweezer-like, above his nose, turned his head to the side, emitted a rough sound, exiting thus, quite effectively I must add, the snot from his nose, and swiped away finally with sleeve of forearm, gentle beard flowing. He then turned and saw me standing, he did not avoid me.

'Well looky there!' he intoned. 'What brings *you* to these parts?'

He had embraced and kissed and begun to lead me by the arm, all before I could reply.

'Come along,' he quipped. 'You must be hungry. Have you eaten, have you eaten recently?'

My mumblings were to form the beginning of an answer, but he had, so to say, beaten me to the punch.

'Of course you have not,' he bellowed. 'I'm all too well aware. Of course you have not!' (He had, one must add, the quite unbearable habit of explaining or stating many a thing twice over!)

We strode along and reached his quarters. He unlocked, we entered: headed up several flights, arrived at his doorstep: he takes out key, bending head, he placing correct key in slot, he

struggling with unsmooth operation, he succeeding, he unlock-
ing, opening, turning (knob—): we enter, he closes behind,
turns lock again, places key on shelf, takes off coat, I standing,
uncertain, he: 'Oh, let loose a little, will you! Here, let me take
your jacket; come, let's sit here,' and he showed me to the cen-
ter of the room, where a set of chairs had been arranged.

'Can I get you anything?' he asked, and while I pondered
(and finally answered negatively), he made his way to the win-
dow, opened it, peered out with torso and all, carefully exam-
ined left and right, finally closed again and mused: 'Nothing
again today, nothing from anywhere, perhaps I shall give the
title up after all!'

'You do know,' he continued, 'not a single verse has come
my way recently, and god knows I have been checking daily
with the supposed agents!' I did not respond, offered no com-
fort. 'But enough of my troubles,' he went on, 'tell me, what
about you, they told you, did they not, the beginning of the
tale, did they not?'

I was baffled once more as my host seemed poised to relate,
I assumed, the rest of the tale of Q__abad. Fearful yet helpless,
I conceded that they had.

'Well, I should have known, I should have known,' he said,
as if reprimanding himself. 'Did they tell you, no they must not
have, I can see in your eyes that they have not, what occurred
after the first raid? Did they tell you?' And before I could an-
swer, he had concluded himself: 'Of course they have not!'

He had just pronounced the last exclamation that a knock
at the door halted the exchange. 'Ah, fer cryin' out loud!' he
shouted. 'What is it now?'

He excused himself, stood, walked to the door and opened.
I could not see, but I heard whispers and chatter. The door
closed, he made his way back, alone.

'Nothing to worry about,' he quipped. 'Nothing at all, it's nothing at all.'

But as he readied himself to sit, the knocks were repeated, same pattern but louder, so that, before sitting, he found himself again walking towards the door upon which a knocker knocked. 'Ah stop it, I'm coming!' he shouted again, this time unamused. 'I'm coming!'

Same chatter same lull: but on this occasion, the sounds of some disagreements also, after which he came back into the room with a towering fellow, quite unkempt: 'O famous walker of the bazaar,' he winked at me, 'meet my good friend, he has been wanting to meet you for a while, he's heard a lot about you.'

All of this as the two made their way in, and as I was beginning to stand, so that by the time he had reached me, I knew my hand shaker, who, one must say, did do wonders for one's sense of, how shall we put it, worth.

'O how nice to finally meet you!' he exclaimed with a broad smile on a bald head, shaking my hand violently. 'How nice to finally meet you!'

Seated, the three of us, in a small circle: to my right the guest, my left the host. Small quarters, indeed, where we sat uncomfortably in the chairs assembled for the occasion.

'I presume that this is not the best place to convene,' he joked, 'but no matter, we will be fine.'

Although I had initially accompanied the poet to his dwelling through the trap of nourishment, he had not, since our arrival, followed through. Nor were there signs that any kind of food was actually being prepared. So be it, I thought, irritated, I shall not take him up on the issue. And as visions of sultry sauces passed me by, I, we, heard another knock. I made the polite gesture but was immediately rebuffed: 'O please,' the

45

host intoned, 'please sit down.'

He stood again and walked the few steps to the door. 'Who is it?' he asked once more. And the voices in unison answered that it was them.

˙He opened and in walked two senior citizens, one the woman, carrying what appeared to be a pot, and the other, the man, a bag. They embraced, one by one (by one), and he showed them in.

'We have visitors!' the woman said jollily. 'Fantastic!'

The two approached the surly gravedigger and myself. We stood, as well we should have, face to face at an angle.

'Mom, dad,' the poet said, 'my guests: here a respected member of the morgue, and there,' he winked at me yet again, 'an old associate who has come to town after a long absence.' Turning to me, he added, 'Quite some time now, isn't it?'

I answered that it had in fact not been so long, but it mattered not. The mother sat the big pot down on the counter, walked towards me and followed through with an unexpectedly warm embrace.

'It is so nice to finally meet you,' she uttered. To which, I: 'And same here, of course.'

The father, in his turn, moved up: 'Pleasure,' he said simply, opening his palm, extending his arm, bringing it close to mine, gripping finally firmly my paw.

They did the same with the gravedigger and backed away.

'We can't stay long, dear,' the mother said. 'Just that… Well…'

She wavered. The poet shook his head form side to side and pressed firmly his lips together in what seemed to be a subtle attempt to discourage her from expounding. She spoke nevertheless: 'Have you told him? Have you told it to him?'

Our host shook his head again, in apparent disbelief: 'Not yet, mother, not quite yet, but I will. Soon. I swear!'

She grew a bit grave, she did not look at me. 'O dear god!' she said. 'O dear!'

The son: 'It'll be all right mother, don't be so worried, it'll be fine.'

The father, only following so far, embraced him and added: 'We'll be going now anyway. Come on,' he motioned to the wife, 'let's go.'

He looked to us finally: 'So long fellows, have a hearty one.'

The mother embraced the son also, looked my way before exiting and repeated her O dear gods. The two exited hand in hand, the host closed the door, the host walked back to us.

He pulled the stool towards him, sat: 'Where were we?' he said. 'Where was I?'

His new demeanor startled me: gone were the cordiality, the amiability, the familiarity of the previous exchanges. He had suddenly, after the departure of his parents, turned cold, staring studiously, as if to prepare me for a variation on unwelcome news. Confronted with this surprising new development, I fidgeted in my seat, took several moments to evaluate his temperament— readying myself, if the need were to arise, for an appropriately intoned response. But before I could let out the first syllable, he surprised me yet again: 'Now, you realize, old chum,' he blurted out 'that it could not have been pure chance, our encounter in the bazaar. That you come along, at this hour, in this ferment, and that among the multitudes on your path, in this awkward fabric of our dance, it is I, one you have not seen in ages, who conveniently drops in! Upon which occasion I invite you to share a meal, upon which you casually agree, and upon which we make our way hastily to my abode. Could this be another in the long list of the accomplishments of chance?' His question was rhetorical. 'And this here fellow, a gravedigger in our midst! What of that? And my gentle parents? Caprice of the beast also?'

47

I felt enclosed, threatened almost, a prisoner of his violent suggestions. Obviously, apparently, there was something to be learned from the barrage. Something perhaps to dread. Besides, my initial tremors had now graduated to full-blown trepidation. The uncertainty in which I floated as to his intentions, the lack of any response to what seemed a casual exercise in rudimentary torture, and in which he was certainly taking great pleasure, the exigency of a helpless Wait in which the potential Coming itself was in grave doubt—all of this contributed to a creeping sensation of illness, for which, once more, I had no cure. Simply put, I could endure it no longer.

I suddenly stood from the chair I still obediently occupied—and in such an involuntarily violent way that it fell, noisily—bumped the poor gravedigger in my haste, and rushed urgently to the bathroom, whereupon I knelt and allowed my overburdened stomach to entice its innards outwards: not a poisoning of any sort, I don't think, but rather from the feeling of nausea that had affected me through the dereliction of my host. He, however, was not satisfied. He had followed me and stood now at the doorway, overlooking my embrace of his toilet: 'This is what you have to hear, O dear comrade! What did happen after the first razing of Q__abad? What was the reaction of the folk? Was it chance, there also, that brought about the decisive catastrophe they had known? Who was in charge? Who ordered it? Why was there no resistance? Further masterpieces of chance? The work of fortune in all its shades?'

I had by now raised myself from the floor, gravely sick, and exited the site of my fall, attempting to elude his unflagging barbarity. A heartfelt punch seemed necessary, but I resisted! O the riddles he heaped upon me! I was merely attempting to walk away, however tight the space—if only he noticed the pain he was inflicting!—that, still unsatisfied, he followed me

48

around the room. 'And why were the citizens spared? Why were there no murders?' He suddenly grabbed my arm, swung me around, and gazed furiously into my eyes. 'This is for sure, valiant soldier, the citizens needed a culprit, they were going to find one: someone to hang, someone to stone!'

He let go of my arm, again, and stepped away. 'Or not? Fortune again? Will you concede so much to Chance?'

And almost as if exhausted from his own cruelty, he slumped back down, with the last syllable, on his chair, next to the gravedigger—who had, surprisingly, redressed himself. As if utterly worn out, he let out a last gasp: 'Now it's up to you, my good man, your turn now, now you have to tell the rest!'

Strange incantation indeed! I saw neither reason nor rhyme in the perfidious soliloquy of the poet, which I readily attributed—for myself in any case—to his recent dearth of solid compositions, coupled with his recurring necessity to occupy center stage. Besides, I had lost all appetite and recognized, as had become my habit, that I cared not at all to respond. My patience, furthermore, had worn quite thin, and I chastised myself for letting the episode evolve even. I saw little merit in wallowing about any longer, but in the spirit of a perhaps senseless politeness, I uttered several phrases excusing myself. The poet, meanwhile, had casually taken out his own eyes, as they had bulged and rescinded and were fiery and sweaty after all the commotion and anomalous excitement, and began to polish them with a large handkerchief, a replica of a magic carpet, with elaborate designs, ready close at hand. Eyeless, he had motioned to the honored guest, and the two mumbled incomprehensibly as I stood several paces away.

They did not acknowledge my salutations, and I made no big deal of it. I turned and headed for the door. As I did so however, as I stood, readied and opened, suddenly appeared before me none other than the painter from the bazaar! Not just that, but face to face, to top it all, turban and long mustache in place, arms folded across the chest! I turned back to the seated couple, who were chattering unfazed, and turned again to the exit: there, before me, it was confirmed, the pained painter of the bazaar, staring, unblinking! Immediately, my neck flexed downward to evaluate the quite unrealistic event. But no, nothing: legless as always, floating! An episode unfolding so far with many improbabilities, and some noticeable implausibility, in which most commonplaces of daily subsistence had once more befuddled me, filled with the unusual and the unexpected, had managed one most delirious dénouement! I turned, one last glance at the careless couple, who seemed not to notice. (In the windowpane, a strange shadow has emerged, a small shadow with wings: tock tock we heard, opened window and undetected entrance, muse of faraway forgettings, and now once more the poet enchanted in a trance...) I turned again: it was not a dream. 'I asked you not to leave,' thundered the thug, 'but you simply turned and went your way! Without even looking back!'

It was true, I said to myself, I had not even bothered to hear his pleadings. But I remained as pitiless as before, not giving in one bit, feeling no remorse, none at all, as I'm sure he expected. 'Now what!' I exclaimed, incensed. 'Now what do you want?!'

The floating painter was taken aback. He froze. I, after the attack, paused also. He stared. I stared. (He blinked, I blinked.) Twitch: twitch. (Poet by the window with companion, wine, cup-bearer and nightingale: exclaiming the anxious cries of the soul: said Anonymous Poet of the Bazaar to friends, 'O how... O how... Ode to a Promenade by Still-light...') I say nothing, he say nothing. And then:

'Nothing!' he answers in retreat. 'I want nothing. Just to have told you that's all!'

'And now I know!' I snapped back, still playing the dutiful role of the angered. 'And this time, I really must go.'

And so I did. And heard nothing thereafter. Poet, painter, pest: I heard nothing from them at all.

———■———

I tried, in vain as it were, to put the debacle out of my mind, but the effort itself proved quite taxing. In the dark, empty streets again after a hasty exit and long meditative walk, I remained preoccupied by the implications of the poet's utterances, and further, by the unsettling combination of a strange solemnity and a scathing violence through which he had conducted his onslaught. The inscrutable exclamations of the mother before her departure, the coldness of the father, the goofiness of the gravedigger, the floating encroachment of the painter: all gave me a sense of terrible, unwanted, uncontrollable, doom. And all as if I myself—and this was the moot, troubling aspect of my derision—as if I myself had generated the tale: both the one I was living—and the one I was awaiting!

The eerie feeling was heightened as I walked about in a daze. I wrapped my coat around as tightly as I could, since it was now a bit chillier, and soon I lumbered unto a popular boulevard, where, to my surprise, the landscape was utterly bereft of animation: no stray dogs, no piercing eyes of roaming felines: only the waning shadows of leaves, projected through the gleam of a street-lamp along the edge... The piers, from what I could see, were also barren. I turned soon into a smaller alley and carried on along the side, walked a bit further and turned finally into a narrower lane, in which I knew of a lounge that I counted among my favorites, and whose atmosphere had certainly suited my tastes on previous visits. I found the un-marked entrance, opened, and entered.

The festive ambiance contrasted sharply with the quietude I had just left. The place was noisy and smoky as usual, with the habitual crowd milling about, entranced in playful quarrels, complaisant conversation, amusing distractions. Some were clustered holding drinks and chatting, while, a bit further in the back, others participated in various games and contests. Upon receipt of my order, I casually marched across the lounge and to the alcove, taken, as I often was, by the spirit of the players and their various skills. I had now regained some aplomb, and I was less disturbed and flustered no more. I whiled away the minutes, soon reckoned that I had collected sufficient poise and rekindled my curiosity enough to actually undertake the remainder of my itinerary. I rested my empty glass on the counter, retrieved my coat, left my smoldering cigarette in an unoccupied tray and began toward the exit. As I proceeded to make my way through the main floor (I was in the back still), a short personage, visibly quite intoxicated, very raggedy and unshaven, stumbled in my path. I held him before he fell, and as I tried to straighten him into a standing position, he grabbed unto my sleeve and struggled as upright as he could. 'Thank you, good fellow,' he muttered half-drunk. And when he had finally pulled himself to, as a token of his appreciation, he dragged me to a table, enjoined me to sit, and plunked down himself.

'Now you see,' he began, 'this here is the reason that I'll never go back!'

He had instantly pulled, as he had uttered the incomprehensible phrase, from his hand-me-down jacket, a small photograph, itself dated, as was evident from the worn-out edges and the general condition of the paper. He held it at a distance, showing it as it were, while he swerved his own body around to peer at the image by my side, although I am certain that he had stared at the photograph countless times, and in the company of many.

'You are the first one who is seeing this!' he bellowed. 'The first, besides myself. I've been meaning to show it to you.'

His first comment already had contradicted my initial impressions, but the second was still more perplexing. Truly, he was mistaken me for another, for I was certain, in my bewildered stupor even, that I had never before in my life seen the wight, nor did I even remotely relate to the image he was showing. He was, to top it all, so minimally conscious that I had little trouble dismissing his words (waywardly out of his mouth).

'You see,' he went on, 'they did this at random. All at random. They did not even know who it was. Just grabbed the poor bloke and shot him. Unblinking. No remorse. Totally at random.' He sighed, his angry eyes swelled almost to abnormal proportions, tiny tears collected on his cheeks: 'Or so I think. But I tell you: no matter what, I'll never go back.'

I was still quite confused, but my instincts led me to simply acquiesce and shake my head in the pretense of solidarity. He was visibly troubled, but I dared not tamper with his condition through any recourse to reason. Nor did I see it fit to enlighten myself, in potential detriment to his well-being, about his arcane pronouncements. I held back therefore, and merely imagined myself, momentarily, the comforting angel of an old decrepit drunkard.

I must acknowledge, though, that the photograph did represent quite a troubling image: a blindfolded man, his arms tied behind his back (one was to surmise, for that was how he held them), simply clothed in a loose shirt hanging over his pants—in what resembled the regular attire of simple country folk—faced a firing-squad composed of four others. Most

53

troublesome was that the supposed fiend did not have his back to the customary monument that accompanies such rituals. No wall, no post, no poles, not even a tree (yes, it's even done before trees): the condemned stood surrounded by nothing at all but the open field. In the daytime also, and with no visible human artifacts in the vicinity. What was further astonishing, it seemed, was that the photograph appeared to have been taken as the hail of bullets had been discharged: for although he was not yet down, he was bending on one side in such manner that can be wrought upon one, that can only be ignited, so to say, by the tempestuous shower of startling forces. Nor had the executioners relieved their shoulders of the pointed guns: still aiming, still at work. My examination of the photograph lasted only a few instants, and when I detected that the old man had sufficiently recovered, that he was, at least, safely seated on furniture from which he could not tumble—not dangerously in any case—I saw the moment fit to stand, pat him on the back, and advise him to be careful. I walked towards the door, turned around before exiting, took a last look, and finally stepped back into the crisp, lively air.

So it was that, without any intention whatsoever, I found myself at what appeared to be a large gathering in an unusually wide expanse. I had walked most of the night, as was my habit, it is true, but it had also seemed that I had perpetually changed directions only within the confines of an unknown maze, subsumed by my own peregrinations, passing and bypassing recognized sites and monuments. It was nevertheless with heightened caution that I stood among them, all of them, in a landscape from which I was fully alienated.

We had all been milling about when a sudden commotion, whose provenance I did not make out, broke out unsuspected. The crowd quickly dissipated, everyone rushing and scurrying in various directions. Confounded by the various alternatives, I decided to head eastward and carried on without significant alarm. I had, after all, no reason to worry: I was a complete transient in a region perhaps long forgotten. The assumption, however, turned out to be erroneous, for I had gone only a hundred yards or so that I was accosted by a group of disguised men along the road. I was suddenly subjugated to a terrible fright, the like of which I had not known for a long while, a terror so intense, in fact, that it momentarily desensitized me, rendering me unaffected by their tirades and the cacophony. I soon snapped out, doubtless through another among the same bantering, and did exactly as I was told. That is: I turned, clasped my hands behind my head, walked at a precisely given rhythm, and did not emit a single sound.

One of the four proceeded to walk directly in front of me. I was instructed to follow that path, without the slightest bit of deviation. I followed all instructions, obediently marching behind the self-appointed guide. We marched for a considerable distance, without the slightest exchange, when the order was finally given to halt. I acquiesced, and then heard one fellow from the back tell me that I could now turn. It seemed to me that I was in a precarious situation through no action of my own, and as urgently as I attempted, I was unable to formulate a means of escape. I was, further, contemplating the very relevance of any pleading or coaxing or coercing on my part, convinced that no interaction would have the sufficient leverage to alter the course of events. Matters deteriorated more than I would ever have imagined when I saw two of the four approach me, one with a blindfold for the eyes, another with a rope I presumed would be used for my hands. The swarm of anxieties and the severity of my trepidation were at no instant more acute, more overwhelming than when the two men applied,

55

one, the blindfold, the other the hand-bind. O insoluble time! They finished the operation and I heard their footsteps marching away to join their consorts. You can imagine the terror that had now engulfed me. I could barely contain my increasing consternation, with the acute coincidences especially, for it seemed that the entire affair was eerily on its way of simulating—O heavens above!—the image that the drunken boor had shown me in the lounge. I was either fully reliving the life of another, I thought, or else, I was retrieving a moment in the past that I had somehow managed to exclude from my ventures. Or, even, I was merely completing a piece that was without its contours. O Caustic Cants! O Gall of Chance! For it now occurred to me yes it did, that I was the first in the long history of our species, the one and only, to have witnessed the slow withering of his soul! Blindfolded, standing in a dreary desolate field, I could see that I had seen myself blindfolded slithering to the ground! It was abundantly clear, it could not be denied: I had seen the photograph of my own death, a privilege deprived all, a feat I alone could claim, and I had not even known it! O Dance of Dread! Take me away, I wanted to cry! Do away with me at once, I ached to scream! Go ahead, I fancied a bark, finally, Q__abad is destined to perish anyhow!

I swallowed hard. Stood silent. I heard their preparations, their rhythmic motions. When, thought I! Carry on, thought I! And sooner than wished, O how sooner than wished, it was upon me! Counting... One. Counting, Two. Counting. And:

'Finish it now!' I suddenly heard unsuspecting. 'Now is your chance, finish it now!'

And a raucous laughter erupted from the four, in such manner that the might of the shock itself almost led to my collapse!

'Tell it to us then, good fellow, carry on the tale!' clamored the other, riddled in laughter still, erupting once more.

'And what happens next!' thundered the third. 'O please do tell us: what *does* happen next?'

O perfidy, O fortune!...

Once more the company raised the pitch, once more the laughter:

Unknowing... Unknowing... that I had told, that I had told indeed:

Allow

then this irrevocable delay in offering the delights of my fancy, for it was not without a good amount of derision that I provoked my separation, not without a hefty dose of admonition and condemnations mercilessly heaped my way that I orchestrated my charmed evasion, not without strong incitation of madness, a few clever ruses and some pillaring that I banished fears, not without some delicate maneuvers, I dare say, that I managed to weave and wind my way through the morass of calamitous propositions, and carry on the tale!

Still, as it appears unlikely then that I will succeed in accurately recounting a most portentous event that transpired before the celebrated puppets, I shall nevertheless attempt to relay the episode, if not in all of the deserved detail, still in such manner that one may arrive, with moderate effort (the foot-clatter of walkers outside windows notwithstanding), at a parallel experience and reconstruction of the unfolding. It is in fact with much trepidation and much exhilaration that I risk this account, for it was there that the most frenetic of riddles unraveled. With such stupendous force all untwirled! With such intrepid tenacity the Unusual imposed itself upon the Moment! Truly an Event of the grandest proportions! Truly a celebratory Occasion for those unsuspecting of the Supernatural! For was it not the incandescence of invisible spheres that now had chosen such a trite, quotidian, silly even, silly, playground, such a marvelous time to intervene and unveil the truths?! Was it not the imponderable Energies that had manifested themselves?! Was the Power of Magic, the Seduction of the Impossible, not sufficient to make those present believe? O clarity of Destiny! I could now carry on! I could go on, carry on and tell, once upon a time, there was one, and there was not! I shall not delay the depiction much longer though, and shall proceed immediately. (Had I in fact ventured far, ventured outside, have I again succumbed to primitive urges of the most deceitful kind, of the most despicable nature—have I sinned in *this* kingdom even, responsible agents save my soul?) I stretched out the hands, the fingers I soothed, my knuckles I readied with an imposing crack. All appropriated elements were gathered, I cleared, and cleared again, the throat—ehem, ehem—adjusted the lighting—and began.

—■—

Knowing not that the day would prove so uncommon and revelatory, but having, strangely, a premonition, I suspended my usual labor of utilizing all devices at my disposition to determine what would occur and how it would all go. No pensive stretches of muted, interior computation, no pure, undaunted, shameless or protracted remembrance: I did not even have recourse to my habitual deprivation of thought, that method of denuding, in effect, of active processes of cognition and the subsequent embodiment of a passive trance that allowed illuminations, epiphanies and solutions of all kinds to flood my humble being! I simply fetched the appropriate volumes and unfolded the desired maps. The conspiracy, I then whispered to myself, is duly launched.

I took to the streets, and, although tempted to make the trip shorter, I concluded that a quiet saunter through the park would awaken my senses, and thus permit, in a little while, a more intense awareness of the intricacies of the performance I was to attend. I quietly confirmed the merit of such a promenade, buttoned up the long overcoat, turned up the collar to protect parts of my cheek, and finally wrapped the scarf around my neck and parts of my head. Stomping an umbrella like a cane to facilitate my steps, rhythmic beats without melody, gentleman hero, a tick and a tock: the entire stroll would, in my best estimate, not exceed, no I was certain of it, not exceed the time needed to arrive before the beginning of the spectacle. I went about without much stimulation, mostly unaware and quite uninterested, as it turned out, in the immediate environment. Surely, the general tumult, the stares, the rhythm of the steps, all merited closer scrutiny. Surely, I would be ever more enriched by an active reading of the surroundings: the rumble and roar of man-made machines, the magnificence of Nature in all its glory, the games of the small animals, the secretive exchanges of the sinful, the prudent strolls of tricky and tricked lovers—but nay, to none of this did I pay the smallest heed. Myself with myself: content with my own obdurate preoccupations, and feeling for it no shame, I arrived finally, only moments before the announced commencement.

A long line had already formed before the entrance, but I, fortunately, bypassed the inconvenience since I held, on this occasion, a privileged pass. I slowly made my way inside and proceeded into the hall. Quite an arresting hall it was too, with an atrium painted in fantastic colors and shapes, with pillars and chandeliers worthy of royalty, and a most majestic, inviting proscenium. I was directed, through the aisles and to my seat, by an awkward-looking and old usher of medium height, of a grave countenance and wan expression, who avoided contact all the while, save for the last instant when, as his final indications pointed to the anointed place, he glowered directly at me, his fiery eyes ever more ghastly on an unquestionably jaundiced visage. Many in the arena were already settled, and I had to excuse myself through various bodies in order to reach my seat. I proceeded to carefully doff my already unbuttoned coat, take off the scarf also and settle. I noticed that the adjacent seat, to my right to be precise, remained unoccupied, authorized myself to place the burdensome vestments on it, until, at least, the occupants were to arrive, upon which occasion I would be obliged to lay them on my knees for the duration of the performance—quite an unbecoming nuisance, considering the financial sacrifices made by most of the spectators to even avail themselves of the show. Impressive as the architecture was, and the maintenance of the hall itself, still the services remained grossly inadequate. So be it, I muttered to no one in particular, no sense in allowing temporary irritations to ruin the grander joys.

The spectacle, on the other hand, soon proved quite unforgettable. Never had I been so affected—so stirred, really!—by such an exuberant rendering. The beloved had been strangled and lay sprawled on the stage. The lover, a handsome knight, stood in the near, in hysterics. The build-up had proven immensely masterful, and I, along with others in the audience, had been on the verge of childish sobs for quite some time when the final scene finally shattered our last defenses. Supreme was our sorrow indeed, and, along with the collective anxiety, surely it contributed to the outpouring of emotion. What's more, the final confrontation, I sensed, was expertly set up, for all were awaiting still the fate of the *other* lover— who had been kept in the dark, as was the counterpart, in regard to the range of the involvements. Duel in the desert? The lament of the Unheard? Here it was at last: the other runs in, stage left. (Whence? How could he have known? To find them here!? It matters not.) Suddenly stops, frozen: sees the kneeling one mourning the beloved. 'And what has transpired here?' crieth the hero. 'Dead!' answereth the other. 'Gone for-

61

ever!' The standing one moves, kneels also, examines the body, approaches ear to heart, makes certain, is just flabbergasted. Beloved surrounded by two kneeling lovers in tears. The second, suddenly overcome with jealousy, stands and pulls the sword: 'And you are the culprit!' The first stands also, pulls the sword, is not to be easily accused: 'I am only the heir to her heart.' And they begin the Duel. Around the stage, sword to sword, unaware! Unaware yes, that each is a son, son born of the same father! The duel of the doubles, it was, yes, the Duel of the Doubles at last! Beloved had been well forewarned, but had not heeded, had not believed, had in no way anticipated a final battle. Would the two lovers come upon the truth? Somehow? Reveal in their verbal swipes throughout their dance of a duel, their provenance? Reveal their names, reveal their lives? Not so, as it turned out: the battle raged, until almost simultaneously, in a most dramatic climax, one enters a sword into the heart of the other, while at once, the sword of the latter enters also the heart of the former. The two heroes that were one fall, but each silently on his own: no sameness in their final bow, never a communion in the throes of death.

The thunderous applause was not delayed for an instant even. An ecstatic audience was on its feet, conquered by the pathos, reeling in approval with a fervor unmatched in recent times. The two actors stood after the curtain closed and opened again, bowing, hand in hand, bathing in the wild appreciation of the spectators. (Then the curtain closed again, and again was pulled, for the clamor had not ceased.) Bows and still more, until slowly, ever so slowly, the cheering subsided. I myself could not be any prouder of my beloved's perfect, literally perfect, performance: an unsurpassed success indeed, in fulfilling the role forever rehearsed! A masterful interpretation! Final, unvanquished glory! I stood (the seat on my right never did find its rightful occupant), picked up the coat, the scarf and the umbrella, and proceeded, through the main aisle, outside the hall.

———■———

With full trust in my passionate perspicacity for such ventures, for such unassuming wanderings and fickle (though harmless, I have always thought) curiosities in unusual locations, in, one might say, sites that appear to the uninitiated as potentially uninviting, perhaps even frightening, given their aura of enigmatic seduction, I decided to do just that: to walk about in the hidden passages—that is, in the endless corridors, in the labyrinthine pathways behind the scenes. Much more productive, in any case, I thought, than idling impatiently the hours away, or passing them in a neighborhood lounge. Without the slightest of deceitful ambitions then, absent all dishonest designs, with no purpose at all, truly, other than to give Time (the father!) a run at its ceaseless monotony, to postpone its unassuming banditry, *bref*, to keep boredom at bay.

I found myself backstage, umbrella in hand, the scarf casually draped around the neck. (It's dark, it's even lonely: carry me through, feet, do not let me down!) I quietly inspected photographs and paintings adorning the walls, I examined the occasional artifact left unattended, but I made, overall, no discovery of extraordinary effect.

It was thus with a dose of renewed excitement that I finally came upon a large, inviting door. I balked, yes I did, and I stopped. My casual promenade had taken me through quite a few hollow hallways, and I would, surely, not have been capable of finding my way back very easily. I was not very aware of my surroundings either, as I had been strolling aimlessly in a backstage that had proven to be not as small as I would have

63

imagined. Sensing a creeping unease, lo, a mitigated horror, I resolved nevertheless to delay panic, to prevent my own abdication to the temptations and to avert the pitiful running about that takes hold of many in such delicate situations. Indeed, while I sensed the turbulence of a mordant harangue forming within my throat, I successfully suffocated its appetency for outwardly manifestation.

Transfixed thus before the mysterious portals, once more I attempted to situate myself. I had come down the hallway, yes, but now I could not retrace: perhaps a few indiscernible turns, a few unfelt penetrations, through one room and into another, lost in thoughts: I could not, for the sake of me, figure out where I had gone! Perhaps only paces away from where I had started, perhaps far from the origin of my first peregrinations! I sighed, I smiled: not a contradiction, for in this netherworld that I found myself, I was not so certain that I wished to know the way back. Perhaps, in a silent fit of rage, I had brought this upon myself: perhaps I had, after all, been the maker of my own destiny (finally, in that most common of evenings): I had arrived, perhaps, where I would have feared to tread… Joyous clamors of Freedom, perhaps… Sweet scent of Unbelonging… Yes, I sighed again, gazing at unseen horizon across the sand and the sea: yes I sighed, wind carrying the fervor of fates astray—yes: here I am, the proud, felicitous, privileged, lucky for god's sake, just plain lucky, owner of a high-tower from which to peer! (I will trade it for nothing, I thundered within, come what may!) Thus and so, I turned again, at the unopened door yearning for me, gasping to myself, I might as well see. I waited, I approached…

Report: inward thoughts and condition, you are aware. Physical demeanor, exterior manifestation: I have justly portrayed. All systems on go then: I, long ago champion of obscure competitions now forgotten, prone to fits of madness and perversion, lauded by some, envied by others, detested by many, down and out at one point like most worthwhile colleagues, transformed into a provider for family no choice, clown by profession, mime by passion, liar by trade: crier by day, wanderer at night: approach, and slowly raise my hand: I hesitate (ah, the pitfalls of the pause), I conquer (the timidity), fist-with grabeth I the rounded knob, I Turn:

I turn, I turn, Impatient Ones: yes, I Turn the doorknob— and the Door, miraculously, Opens...

Creakily, granted, but opens nevertheless! And towards the inside: which translates, as concerns my motions, into: a step forward, an elongation of the arm (rather than the more inconvenient pullback), a forced nudge: a peek in, so that I confront the numinous darkness. Hesitation again, doubt again, dread, potential chagrin. But I persevere: another nudge, I step in, knob still in fist, look, let go, door goes its destined direction a few instants more: I find the switch (somehow), click, turn, lights coming on, I see: Oh the marvels, the marvels...

I take a few steps and begin my inspection. Captain U. at the helm, Captain R. to the task. And I shall be up to it, I shall: no regressing: carry on soldier, carry on, be not afraid. I shall discover and tell, massacre and yell, bang—not dwell. And before I could even attempt the more independent inspection, I had come upon several figurines, lying chaotically on the floor, on a leather lounge chair, by the casements: one, another, and still another, lying helplessly, open-eyed. This must be the room, I told myself, it seems like I have reached the very chamber! Could it really be, I pondered, I am destined to this, I mused, I should have known, it was inevitable...

65

———■———

It was a large room, and in such shambles, in fact, that it was quite onerous to define any borders or to make out any shapes. Tapestries were draped on furniture, costumes were haphazardly hanging, books, sheets, boxes, folders and musical instruments lay in all corners, open cabinets and files were strewn about, closets overflowing, wooden statuettes, bigger, smaller, an extraordinary amalgam of things known and not: ancient maps, drawings of imaginary cities, sketches of unknown lands, unfinished works: letters, typescripts and ancient manuscripts, a book on modern tales, and another called *The History of Perfidy*: chimes and vases and a decanter and a casket along the wall: 'I cannot possibly attend to all of this!' I told myself. 'I cannot possibly get to all of this!'

I was succumbing to an overpowering sense of helplessness when, as I had taken several steps, I stumbled upon a figurine in the shape of an awkward monster (many-headed at that) of much repute. I paused momentarily, bent down and picked up the object, examined it and noticed quickly that it was constructed out of a rare wood whose provenance I could not establish. It was still in good condition, and so I surmised that it had served either as a mere decorative artifact in a large spectacle, or else as the central focus in a small-scale puppet show. I decided to amuse myself by imagining the effect on an audience made solely of children, believing, unbeknownst, the movements of the grim monster. 'How may I help,' I imitated the potential voice—this being, of course, the puppet-monster blocking the way of a puppet-hero, whose adventures would have, up to then, been depicted for the group. 'Where is your destination,' I said, suspecting that my facial contortions matched the imitation I had undertaken. To which, the cocky one: 'Out of my way, I am the Conquering Hero, I let no obstacle stand in my way!' (I pictured the wide-eyed muteness of the children, agog with the pronouncements of the figurines!) The monster then lets out an evil laugh—'We will see about that!'—attacks the hero, and temporarily knocks him down. He lies, unmoving, as the hands that guide his motions remain inert behind the stage of this world. The audience gasps. Potential panic. Fear and uncertainty. But he will get up, they fathom, the evil monster cannot get away with it. Not so easily anyway. He must move on. He must! And indeed he does! The puppet-hero miraculously rises again and confronts the challenge before him. He backs off slightly, draws his sword. The monster comes towards him, the hero swings: no match, though, for the strength of the monster. He is helpless, retreats: but does not retire, dares not abandon. As the monster traps him, with miraculous credulity, counting on the voracious desires of his adversary, suddenly, the hero slips away to the other side. He turns again, slowly, faces the monster. But his gesture is only a bluff. He quickly turns back, scampers in the opposite direction, crosses finally the gate that his enemy had been protecting. He enters and the reeling monster can only sulk in defeat. Ruse over rage, the final verdict. And the hero has conquered again! I did not surprise myself of course, it was expected that my hero, also, conquer.

67

The episode duly completed, I carried the piece and placed it on a shelf—it did not have a string, by the way—fearing that the floor might jeopardize its survival. With my monster overseeing the rest of the operations, I continued my exploration of the playroom. I leafed through an imaginary map of the planet, skimmed inattentively through the previously mentioned *The History of Perfidy*, and subsequently picked up a thick, dusty volume which seemed to encompass a vast range of experiences, all arranged conveniently in alphabetical order. I browsed at leisure and stopped haphazardly at a passage entitled, uncharmingly enough, *Albatross,* whose contents did at least bring a smile to my face and set me off, momentarily, into a fantastic arena I was not sure I deserved. I went through the book some more and bypassed, under B, *The Bewitching and Hazardous Nature of Masks, Mirrors and Metamorphoses.* Leafing to the left I was, the volume having assuredly been written in a language of such logic, that I glanced quickly, under N, at *The Narrative of I. Avaré, who in the year 19——*, went backwards again, skimmed, under C, *The Cry of the Masses* and back again: under K, an interesting title that caught my attention, *The Kava of Freedom,* which I ignored anyway. At last, under Y, *The Yearning of A., known only as such, believed to be an alias.* It appealed to me immediately, and the entry became only the second through which I actually read. It was most intriguing indeed, so much so, in fact, that I deem it charitable to share the pleasure of at least a fragment. It read, *The Yearning of A., known only as such, believed to be an alias. Dates of birth and decease unknown.* In smaller print below, there was a brief biographical blurb: 'Heretic during the revolution, who attributed no specific reason to the uprisings. Known to frequent gaudy locales, to possess a villainous smirk, often pitilessly unleashed upon his enemies and his irritants, and to espouse an unwelcome style of circulation. Musician who, during the raids, stood alone in the square and played the violin, counted among the most cherished in the history of the city, for citizens from afar and from near congregated, to listen to the deafening sounds of the planes. Puppeteer extraordinaire, prone to hallucinations and multiple personality disorders, who charmed old and young with narratives of hazardous voyages to haunted homes and seas.' I closed the volume, motioning an appreciative salute to the brotherly bloke.

I finally unearthed, under a pile of sheets, a number of marionettes, each of which bore an uncanny resemblance to characters portrayed in the thick tract, whose biographies I had either read or scanned, each deliberately carved and constructed, clothed even, as would be their more animate, and obviously larger, models. Yes, I concluded, this was the marionette room as I had earlier surmised, and these replicas were perhaps purposely hidden to protect from the intrusion of outsiders such as myself. No matter: the fiery lads had their strings attached, almost begging for manipulation. How better to occupy myself, I thought, than to toil away in pleasant idleness: do something wacky, and daringly too: constructive idleness, say. I took off the coat again—it was getting quite warm in the midst of such a throng—put away the umbrella, and left the scarf on the crowded sofa. I then assembled the marionettes, fetched a miniature stage and kneeled in front. 'No need to hide!' I mused. 'There is no one here but myself.'

Indeed, indeed: I was the god, the player and the befuddled spectator all at once, and this was my playpen.

'Well then!' quipped I to the silent dolls. 'Are you ready to perform? Move those arms and legs, now, little ones, don't disappoint me! Twist that neck, open that mouth, don't look where you shouldn't! And remember: don't disobey your master!'

I readied my fingers, cracked up the voice, took a deep breath, and let it loose: 'Good evening, little ladies, little gentlemen: we have quite a show for you. Are you reeeeeaddyyyyy?'

And I cheered the cheer of children in awe: obediently they chant a marveled yes, and so I go on. 'Well then, let us delay no longer. This here,' and at each of the presentations, I made bow the appropriate puppet, 'this here is the father, this one here is the mother, this the young son, and this the daughter. This one is the tyrant, and this one the rebel. And the rest of the band, well you'll meet them in all their glow.'

I simulated a thunderous approval, I cheered a loud yeay. 'Our spectacle is titled: *The Revolt of the Marionettes*. Hope you enjoy the show.' Clap again, yeay again, let the first act begin!

The Revolt of the Marionettes

Act I, Scene 1
The tyrant walks in, surrounded by two ministers.

Tyrant: The times are bleak. The populace is agitated. I have instituted all the policies. I have attempted all tactics. There is a foul smell in the air. I tell you, I do not like what I sense.

First minister: It will pass, Sir, this also will pass. The excitement is temporary. They cannot fathom a better reign.

Second minister: Sir, there is no danger. The restlessness is an illusion. The widespread discontent—that is only a rumor. You have nothing to fear.

Tyrant: Perhaps you are right. I can only hope that you are. Still, I will take the necessary precautions. Let's see... Hmmm... Have the son of the barber arrested. He has been most unruly in his neighborhood. Have him rest a few nights in chains, in the haystacks. That might change his mind a bit!

First minister: Immediately, Sir.

Second minister: Immediately Sir, we will get on it at once.

The two leave hurriedly. The tyrant stands alone.

Scene 2

Tyrant: A darkness has swept upon this land. Will I vanish Satan or Saint? What I would give, to see the nights ahead!

Scene 3
Two soldiers rush in, dragging the older son of the barber.

Son (enraged): You will perish like all the rest! Your days are numbered, you worthless tyrant! You are a beast!

Tyrant (to the soldiers): Take him away. He will learn to speak as he should. Go now, away with him!

Scene 4
Two other soldiers hurry in, before the others have left.

First soldier: Sir, there is a crowd assembled in front of the palace. They are restless and chanting for the downfall. Shall we fortify the premises?

Tyrant (to the audience): Night is upon me at last! The hour to perish has arrived! I am doomed! *(Turning to the soldiers)* No, no! No, don't do anything... Do not act hastily, I mean. I will go myself. I will address them myself. Prepare the pulpit. I will be out shortly.

I was still fully engaged in the first act of my play that I noticed, across the room, another marionette lying on the ground. Taken as I was by the appearance of the forsaken statuette, which I had not detected before, perhaps because of a superficial scanning of the area, I considered abandoning, momentarily anyway, my improvised play. I thought better of the rupture however, and so decided to carry on. 'Quite a packed first act!' I chuckled to myself. 'I hope the children are liking it!'

Act II, Scene 1
The tyrant stands before the masses in the public square.

Tyrant: I too, am weary of these conditions, my people. I too, am weary of the lies. I too call upon you to shed the veils, and to build our world anew.

Voice from the crowd: You're nothing but a monster, you tyrant! Down with the tyrant!

Other voice from the crowd: Your time has come, old rogue! Better go peacefully than have your head cut off! Down with the tyrant!

Crowd: Down with the tyrant! Long live liberty!

The father of the captive has come forward.

Father: Free my son, old tyrant! He has done nothing to you! He is a hero of this land! Don't be a coward, free my son at once! Your time has passed!

The mother, by the father's side, is weeping.

Mother: Free my son, old tyrant! Let go of my son!

Crowd (in unison): Let go of the barber's son, old tyrant!

Tyrant: I will do as I must, my people. Fear not for your lives or your liberty. I am among you now, and I will stand aside when the time has come.

Another voice from the crowd: The time is now, you old tyrant!

Crowd: Down with the tyrant, long live liberty!

Exeunt the townspeople. The tyrant stands alone.

Scene 2

Tyrant: And now I stand alone, above this bottomless abyss. They will not heed my call. The hour has passed, they will not hear my words. (*Mimics a speech to the crowd*) I am not the one who held you captive! Not I, who brought you this calamity! Not I, who fashioned this fate! I am not the one who brought forth the Night! It is not I! (*Speaks slowly again*) I will call for a world without the night! But they will not heed the call. The hour has passed...

73

——■——

I still had time before the final spectacle and decided to carry on with the play in front of my invisible audience. Undisturbed by any structural (or cultural!) obligation, I resolved to end the show in the next segment. I brought out the tyrant and recited his final plea—'The Last Warning of the Tyrant'—in which he warned the citizens of fatigue and of easy seduction. Therein also, he claimed to have been a benevolent tyrant, a man of good intentions, of wise principles. Little, he added, would change in their lives, unless they awakened fully from their essentially inanimate state (this one amused me to no end). Still, he is driven out with a chorus of admonition, and the crowd rushes to the pulpit and hails the dawn of the new day, of the new order, of a world without the night! The bold one stands and leads. He sings the new song and warns of complacency. 'We must fight and struggle!' he proclaims loudly. 'We must free ourselves from the tyranny of our lives. Each to each, and one for all! And the burdens off our backs!' The delirium then ends with the chant of the crowd, and, I beckoned, the swollen crowd, those other witnesses, the other accomplices, yes, the audience itself, the sure-fire glee of the children-spectators!

Phew, I let out, that was quite a trip! I then slowly detached the marionettes and walked towards the sofa. I put aside the many objects scattered atop and plunked myself in, now ready to truly idle away some time by the Judicious Doing of Absolutely Nothing, my efforts at improvisation and the constant shift of the voice exhausting me to no end. I surveyed the room, alone, seated and unwilling to budge for a moment even. My attention was soon cast again upon the marionette I had noticed during my performance, but which I had quickly put out of my mind as I attempted to finish the work at hand. Strange it seemed that, it lying so close to the door, I would have failed to notice it upon my entrance. Stranger it would have been though, I granted to my own silent doubts, that this was not the case: for only two options remained: that it had materialized willingly during my presence from parts unknown, or that another object in the room, perhaps even another puppet, had

cunningly transformed! 'The Metamorphosis… of the Mario-
nette,' I laughed! As I was unwilling to move, curious yet still
lacking in that brand of demonic obsession that at times drives
me, I judged that rest was foremost among my desires, and
that for once, I would honor the pleadings of limbs and mind
alike. 'No rush anyhow!' I ruminated, as to the matter of the
puppet by the entrance. 'It can wait.'

My playful fable temporarily halted, I recalled that the his-
tory of the string and the birth of the puppets had not gone
uncontested. Had, in fact, sparked some impassioned debates
in the early parts of the eleventh century. One most zealous be-
liever, to begin with, had vociferously argued, and this without
shame, that the original idea for the marionette and the subse-
quent development of the theatrical medium had come about
in the earliest of societies, and that, in fact, this was an extension
of the theological monism that had been embraced by the first
civilizations—by this he meant, tautologically enough, those
very monist societies—in order to celebrate the controlled des-
tiny that they professed, their intimate love of god, and the
unbreakable bond they had with their maker and their guide,
without whom their slightest movement would have been im-
possible. Man was free, he asserted, but only so far as he rec-
ognized the limitations of his capacities, only inasmuch as he
willingly accepted, celebrated in fact, his prescribed fate, the
one and only. Although this line of thought had acquired quite
a following, it was just as vehemently opposed. The *maître-à-
penser* (clear the throat!) of the second group proclaimed that,
far from reproducing the willing submission of humanity to a
god omniscient yet unseen, the play of the marionettes, having
its origins in the earlier primitive societies—and not, as his
rival would have it, in his own 'civilized' version—enlivened
the perpetual need of the populace to renew itself, to contem-

plate its own condition, and to constantly measure the merit of rebellion—a liberty from all shackles, visible or veiled. The very opposite of the first line, it could logically be argued: to promulgate the fallacy of Fate. 'Nonsense,' responded a third group, with a following inarguably minimal compared to the other factions, and whose leading theorist was known to be a drunkard himself. 'It is neither an embrace of the determined path,' he claimed, 'nor the perpetual call to a willed destiny. No my good men, it is plain and simple entertainment. I come, I watch, I cheer or I hiss, and I go home—if I have one! That's all there is to it: no morality play, no message, no lesson, not an illustration of anything! Nor will it be able to sustain its current level of popularity. An art form destined to disappear, bound for extinction, and there is no merit in debating the case. Besides, children seem to get much more of a kick out of it than we do.' The prediction had not come fully to fruition, but it was true that in subsequent eras, the genre lost favor in most parts of the globe. It did not die out fully anywhere, but it was indeed constricted to small showcases, with audiences comprised mostly of children.

76

The debate never raged again as it had in such distant regions, but the aesthetic of the marionette play was taken up again in 19—, when one most ambitious and provocative scientist, researching the topic in his off-hours, an avid fan and a healthy enthusiast—he was, by profession, a heart-surgeon—had fashioned a new interpretation, with evidence culled from various sources and gleaned from various archives, not all of which could be verified—and which, predictably, provided the opportunity for the skeptics and the naysayers, not to mention his personal enemies, to ridicule and vilify the good doctor. He claimed, in a paper published surprisingly in a leading scholarly journal, that the significance of the marionette play had been established, from the very beginning, in the paradox of 'The Tail in the Tale'—as he had proudly, bemusedly, coined the pun. (Carried away in private, he seems to have been highly tempted to present his case in the lame name of 'The Tail in the Tale of the Tale'—only to be discouraged, at the eleventh hour, by a wiser friend.) In other words, of the story, imaginative, free, unattached, and the medium: where the mechanical control and the manipulation of all gestures, contradict deeply, the fabric of the performance. He had, furthermore, insisted on the singular importance of the imaginative and the fabulous in that fabric. Contrary to popular belief, he had argued, neither the first plays, nor any of those that followed in other parts of the planet, had ever merely played out, performed, as it were, an already ensconced tenet of one doctrine or another. Far from depicting the primordial dogma of any faith or a crucial episode in the genesis of a sect, far from demanding the rejection of any edicts, and far more than mere entertainment, the plays enlivened the central paradoxes of their own artistic creation: 'Bound and made, malign product of places and tongues, still the artist never ceases the story,' he had argued passionately if not wholly convincingly. 'It is senseless and it is not. There is a dance, and there is not.' The marionette play, the generous doctor had argued, perhaps in haste and in uncontrolled enthusiasm, was, *in itself*, in essence, 'already an aesthetic principle, an entire vision, in fact: no summarizing, no explaining, no translating, no transferring. It is One, or it is not!'

    The valiant efforts and the tireless ethic were easily silenced. The issue subsided, without so much as the origin, the history, the significance or any other relevant detail about the medium itself truly revealed. 'If only I could give them one,' the doctor had murmured in defeat (or so the rumor goes), 'but alas, I am only a repairman of hearts!'

———◼———

I finally deemed myself rested enough to stand and walk the few paces to the puppet by the door. Inquisitive yet inexplicably cautious, I at first merely bent at the knees and looked at the small statuette from above, whence I detected a kooky feel, and an uncanny resemblance to a face, an image, that, despite my best efforts, I simply could not place. I rotated my head, a different angle, still at a distance, still bent only at the knees, but was not better informed. I finally crouched next to the doll and proceeded to pick up the curious object. It appeared to be a bit smaller than the others but remained as well constructed and clothed as the rest. The string was attached, and it seemed as though, for reasons I'm unwilling to describe in detail, this particular statuette had recently been used. It may have been the less dusty cover—was there in fact less dust?—or a dampness I felt that may have derived from the sweat of a previous purveyor. Of that I could not be certain, since my own hands had perspired a good deal themselves. Still, something was askew about this particular marionette, and my irritations, as well as an atypical sense of urgency, were both increasing as my inability to place the source of my agitation, and my inability to construe the provenance of the doll itself, both grew without respite. What had I seen that I could perhaps link to my troubled judgment? What had I witnessed as of late that could awaken such deleterious sensations within me at a most unexpected hour? Or was this written after all? Had I not premonitions from the early morn? What was so particular and peculiar about this day that after a life in the theatre, I could not place the sources of the disturbance? Is this where I was meant to be?

Troubled and increasingly perturbed, I paced around the room, grown man with a doll in my hand, and a string on

78

its back. Another relapse into old childhood habits? I wondered. More delusions? Or was I experiencing, unaware and undaunted, in this backstage of the great hall, the equivalent of a mystical revelation? I could not tell for certain, but what I was sure of was this: I was pacing faster and faster, my senses on the edge of unencumbered flights. My heart was pounding indeed, the limbs were shaking, my hearing ever more acute. It seemed as if the walls were tightening, as if the ceiling was inching closer and closer to the ground. I felt a coming calamity, an unstoppable force. I turned, and back, seeking a hidden savior, my feet on their own, running around the room: furiously around, there was no stopping it, no way at all, it was, yes, again, inevitable...

'Faster!' I yelled suddenly, not knowing the provenance of my exclamation! 'Faster, go on, faster!'

Thundering it was! As if the coaxing of a charlatan! And yet, I had not willed it, not willed it—that much I knew! Was I possessed? Haunted? Overtaken? Quivering now a maniac in unnamed labyrinth I? 'Can't delay it again now, not this time, not this time!' Surely the first symptoms of folly creeping upon me, I thought, sliding within my soul, pitiless, demonic! Which was my heresy that I among *these* dolls would burn, I asked? Whence the blasphemy that summoned *this* punishment? All luster was now gone from my visage, to be sure! Pallid as a ghost I stumbled across the room! Like an aged, vanquished buck tottered I in that vault! My own sepulcher among the dolls, I cried! I like them among them in death, I cried! Dormant proctors of mirth, assemble and rescue the feeble knave! I let fall the marionette, rushed to the window and pulled the blind. A strong gust came through, the wisp of the wind as if a scream had entered also. The sheets flapped, the pages of *The History of Perfidy* turned wildly. Maps and

79

manuscripts flew across, and my monster fell off the shelf as the strong current raced to the other side.

'It's now or never!' I heard again. 'Now or never, don't be a fool!'

O spirit of Satan! O Dawn of Darkness! What were my follies that such a fate was bestowed?! Had I forgotten anything in the book?! Did I not stay true enough?! I have been a wanderer all of my life, I yelled, is this the terror I must suffer!

For I wish not to burden you any further with undue suspense, O guiltless, O gritty, O hapless reader, I wish not to misguide: for I knew now, I knew, it was none other than that throaty Pest, the ubiquitous grit and traitor to all solitary souls, that shaky instrument of the gods and breath of bawdy spirits, say it loud, say it clear, that guileless soldier invading again, fomenter of discord, charmer and provocateur at once, anarchist fiend, collaborator supreme, it was, it was the one, the only, none other than the voice, *the* voice, *my* voice, clamoring unclad, my own voice, clamoring, uncalled!

Prompting this capricious soul to pace madly around the room, searching in vain for the appropriate dagger! I paced, dazed, knocking down the statues, tearing apart the sheets, throwing the dolls at my feet! I lifted the imaginary map, the only one of its kind, and tore it to pieces! I tore the pages of the dusty *Dictionary* and ripped apart the volume! With one swipe, I had cleansed the world!

'You're being a coward again!' I shouted unwillingly. 'Did you not launch the crusade? Did you not summon the scream!' Unrecognizable to myself even: but there was no doubt, no doubt at all, I felt my lips quiver, I sensed my throat in thrall! Incomprehensible syllables rushed out of my mouth at speeds unfathomed! Unknown words clamored, the breath of another through me! I am possessed, I thought, truly possessed!

Faster and faster I went, sensing the end, flapping of arms, tap-dancing feet, blubbering and wailing, murmurs now, now the maniacal thrusts of the head: uncontrolled, uncensored: madness is upon me I'm certain of it, I shrieked, madness is upon me at last!

Exhausted and draped in sweat, surrendering to a dominion I could not recognize, I sped to a scythe I had noticed on the wall, clung to it as if my own, and began swinging wildly, swinging the arm and the scythe, twisting as I stumbled from side to side. But there was only laughter in the room, only laughter, laughter of my voice as I swung the scythe like a warrior in the desert sand alone. And then, finally, as a moment of respite somehow came upon the haunted chamber, I fell to my knees. No screams, no laughter—I had merely ceased all movement, I had ceased all mumbling.

Teary-eyed and in shambles I was. A monument to cowardice I was. I loathed the next step even, weary of the next world's designs. But I managed a heave, I slowly pulled myself up, I examined the surroundings, I inspected the destruction I had wrought. There was not a sound. I glanced right, glanced left, glanced around, then looked at the ceiling, and finally, took a few moments of rest! But then, again, suddenly, faster even, I felt once more the quivering of my lips...

This time however, emboldened by a strange resolve, with a scythe in one hand and the invisible sword in my grip, mad as I was, with silence I clamored back: by somber alleys, memory before the war before the birth before the fire, buried among sand-dunes among the clouds of refuse among: the hand, in the breeze blowing the veil, by a roadside with rising dust: Ahhhh, I gasped, now silence saddling the voice, I will not take heed, shall not take heed, I must go on, I also hold a dagger in my hand!

Relentlessly though, pitilessly, louder still, ever more cruel, ever more, my voice carried on, ruthlessly on, endlessly on! Banter and bull! Loud and crazed! Tataa, Tataa! I walked and stumbled around, pacing, looking for the marionette I had dropped upon the first assault. For now I sensed it, I saw what it was, I recognized the cold, dour gaze, I recognized the familiar grin!

Voice: You'll never find me, you'll never get me, never do without me! I told you, I've told you! Always with, never wither! Always with, never wither!

Silence: I walked alone in desolate streets among the unseen, unfazed: I saw from afar the halt, the march, with sorrow at the altar of dawn, how to tell those unknowing: hail and hollers and hair flowing arms like wings extended demanding the presence of the gods: here, now, on a bridge aloof over a river that flows, a city that drowns at the fall: with the streak of light on water, a stranger in the mist, peering, staggering, through poles and railings and wires, at the masts of ships, at the waves and the swaying boats in the port, crumbling...

I was whisked away from the urban boulder, blinded, led into the secret chambers:

I wondered who they were, frightened again, pleading, but no one hears, no one sees, their songs, among them not of them...

Another enters the room, I felt it, the hush, the beat... Slides in the room, tenebrous chambers, inspecting them all, us all, ordering the beheading, no other way: to the cliff, the abyss, the yards, all were taken in turn: commotion and shifting loci, boisterous howls, offerings to pavements and to walls: the echo reigns, drumbeats and heads buried in hands, opening wide face of the scream a sigh its muse: along the riverbank they gaze, all in line, their horizon a grainy hue of gray, along the river the fever of the lost: suspended held, praised or plundered, here, now, surrounded: the ordeal, the ritual, the seven tasks! But the silence was never raped—and so I passed!

I was spared then, hailed, lauded and cheered: the blindfolds came off, greetings all around, they congratulate, I am among them, unnamed and saved, above the river atop the bridge, in the fields and the roads and murals of the city under the sun, in this private hideaway, after dusk, in these quarters, forever more and immortal, a brethren in silence: another shadow is born in the night...

Voice: They remember you, they know you, they'll want you again, again the ship, again the sail, again and again: tell the tale, stop the barter, tell the tale!

O Spirit of the Night, a Rage in the Room of Play, a Rave in the Room of Chance: madman that I am, I will carry on, I will, I will!

I had now arrived at the marionette and picked it up. The confusion within me swirled—that sinister pose, that treacherous smirk! I carried the marionette to the stage I had earlier used (how long ago that seemed), I pushed aside, violently, all of the debris, all of the scattered pieces, all of the shattered pieces—ah this stage on which I had earlier played out the drama, played out *The Revolt of the Marionettes*! I found a random handle and placed it in the front of my stage. I took one of the dolls and snapped off the string. O metamorphosing marionette, now is your hour finally come, I sang in revenge. I tied the new string around the neck of my standing puppet and raised the doll to the stage of insurrection: all was set again, all was ready, here we go. Silence. Voice. The Quarrel, the Duel. 'In the name of the father,' I thundered, and paused. In the name of god, the compassionate, the merciful—and I pulled the bottom from my ravenous raven! O my suspended marionette, I feigned in tears... But the marionette, to my astonishment, on the string, dangling, seemed alive, alive still, still alive…

A frenzy unfathomable charged through my veins. A fear unimaginable. A jolt inconceivable. Distress unspeakable. It cannot be hung, I mumbled in dismay! It cannot be hung, I shuddered again! It cannot be hung, I clamored louder and louder, it cannot be hung, the marionette cannot be hung! And as the tremors increased, and so the furious pounding of my failed heart, terrorized, once more I heard the quivering of my lips: 'I'll never die!' bellowed I. 'I'll never vanish, never go, madman, never rid of me! Always be there the voice always there the voice I'll never die!'

But this same barter enveloping the air, in an instant had quickly waned. I ceased also, peculiarly, strangely: and, as a curious calm invaded the room, I quivered no more…

I raised my head, which I had bowed in defeat, and saw, before me, a marionette dangling as if dead. Quietly, I approached. I untied my makeshift noose, I strung the marionette around my fingertips, placed it on stage and began to play: 'I'll never die!' I imitated the voice. 'Never die, always there the voice, never die, always with, never wither!'

And as if overrun by some potent force, I burst suddenly into an uncontrollable laughter, wriggling in pain, holding stomach and bending knees, on the ground rolling in the room, stumbling by windowsill by the monster and the maid, the scythe and the stage, in the great hall, by the wall, the door and the shelf, through me my own devilish roar: I will never die, I repeated, always with, will not wither, never will wither—always with, never wither:

So

I hovered above the statue in the public square, circled around and descended finally, leaning, sulking, one arm, one wing, raised, in the portrait of the peering angel against which I rested. As if Orpheus captured in a photograph at the moment of the turn, before the crumbling, revealing the sites of past lives: before the fall, speaking mask, before the fury at the ancient orgy. In fanciful flights again, blasts from the past (if you will): framing the ties and the binds, landscape and belonging...

—■—

I sat here a fortnight ago, I whispered at the site of other gazes, I remember: there were no windows, no entryways, no statues. I sat on an old bench, straight-ahead my glacial stare: these people before me, I pondered, crossing in all directions, the chatter among them unheard, sounds of engines, the motorists, such common surroundings: no secret lust, no esoteric characters, no chance encounters: no illuminations or prophecies, only tremors. I sat there as I had walked in the other cities' streets, thoughtless almost, it was already decided, it was already known, there was nothing to make of it...

Leaning against a wall with neon around and peddlers amidst the noise of the cars and trucks and the horns, in the magic choreography of chaos: looters dormant in the angry eyes, the hurried gaits,

the sudden shrieks: bustle in the circle,

the sidewalks, the side streets,

the running, the rushing, the shoving, hidden beasts within, skipping, longing, gentle souls, bereaved, climbing steps and holding hands,

how the seducers slide among them revenants, lying helpless

on pavements,

ruminations of the dead, or the dying.

On rooftops the tilt of the corbels,

the graceful glides above of the cirrus:

a woman who walks with a cane, alone, a merry singer who

whistles hip tunes, a widow on a rocking chair on the balcony

back and forth: the hookers

and their pimps,

the beggars, the players,

on park benches the neighbors, the snorers,

the snorters: a simple whirl,

arms extended,

and the world about begins to turn,

maniacally turn, as on any other night,

around me the lights, flickering, circling

the endless dark,

around the fountain, by the merchants and their pleadings,

the high-rises and the tenements and the projects all into one,

lifting one leg, swirling on the other, quickly crouching in

the pose of a made-up war dance,

twisting, all of the stars, the chimneys, the domes and the

flags atop flagpoles, red heartbeat flashes warning planes or

remembering martyrs,

the echoes of ancient commandments,

the calls of the muezzin,

all into one,

a kaleidoscope of motions and sounds, of shades and hues:

of untold tales, and unnamed truths—.

In those hours of silent musings and mazes afloat, in the

saunters among night shadows and festive spirits,

with those frivolous songs in unknown tongues, with strangers of faraway worlds and imaginary bands:

awkward in the city's fogs: sitting on stools guiding forbidden plays or perched guarding from high above:

from high-towers and vaults: from the windowsill spying on the creatures below:

I see myself in daunting flights, with muted verses coalescing into traces I had only to unleash, nourished by another gaze, another's glance:

I hear the proud scream of a crier rebelled,

I hear the echo of abandon, echo of restless wanderings, of lightness and laughter, of steps in the alleys, by the wharves, surrounded by silhouettes holding hands, encircling, in a dance...

———■———

Above the rooftops again and the river and the cupola, to the site of another landing, of long-ago into stranger lands, of the first paces, the early signs: the descent, finally, on a carousel, a giant carousel in all colors with horses and elephants and antelopes and giraffes moving up and down and all around: up down and all around they went with happy tunes blaring, bathed in red and pink and green and blue, drowning the noises of nature in their mirth: I descended straight unto the saddle of a white Persian horse (wooden, granted), held one hand on the giant pole crashed into the horse's skull and into the arched roof above, the other held apart as if a showman on a stage with pizzazz.

A boy adjusts himself on the swing—tries to, anyway, can't seem to get the handle even though he is the only one in this whole playground. A football game in the courtyard later on, that's the word, a miniature game of baseball: with four bases all close to each other, no one knowing what to do, a racquet-bat, throwing the ball. Hoop deals, hook shots, fake dives: kicking again and again a dumb ball against a small wall, searching around for the wrong kinds of gloves.

'Hey,' the others shouted at times when I sat alone on the slope, 'wanna play?'—

…but I waived my hand and shyly looked sideways… not even understanding what they—say!

Such empty spaces, expanded fields so flat and green, the roadways so wide…

Fast-moving cars on multilaned roads and big highways go Vroom! Vroom!… The land where the deluded think they have been saved, the exiles, only because they have left these hollow sites, these grounds of first refuge… Still pathetic all of them, but on the deathbed they will groan and wonder, sigh and mumble: this blandness so marvelous to us, these were the fields outside the garden to which we were pointed…

I: was the one newborn in the margins: dangling on tears their screams, the fate of us, far away from doom, but here the most wicked gloom I've seen…

I am the one now in the darkened cities and alleys where the ravaged ones walk hollering to the heavens unforgiving: I am the one whose portrait of glass is painted on the sidewalks of Bazaars and the atrium of unreal Halls:

I am the child of the wallclimbers and flagbearers and chanters and rhymers and postercarriers and fistraisers and killers and the killed: on these grounds why these grounds I tread: alongside a heathen, circled assembled dazed—babbling the smile of buffoons fixed on my face. Which alleyway which: is the dust ridden path to the savior's shelter? Where are the ravens and the maidens? Where is the tavern of imagined souls, the haunted gambling house of merriment among the damned?

A wanderer, at last, sitting, behind the mirrored doors, on the sand? Where?

I, am the child of the fragments and the torn. In infancy silenced now disciple of the gaze: I am the child of the fire of the flame, I am the child of the shrieks before the antelopes, I am the child of the fallen at the square, the first bearer at the morgues of paradise: I am the blinded but the vision, the muted but the cry:

I: am the child of the revolution!

Here, I stand, again, of memory—telling: *here,* is where I know: a glass veiling then's whispers… What a silly place to have come, really! Even the shopping center and the mart and the road and the trees haven't changed: no structures of centuries ago, no sir! Just an open expanded field and the pointless complex which if it didn't exist would change absolutely nothing! Say it just like that, that's how it should be said: what bland and boring and bare locales that make up our birthplaces! The little boy will be lost, the little boy will be gone: new era with the phrase, how to talk, watch the brothers on the tube, the beginning of the new! Still, no one predicts, not yet, that the world, that world, is falling apart: this is where I know…

89

I, am the child of the revolution…

Now these kids who giggle, who are giggling… On the swing, tummy on top, one lets fall his slippers and kicks them as the swing goes back and forth. 'This is too funny,' says the partner on an adjoining swing. 'You wanna do it again?'

To which the first responds by doing exactly that! (They're about seven, eight, I should know, and the mother is here, reading her… novel. If she asked me: who are you, or if she said, hello, I would mutter simply: I was born here—again—did you know—a long time—ago…)

'A fir tree stands now,' I mutter aloud. 'Was it there—in the front of that room that was my first, here?'

A stranger had now appeared as the carousel went round and round without a whimper. A stranger sitting backwards on the elephant in front, going up as I went down, and, you guessed it, down as I went up. He had appeared moments before, chin on hands, bespectacled, his bent elbows resting on nothing.

'Let's go,' he said finally, as it seemed the monologue had come to an end. 'It's time to go.'

On a first floor terrace giving into this dull parking lot, an old man plays a guitar and sings: seated before him, his private audience, the members of his family, doubtless... There was a guitar player there too, a guitar player... I remember him, he played on a bench alone, I watched him, before—and now...

—I, am the child of the revolution...

The stranger interrupted again, insisting that it was time to go, really, that it was better to go.

'Fine!' I replied. 'Fine!' And as we walked away, I could not avoid, the last look, at dusk, did not avoid, a last turn.

———◼———

Now from dome to dome, from the gravestone to the archway of convents, from the cradle to courtyards of prayer and worship, from the crest of vicious waves to the swirling storms, from the lamps hanging to the bells of churches, from the sacred terrains to the peak of minarets, from balconies to belvederes, swinging chandeliers and majestic cirques: the skips and flights, giant steps and flapping of wings, the swooning, the carousing, the glides:

January 15: This morning, under the roof of the courtyard, a bully confronted his daily prey. His friends stood and joined

in the teasing. Administration of head slaps to the poor help-
less lad. But he did not cower anyway, even though he gave
away some coins and all his food. Cruel rite of passage, I guess,
and no one dared intervene. I watched them too, the shameless
thugs, and the pranksters around the corner delighting in clev-
er ruses. Later, some young rebels were hoisted with much fan-
fare after a hard-fought victory: cheers to them and their lovers
in their arms, hip hip... Some kept shyly to themselves, a few
huddled by a pole, I looked at the scene from afar, alone...

January 20: At noon today, everyone came together outside the
cafeteria. A big football game in the snow. The snow and the sun,
everyone in good spirits. And the exam? I thought hard, what to
do, hadn't studied much. Forget it and play, I thought. Play the
great football game in the snow, that's what you'll remember ten
years down the road. And I did. And am glad. The exam came
and went. But the game... More than twenty of us. Everyone
laughing and yelling. Unforgettable, frankly... I have a sense
though, that the consciousness of future penchant for remember-
ing, might... spell the downfall—wherefore? I wonder...

January 29: Memory up to old tricks, I can sense it. The im-
ages loom, from so long ago. The fields and the court, the gym
and the hallways, the classroom even. Shooting paper balls and
real balls, paper planes and toy cars. Merely walking in the
corridor and the sudden detachment. As if I were not here
anymore, not *among*... The sounds, their voices, their eyes,
the movements... The contests and the challenges, the lies that
are told, the desires unsatisfied, the lust ignored... As if I were
summoned to witness—and one day... To hear their grief...
But I'm going off... Drivel probably... (Divine watcher walk-
ing in school corridors I...)

February 3: The detachment of a few days ago has not
dissipated at all. A sense, in fact, that this is the chosen lot.

91

Without being chosen of course, the irony. (Fate, for god's sake, and I can't believe I'm even pronouncing the word!) A sort of perpetual conversation, *and* evasion *and* battle— with Death and all its incarnations, all its cloaks. And yet, as if it were this same perpetual duel, coexistence maybe, that allowed the Work. From beginning to end and back, and again—that allowed the burst into the adventure—the transmutation of all—as if the burden and the farce. (What burden, what burden!) And they all coalesce. An answer of sorts. Ultimate triumph of a *theory*. The accompanying levity. After the fall.

February 5: I tried to explain it, but it didn't work. And I won't try again. Nothing to say. It only confirmed my worst misgivings. It seems indisputable to me and I shall perhaps reap its (fiery? thankless?) consequences. Where to, this cult of possibility?! This worship of ambiguity?! To oblivion, I know... And beyond! Add to the volatile mix the insufficiency of existing classifications—this obsession with categories!— and the picture, as they say, ain't so pretty. The seduction of the genre... Soothing melody of partnership of course, of prosperity even, *and* posterity! How to combat this? Or, is it, after all, a *battle*? (I'd like to think not... There must be a lightness, a peace, within... Stranger to all tongues, inhabiting them nevertheless... Allow them to traverse *me*... Pluck them away, petal by petal... In their center, not only at the margins, into a whole... And the impossible verbs, the nonexistent verbs, all at once...) What the answer is? Masks and selves—masks and selves—masks and selves! (Prosopopeiaaaaaa! Hold back the ecstasy—The Speaking Ones...)

February 7: At V.'s—Parody of a secret society game. A competition of sorts. He dimmed the lights. We sat around holding hands. His room. Sitting in a circle close to a candle, in hushed voices. 'Against poetry, the novel, the play,' chuckled the good host to start us off, 'and all their brethren!' Everyone gasped and the game began. 'Thank you O deities for disallowing the acquiescence to the foolishness,' the first began, 'and for disallowing belief in the hideous idiocies and the forlorn rituals,' uttered the next, 'and obedience to the laws and the mantras and the path,' said the third, 'and entrapment by your creatures or your monikers…' And so on until the last—whoever is stuck or can't find another phrase is out, until there's one left, the winner, of course! New games, that's the ticket. None taken too seriously, vagrant chaps, gypsies at heart, pure kingdom of blasphemy.

Sometimes, after the improvised drudgery, I would stumble to concerts and halls, to drunken eves in forbidden places, resting in gaudy corners: dreamful days painted with glee, bellyful of laughs or groans, gratitude galore, admonition too, landscape framed with—funk.

February 9: I watch the big band play the swinging music. I see the couples dancing. They stop, but the band keeps playing. A drunken man, stumbling, in coat and tie, goes up to the dance floor alone at the next song. He dances alone. People look at him dance alone. No one knows why drunken men dance at the music of big bands alone. No one knows whether to ridicule him, to pity him, to admire him. To like or dislike him. But when he's finished, everyone claps and the lone man of the dance floor takes a few bows. (And then there are those who stare at him, stare at the drunken man on the dance floor alone…)

Later, I walked to the diner (its neon lights shining in the night): open around the clock, with the waitress and her greased-up hairdo and her white apron over pink blouse. Money on the counter and I plunk down on round stool. Quickly

93

served. Sitting, blank, again, alone. At the open all night diner, the *Say 'n' Sigh Café*—my kingdom, my home.

———■———

I stood now, incredibly, for it seemed impossible indeed, I stood, on the edge of the pointed steeple itself, both arms expanded as if to embrace all of the sky, back arched, hair flowing, as if offering or singing paeans, to air. The stranger, meanwhile, had followed, motives fuzzy still: holding on with one hand to the eaves suspended in midair, he smoked, coolly, with the other, his cigarette.

'And yet,' I continued from the outpost in the clouds, 'there is no one here now... No one at all... Not a single soul... Not a single soul...'

What if someone found us?

What if someone like me, from then, came, at this same exact hour, here, to stand, stare, and breathe?

What then?

What light gleaming through the trees and the frame of the window...

February 12: Dashes through streets, quick lunge, sharp turns, big grin. Arms pumping, feet a wee bit above ground, smitten sprinters floating, rapidly changing clothes, flashes of former selves. Down Memory Lane, marching, mocking, greeting: slowed to a stroll, darting and back, skipping two-footedly joined at ankles hands down by the side touching all the way that's the rule. I look up, not a cloud in the sky, hey hey, bright shiny day:

Ohoy, Ohoy! They clap in the stands! Hugs and kisses! We've won! On the last play! At Homecoming! Believe it! Out in the parking lot sure they're having fun but then again they're missing this! The most avid fans have rushed the field, too many of them to hold back, hanging on for dear life...

On to the party, everyone, on to the feast! Boom boom boom, dance away, dance away the night night night! The hip movements, the twists, hold me by the hand now don't let go, waltzing and schmoozing, cheers and sneers, chug chug chug: tubes down throats and barfs down bins, crawling fourleggedly doing shots shots shots, naked prancing around with a necktie on mind you, quite a proper prim one too for the future executive baring all on this eve! Smokes now, grass hash and speed which will it be which will it be none for us thanks, fun while it lasted, leave the perimeter, pass out as they say, where to, to the room, best refuge, morning high. Haze in between, don't look now. Pass barely, groovy, get out. First tremors again, agitation of long ago, lonesome strolls in the halfcity capital of the free. Sinful calls to seductive hustlers: on rooftops again behind railings dangling. On benches extended legs crossed arms chin in chest toe to air zombie-like staring: what the, what the, what the—where to: climb that pillar, jump the mother, mug the sucker, shoot:

A memoir (—fragment): I arrived through what seemed an unreal landscape. Barren for the most part, through vast, empty fields, with steeper hills in the distance, a countryside drowned in mist by the time dusk came around. The other passengers were quiet, their eyes cast straight ahead or closed, their own brand of revelry, I surmised. I stepped out at the appropriate station, out and into the tiny square, where I sat on my bags with my hat on my head. They finally came, the two, one I knew, the other not. The weeks, the months, by the river in the coffee shop, in the homes and through the byways and the grand street, the only one. With sisters and mothers, neighboring aunt, daughter and grandma it's true. One afternoon, in the yard, the dog ripped down shirts hung

95

on the clothesline, ate also the socks, chewed them, rather, out of recognizable form, and, obviously, function. He then managed to work his magic on the fence, ripped that apart, and darted suddenly into the wilderness! They ran after him, a fat short woman, a tall young one, an old crippled one, a deaf bent one, hands in the air shouting at the top of their lungs… They finally caught him, for the record, dragged him back and gave him a long, cruel, whipping. Quite a sad scene, what with the huge puppy dog eyes…

I remember well, it was right before my own farewell, the morning of my own departure. With the sister next to the car, one by one the embraces, last hugs, bending and lifting with both hands finally, the suitcases, the illusion, once again, of displacement. After the strolls down fourteenth, after the torn sidewalks and the broken homes, all littered with junk and dreams, febrile fabric of our passage. After the aimless stand-around and the lazy obscenities, and the rambles unceasing and the crazy shouts of the not-so-empathic neighbor, after the fall, after the bombs. After the screams how dare I, in the company of the damned, after, the merry troupe like a carnival in the street singing beating their drums with their sticks. After the strolls unnoticed in bars, occupying a random seat, don't chat don't cry what will I do, sudden inspiration baby, show me, the way, to, the next…

Majestic city sitting in absolute quietude: inviting its con-templators to these perverse ways. There is simply no way to dodge it: I'd said my good-byes, I was gone, again. Have to constantly remain out to remain self, to forego the inclusions, for the necessary pause, to be free, and there is only one word, before, during and after, only one, what one can mean by rev-olution, revolution, in, *in,* the word. The great illuminations, here, the uncanny contemplations, the odes, the magnificent

unattachment: the train station, the glacial gaze of an exhaust-
ed bitter worker forgotten, his skin rippled by the suffering
and his cigarette how he turned, suddenly peering at me I'll
never forget. (In the staircase, the winding staircase the refuge,
the swirl into otherworlds, the slow step into other places.)
In the filthy basement hole, no heat no light no place to pee.
In this city now, this (Maria help me) street, in this city, this
snow, how does one, end up, where one, goes!

On a wintry morning in the park, while the snow, another,
covered a timeless man seated on a stoned horse, I thought of
a portrait for the spring, summer and fall: of a walker standing
before the statue of a rider on a dawn of each season, painting
the wall: despair the companion, shadow loyal still: peregrina-
tions all, wondrous, into the First Silence.

———■———

And bang! A sudden shift, a quick launch, and there: jumping
both at once unto the trapeze, flinging up and down, tumbling
through, a giant trapeze that hurls us both, high into the air,
quite a long while before it's reached again, twisting and yell-
ing upwards as we go and downwards: on the upswings and
the crashes uttering speedily this next one, a harsh one, not
easy to sing when propelled rocket-like into the beyond and
plunged back mercilessly head and heart both torn apart on
the way, but it must be done, must be done—the stranger a
parallel floater on this trek: in these worlds:

dust-tracks on which a ball rolls swiftly as young yellers dash
back and forth—

fields: strewn with grasshoppers and butterflies crushed or
caught—

walls: still unscribbled without guidance or desires or com-
mands—

streets, with names of otherheroes, nights, without shelling without flares without screams—

windows without secret watchers—

songs written and sung—strippers in gaudy places—sloped alley with abyss:

desertland between our abode and the next: it can take a lifetime recalling, but there's only fragments on this voyage, only that—and so the highwalls: before the entrance to the mausoleum, touching the arch, reaching, reaching, on the pilgrimage, shoeless with hands above the shoulders reaching desperately also to be saved: once upon a time: when the news of the first death came, I remember where I was: the young mother in tears with only one consoling friend by the side…

And the first shrieks when abandoned with the masters, the terror when stripped, for all stood and laughed, ha ha, ha ha… Fingers pointed, eyes protruded, demons inside those innocent babes… Jumping over small bootehs ablaze in corners of the city still untouched by the rage. Now I sit but mostly I stand by windowsills watching the passersby… Now and in the near future I fathom.

Convention of timid villagers surrounding incoming automobile sputtering up stone-strewn hill…

Assembly of the wicked seated in room on the pillows tea-sippingly discussing the deal…

Knockings on doors, first versions of future trick-or-treatings, after a new year…

I had arrived and gone through the gates, everything seemingly so common still…

A bearded man with a tired but joyous expression, as if victorious, as if the battle had finally been won, was heading in the opposite direction. I'm not sure what happened, don't know how we set on the topic. It wasn't even much of a conversation really, just quick exchanges, him on his way back in, I on my way out. 'How long has it been?' I asked. And he answered that it had been almost twenty years, that he kissed the ground when he stepped out on the tarmac, that he was finally home! 'Home,' he repeated, 'home!' (How could that be, I mulled, secretly, how could one stay away so long?!) I saluted and exhausted-but-victorious-so-he-thought marched his destined way: this is the last, it may be the last, memory... Before...

'But that can't be it!' the stranger dashing next to me at samespeed looking up arms pumping like his counterpart said. 'That can't be it, can it?'

'It can't!' I replied. 'You're right. It's not!'

Thus the next, the last... Remembering: a witness, of black-blouses and blackshirts at the processions with the wailing: a teller, early on of innocent tales and stinging aphorisms: a de-nier, of simple tasks and childlike obligations: desiring a few volumes more, of alchemy and mystery, of reverence and rib-aldry, of battles, illusions, and absolution: a waiter, by seasides, lampposts and yards—dangling already, maybe innate, disci-ple, always, forever, it seems, of that cunning beast!

The trapeze, on the last fall, has vanished. With a thump but incredibly without breaking the neck, whoopdeedoo, lying on the back with knees bent, pulling myself up, arms around knees for some respite, thinking suddenly, whatever became of, wondering about the tagalong stranger, who knew better, knew better than to take *this* plunge! Doesn't concern him-self with these matters anyway, that's for sure! Will come back though, promise you that, he will come back!

The task before last now, it must be done: two masked men carried me to the chambers where I sat before a faceless mul-titude. They were in darkness, they could not be seen, anon-

99

ymous silhouettes in what was a tribunal, a scaffold, a booth, an interrogation room: and a private hall, where I confessed, or so it seemed...

'There was a scent, a lure, a singer: in the night the source: muses afloat, in the street the crowd, the noise of the shots, see them scurry away, lurid, senseless, frenzied dash of the many, dance of chaos in squares in alleys the Cry: a fallen figure above away from him they flee. A fallen figure above away from him they flee. Must repeat. Vertiginous visions of the unheard, even the sky trembling, weepings in solitary alms by the riverbank, signs of storms ahead, thunder across, devoured children battling in corners in private hideaways now aflame, scrawlings of their names on their blood: Revolution Come, carry on:

'With ashes in heaps in eastern town with sprawling mosque and borders in the near: cramped watchers from doorways peering: silent accusers of marching commanders, surveyors of ghastly scenes: of lust: in streets and alleys—north, south, east, and west—beyond rivers across hills and prairies from sea—to saltless sea: blood trickles on sidewalks, on pavements, on the friends' shins and shirts: desires unfurl as they go riding carousing mindless howling horns unleashing the thirst to watch, to lick, to lap, to hurl: halted gaits, hidden faces behind the banners: the portrait of the sullen departing ones above the horseman toppled by machines, with the snarl of the hungry adrift among burnt-out buildings in backgrounds. Barracks, sirens, helmets, shields: the roaming, the rampage, the roads, revolution come, carry on:

'Across the courtyard, a silent scream: he went to the window, he watched, he saw, he must. Sped to the door, he opened, swiftly down the winding stairs. He pulled the gates and crossed, racing to the next building. He hurried up, quietly to the door, the pause. He knocked, he hollered. There was no response, not on this night, behind these closed portals: no response. He crumbled to the floor, against the steel portals, helpless: no response, only a laughter, a fiendish laughter rising on the other side, a laughter behind the door. He rose slowly, gliding along the surface, ear to steel: an evil laughter rising, unmistakable, the same voice. It was not the first time, he had seen it often, the silhouette on the wall. Now unbearable though, this laughter, he had never heard it, never stayed long enough, perhaps, never watched long enough, he would always turn away…

'Shall he knock again? If only he went back… Back down and through the main gates and across and up the stairs and back in his chambers, then perhaps… Why knock again? Go back the way he'd come, watch again through the window, he'll know something. When all is done, he'll know something. But here, as he stood behind the solid, steel doors… And the laughter had subsided… No laughter, no scream. Behind the door, there is no laughter, there is no scream… What transpired in my absence, he wonders. What happened when I furtively ran to save. Should I have stood watching, my eyes unblinking no one daring to flee… Fear alone of my eyes… But he had rushed just the same. Who was the shadow… On the wall… Was she at her desk again now? She had walked to the balcony, that much he knew. She had watched the assembly, that he knew, for he also had stood transfixed, peering below. Watched her watching even. She had gone back to her desk, this much he had seen, then turned away. And then the scream: then the shadow, only the shadow, on the wall. He must go, must hurry, he thought, cannot abandon. So he rushed, through the gates and the staircase. And now he stood behind the solid doors, wondering: wherefore the laughter, wherefore the silence.'

101

The anonymous ones sat, still, glaring at the confessor. 'Needless to say,' I concluded, 'he did not knock again. Nor did he rush. He simply descended the winding staircase, slowly… How quickly he had climbed, he marveled! In his own courtyard, the mandolin player in his torn clothes sees him but says nothing. Up his staircase exhausted to his own portals. He throws in the keys and opens the steel doors. He enters, but dares not look, from his window into hers. He does not look. He stays away. He cannot look. He will not. Carry on.'

———■———

Shelling and burning: the fire: the pillars and the portals and the halls are withering: the chandeliers crash, the galleries crumble. They stand alone amid the ruins: she stands holding aloft her arms, around her spinning in a tornado the columns, the shards and shattered glass, the bricks and bones, arches and pedestals of the monument behind her collapsing. She stands as burns the lone repository of all of this world's archives and documents, all of its manuscripts and collections, the registers, records, epics and portraits, the dreams and cycles, the myths and miniatures: volumes of wisdom and of humor, hymns and allegories, and a small book within which was contained the Whole!

Darting in and out, they braved the torches, rushed in to save all they could. But as there was no respite from the ever-rising flames, they gave up the futile effort, stood idle and bitter holding back their shrieks. A long line was made, a chain of sorts, from within the edifice to a safe distance: where, one by one, the pieces of memory exchanged hands: passed from one to another, to rescue from oblivion, stacked into a pile.

As the roar of the blaze magnified, the unbearable heat and the unsparing sway of the flames soon drove out the most dedicated of the saviors. They all stood helpless, watching before them the collapse of this great citadel, the slow crumbling of the great library. I was summoned again, the scribe, the same one, with quite a reputation to back. I waltzed in, alone, and walked to an old, rustic chair placed before a small, wooden, decaying desk, surrounded by the flames reaching into the celestial spheres, this grand coliseum of ideas, this hall of fantasy, the theatre of daring and house of affliction, all into one, all ablaze...

I approached coolly, the leather jacket came off and also the fedora, placed gently on the desk. Slowly, I sat, unabashed, unexcited. 'I cannot be untrue to myself,' I started, 'however startled I may be by this account or that, by one tale or another. I have taken a most benevolent risk, and I shall continue on that path, but I must also attend to my own duties. An unholy alliance, then, this too? Such melodies, stories after the telling, verses and seduction of strangers? The same prayers as those chanting? Occasion to be sent to the hellfire still? Again?'

I stand now and pace in the wasteland fashioned in the midst of the pandemonium. Look up and down, hands clasped behind the back, one moment thrown up in panic, the next gesturing wildly. Shaking hysterically, profusely ashamed, seething. Wind down again, sit, one leg over another, elbow on table, grasping pulling the flowing hair, peering into the flare, last sigh before the end, silence after the sigh. It will be my intention to deduce the very odyssey of the word—and it seems to me that the story of the word lies in the accumulation of its readings. It thus appears that the story is in the following catalogue that I now offer to barbarians of old, the authorities of today, and to posterity: from one universe of letters to this one, the story is the same. And then, giddy as a child, in a mood that all but banished the inferno from my thoughts, I went on to propose a Taxonomy, which consisted, in fact, of three minor variations. 'The first,' I began, 'expounds on the classifications of methods of poetic creation, inasmuch as the work is a complex web formed through the weaving of parameters, taking into account existential circulation, experiential documentation, modes of research, exploration, collection, and the scores of personal manipulations and deviations wrought upon that most cunning illusion, *reality*—offering, all the while, a compendium of cries and gazes, a veritable gold mine of turns and murmurs, an elaborate study of motions and stillness, along with, perhaps in a detrimental manner, a detailed analysis of the necessary behavior among one's own kind. The second,' I continued, briefly, and not so seriously, 'consists of a classification of readings of volumes that explore the very topic of the nature of reading.' The third and final classification, which enthralled me to no end, provoked gleeful shrieks and incited a most wondrous inner turbulence, consisted of a smooth fusion, enjoining, call it what you will, of all imaginary taxonomies and real taxonomies, impossible taxonomies, most probable or obvious taxonomies (two separate categories), pedantic taxonomies and audacious ones, encyclopedic taxonomies and taxonomies of singular, incomparable events! 'I shall in this way construct a most glorious Book,' I laughed, 'containing them All!' Then, all of a sudden, mindful of the fires raging about, I turned grave again. 'And I shall do so without dismay, with passion and without delay—for, surely, unsurpassed reverence, unchallenged as it may go, cannot fulfill one's deepest desires to determine the provenance, existence, or nature of things, or one's perhaps even more worthwhile effort at fully ignoring these! For although it can be quite fulfilling to carry on with false notions and attributions, I am convinced that such practice is contrary to my, and my people's, earnest curiosities!'

And then I began to read, read my own words, conspicuously absent from any page, this page or that, any page at all, as with each of the utterances, each of the defiant lines, the flames reached higher, surrounding even more, ever more…

'What to make of the proposition that neither I nor anyone else shall undertake such a feat,' I went on, increasingly intoxicated, 'if unguided, alone in such a battleground, powerless, merely led astray, in such a wilderness, worthy of the most abysmal of tortures and punishment?!' The flames reached higher as I carried on, daring again, unabashed: 'And what of the proposition that the ecstatic chants of the poets and the silence of the tellers, all of them shall be once more muted, for none shall follow them, none must pursue them, for they travel long and hard through the hills and valleys, seducing the perverse?!'

The flames reached higher again, higher still, an unforeseen fury, raging, raging…

In heightened stupor and in heightened rapture, in an almost trance, I rested the quill, stood and opened the book, opened and read passages, thundered and recited passages before the edifice in ruin.

'I have explained it perfectly well,' I cried. 'I have reduced nothing! In a most glorious way! I see no other option! This or nothing! I have written the Book! I have explained it perfectly well! Those who wish shall be enlightened! The ignorant will carry on! Convince without a holler! So be it: I have done my duty! There is a story and there is not! Hellfire for me if they wish! Only I cannot burn! I cannot burn!'

And I thundered and recited and the fires raging, the flames sweeping, I turned the pages and hollered the lines, a prisoner of the walls of flames, hollered and turned furtively, turned the pages, accursed and reeling, uttered the phrases and sang the songs, blabbered drunk and shrieked wildly. And as if in a most glorious show of defiance, suddenly I sprang again and turned up the head: I lifted the book, lifted the book higher, in one hand, higher and open, as if an offering, a majestic Offering, in silence, and stillness, with the fires ablaze: and the open book held before: I leafed through its pages holding it aloft, faster and faster, the book aloft now turning rapidly with the winds of the fires, the slashing winds of the fires themselves! 'You will write in your rage the tale of your own doom,' I thundered, the winds turning, turning wildly the pages of the book... 'And I will know only penance! No punishment ever! No scaffolds! None for me, thank you!' Holding aloft the Overbook in which all the lines were untraced, I began again, heretic in a trance, Heretic indeed, summoned on the occasion to save!

'Scattered!' I then cried. 'All are scattered! To the outer reaches of every isle and the farthest points of no return, all are scattered! With your own winds, to be heard and cherished! All of the words of my book scattered and held aloft, with the winds of your wrath!' For indeed, all of the pages of the book, all without exception, every single one, all of the pages were unmarked! All without a single sign!

'Scattered!' I repeated. 'Alive, always alive! Never wither always with! All there is think no more! Blasphemy, ecstasy, loony tune in a cartoon! Sing along now clap your hands, freedom is here, one for the band! Cannot wither, never wither, always with, never wither!'

And before I had closed the night, I thought again, how there was, no more all it is, no more, revolution come carry on, onward ho, carry on, never will wither, revolution come carry on, revolution, gone, carry, on...

———■———

I stared silently at the door. There was a knock. I had been waiting. The door was flung open.

'Come in,' I said, pallid and exhausted.

'You have to come out,' the voice said. 'I'm supposed to wait out here!'

A heretic, savior of memory and all of her offspring, of the self and the likeness, peering, perched and turned on the statue in the square, I, stood uneasily, marched cautiously out, the small cabin as always on the brink of a turbulent collapse, halfway on land, and a little less than half over the edge of the cliff. I stepped out, I saw no one.

'Well?' came a voice from parts unseen.

'Well what!?' I shot back, angered and threatened.

'No, no, not 'Well!', 'Well?',' the voice tried calmly to correct. '"Well?"!'

I made out the provenance and walked toward the ravine. Two hands visible only, arms outstretched, fingers gripping firmly, tight, the edge, holding on, extremities of a suspended body. A bald head was hanging down.

'I guess you can say she won,' the voice said with the head tilted downward. I bent quickly, on one knee, offered my hand to help up the hanging partner. 'No, no, that's all right, that's all right!' came the reply. 'Fair is fair, I can take it! That was the deal, I can take it!'

'What do you mean?' I shot back naively, almost innocently. 'You're not going to last long like that you know!'

He was looking up now, struggling to catch a last glimpse of his former companion. I recognized him immediately, it was he, the stranger himself, the tagalong who had accompanied, tempting me all along, dragging me away: on the carousel, in our voyage from dome to dome and roof to spire, throughout the floating dashes. Saddened enormously at the sight, I moved closer, hurled my legs over the edge, the feet playfully swaying, sitting at the edge of the cliff right next to the forlorn fellow, wicked tempter that he had been, still hanging, and whose extended arms paralleled my sitter's legs, fingers gripping still, firmly, a voice ever more sordid as the minutes ticked by.

'It was meant to be perhaps,' he let out, sarcastic and hopeless at once. 'Not of your lot to so easily take us in! I really did enjoy it though, you know. All those moments… in the streets… pumping arms and all. The time you stood on the spire of the cathedral… I wanted to… I thought you did too! That's why I volunteered. I had a feeling. Besides, I thought we got along pretty well…'

'No joke now!' he said again, struggling, his fingers sliding, his head bobbling up and down, a painful grin a fixture on the tightening face. 'This is getting pretty tough!'

'Look here now old pal,' he quipped again, 'I can't take this anymore, you gotta help me out!'

One hand had fully let go. He was hanging limply by his side, holding on with the other only, desperately clinging to the edge— desperate, futile…

'You're just sitting there!' he said again. 'Be helpful will you! Just rip the other off too and I'm out of here! Show some mercy!'

The pitch in his voice heightened, a pathetic but cynical mix of relief and sorrow…

'Make it easy now old pal, come on!' he cried anew, almost possessed. 'Come *on*!'

But then, as if a shameful confession, as if admitting to an emotional longing, startling him even, I shot back: I can't, I'm sorry, I just can't!

'Just a little *nudge*, no?' he insisted, undeterred. 'Repeat after me… One by one his fingers lift I from this edge, sending him tumbling into the endless abyss, the last spoils of my victory, my salvation, my spring…'

My hesitations revealing perhaps what I had wished eternally concealed, this time vehement and unrestrained, with no regard whatsoever for the condition of the helpless chap, in a most unseemly manner, I shouted at the old soldier: 'I can't, all right! I can't!'

And O how painful! For it was not long, not long at all, before the stranger's other hand slowly gave way, his grip gradually slipping from the cliff's edge…

Sitting next to him, unwilling to leave, unable to end the agony, I merely looked on in disgust, in private and profound grief at the unbearable ordeal.

The grip was lost, finally, the last screech and the nails scratching the inches, tumbling down, into the abyss, echo thundering then, echo thundering now, of a terrible cry, an unseemly scream: the saddened savior of memory by the cliff watching, helpless, the fall of the beloved companion, the stranger that had appeared, the one and only, the elusive one: the Angel of Forgetting…

rose from my watch-post and headed back into the appointed Hall. A most magnificent palace, one must say, with chandeliers and marble floors, with priceless ornaments and works of masters aligned on the shelves and the walls. I walked into the Hall, sat behind the desk and looked through the shutters of the window unto the sea: to which spirit must I be thankful, I thought, surrounded by such scents, by such tranquility, such silence, of the kind I have always sought! And before I had fully settled, I took in, again, the soothing sensations, this kingdom of comforting aromas, this marvelous, unequaled, dais of perfection and beauty.

I peered out through the window at the sea and the horizon: today, I thought, I must tell of the wind that was carried on the waves: I will tell of the wind that was carried on the waves...

It is possible that the morning's wind was lost at sea, I began, and that the waves of the shore rescued the wind out at sea, and that the journey to the shore of the wave that carried the wind is quite uncommon, and that we have not heard the laments of the wave, or the laments of the wind, or the laments of the sea. It is possible that the historians and the biologists, the seafarers and the voyagers, all have neglected to record the laments of the wind, the laments of the wave, the laments of the sea. I then opened a book that lay on the desk, the book of longings, the book of questions, the book where rested the meditations, where will lay to rest my world. I opened to the first page of the book and began to inscribe: *The Tale of the Wave that Rescued the Wind*—: *in which will be told the hazardous voyage of the wave out to sea, the battle of the wave with the sailor, the rage of the sea, the thunder and the storm, and the journey of the wind and the wave unto the shores of the sea.*

I paused and raised my head, a bit queasy and doubtful: maybe waves save winds out at sea all the time, I thought, and only *I* have been blind to the motions of the sea! The fishermen, at the docks, they must know: were I to ask, do you know that each day a wave, surely they would smile, backs bending, laughing, saying that of course they knew! And the barkeep, at the saloon by the sea, he must know: were I to ask him, do you know that each day, surely he would mock me, in his roaring growl, that all have known of the heroics of the waves! Each day's journey begins with this treacherous trek to the wildest waters and back to the shores of the sea, I thought, and today marks only the day of my witnessing! 'All my work is a deplorable inaccuracy,' I blurted out suddenly to no one, 'riddled with falsehoods and fabrications! I have merely come upon my own blindness!' Then I turned again to the book and wrote the tale of the wayward scribe of the sea, on the day he had learned of his blindness and recorded the occasion in his book. And thus, *The Tale of the Wave...* was transformed into the *Ode to a Chronicler of the Sea*, in which, in an elegiac tone, I revealed that I knew, in fact, little of the flight of the seagulls, of the rescue of the waves, of the story of the sea...

And with the confession came a new resolve, in the majestic Hall on the day that I had been summoned alongside the muses, the masters and the doubles: I have told another in the boundless treasury of the tales of the sea: I must cease telling of the sea: I will peer out from this day forth, on those grandiose hours where these portals have opened to invite my wretched soul, and I will tell of an impossible city. Yes, I proclaimed with increasing joy, I will tell of the city and not the sea: *The City of Enchantment*, I wrote in the book, *in which will be traced the*

111

motion of the scribe to tell of an entrancing city! I will tell of the lost city, I mumbled again gleeful, of the transparent city! I will tell of the mutation of cities, of vanishing cities, of exploding cities and unreal cities! I will tell of the city of alluring glares, the city of the mutinous jester, the city of lust! The city of forgetting and fragments, of ruin and remembrance! I will tell of the city of cries and carousels by the sea!

Decidedly, I smiled, this *is* the Room of comforts and sweet sensations! At the brink of insanity, in the midst of distress, I am rescued by a magnificent Illumination, by Divine Intervention itself! There can be no failure here, there can be no doom! Only triumph and contentment, only radiance and serenity! Ahhhh, I marveled, what bliss indeed!

But now, set to abandon the exploration of the sea, I pondered nevertheless the last tale of the wind. What of the call of the wind, I thought, have I told of the birth of the wind: and knowing that I had told the last tales of the sea, I mused that I would depict instead the sounds of the wind in the enchanted city: I will tell of the enchanted city and the wind: I will tell of the howls of the wind in the corridors of the enchanted city, of the wind in the streets of the city, among the echoes of the city, among the shadows of the city! Of the wind the savior, and not the wind pleading out at sea. And I smiled the final smile of a triumphant bard. Time, even, has dissolved here, I mumbled, in this great Abode, in this great Peace, where all my songs are heard, all my hymns celebrated, all, Understood! Here reigns eternal glory, I said, here reigns Eternity itself!

———■———

I rose from my seat after a last glance through the window, closed the book and walked through the pillars of the majestic Hall: on these marble floors where many of the brethren have come for the peculiar brand of worship, where many have stood pensive leaning against the sculptured columns, where the busts of visionaries past sternly scrutinize, I, promulgator of fantasies and historian of the sea, the sand, and the Hall from which I peer, on these historic grounds, through the pillars, I walked.

In an adjacent chamber of this same Hall, I eased unto an exquisite divan built with the expert hands of master artisans, sculpted to perfection, woven with the same delicate knots of the mapmakers of its land of origin, covered with the rarest jewels of exotic kingdoms. I lingered, knowing that this would be the site, this the night: in this last of the venues, in this historic Hall, in this last hour that the battle would begin—and end: between the author of the *Divan*, and the progenitor of that most ambitious of projects, a work conceived to be expanded and completed throughout the ages, a literally impossible endeavor, *The Encyclopedic Dictionary*. With this creator and all the illustrious heirs, the very last challenge mounted, the greatest of feats, in this Hall and no other, where the edifice itself would be at risk, and the insistent echoes of warriors past, and the scars imperceptible on the busts here victorious, the very last hurdle: to prove, to confirm, once and for all, that the revolution, nothing less than the revolution, could be held to the same whim, to the spirit of collection and organization, to the particular painter's pallet, so to say, to the chosen mode of circulation, to personal driftworks and knotgraphs, to the same subservience to contours, enchantments and tone, lo, to the parameters of the forms—and their displacement: to play, and fancy.

This was the time, this was the occasion: the rigorous author of *The Encyclopedic Dictionary* (first): the ecstatic author of the *Divan* (next): in the mirrored chamber of the Hall:

'Forty-second day of the year 19—. You must remember… Fists in the air, arms swaying, rhythmic cries, after the fire…

'The charred building stood still, in her flower-plaited veil biting her teeth a bereaving old woman…

'Banners floated in a river of gazes, discontent darted about, quiet commotion of the invisible. Death to, was the chant: on the walls, the statues, the railings, secret longings of the restless and the lost: at dawn already they were assembled, at dawn, in the public square. They had come in the night, in small groups or alone, through the boulevards and alleys, on rooftops now, on lampposts, at the feet of the ancient savior, in all corners, through the labyrinth of the city now a new maze.

'Messengers were sent everywhere, to spread the word: into homes, schools, small shops and prayerdomes. They have gathered in the public square, hey ho, join your brethren in the center of town… Death to, they cried—and families braced for catastrophes unknown…

'Excited children joined in bewildered, while the crooks and the scoundrels left without a sign, without warning…

'They poured in from every direction, as if choreographed: I could see it from above, in the center, they were growing enamored, stronger with each step, their will unsurpassed, undaunted…

'A boy is crouching. There is no one around him, an island of perplexity behind the shrieking marchers dispersed: dashing away or standing tall, seeking: next to a comrade, watching over, one tends to the wounds, the other weeps, a last is pressing his head on the lying one's chest: austere expressions—a variation on coming darkness, on darkness and grief.

'Branches of naked trees and rooftops were covered, lampposts coated, a kindly sheet of whiteness over a city in need of repose. With clashes of the weeks before, the dead in the streets among them their brethren before the spiral into char into dust: they stopped, they marched, they waived, all on the helpless statue of the toppled idol, necks of the climbers bowed down looking at it as if a corpse. What to do with an inert object—huge, granted—made of bronze and all, that's been worshipped and spit at, and manages, in the final analysis, to be quite useless!

'The victorious, of course, were held, carried on shoulders. Sagging chins of old men in the foreground, who stretch their necks, above the masses, to see: a serious, strong and unrelenting fellow sits carried across on tops of hands and on shoulders, smiling—surely praising those who have made him a hero, if even for just one day!

'It was a wide area, I remember, surrounded by the ancient towers, overlooking the square—with the monument, in the center, of a winged angel floating, almost falling. I did not join, of course, I had merely walked to the window, witness now to the unfolding events. Not a single stone of the concrete under the feet was visible, last drops of blood, 'death to' under breaths no more. I returned to my desk, I began the heading, in *The Encyclopedic Dictionary*: *The Cry of the Masses, insofar as it is an account of the events unfolding in the year 19—*. I paused and walked about the room, yielding to the urgent sensation. I returned, shortly thereafter, to the desk and, when I began, so too, at the precise moment, you wrote, in the *Divan*, a fragment entitled, *The Cry of the Masses...*'

There was a silence in the Hall: a momentary silence, and then the echoes carried on: this now, from the author of the *Divan*:

'Foreboding, foreshadowing, I could not tell. But I had sensed it, I had sensed the coming tide.

'It all developed quite rapidly of course. A multitude had

115

gathered, defiant, triumphant, already. I approached also, my window giving unto the square, I opened wide the shutters, I stood staring, in a trance almost… I was nervous and anxious, but I also knew… I knew that this was not a moment to shun…

'The raised arms, the swaying fists, no other way to tell it, really! Open palms or fingers bent, the toothless one with the hat, the bearded one with the funny mustache, a young dreamer now dancer in the middle who has twisted to call a friend—or foe, lost in the herd. In the back, behind a fence, the outline of a fat bureaucrat with his hands in the pockets, ragtag pants, humble jacket. Impromptu parade before the next, jubilation in which join the bored also and the idle, innocence writing the script of doom.

'I saw them riding tanks holding the gifted rifles of the mutinous: a cortege of moving vehicles, them atop shouting upon command, coercion or pure boredom, who knows, everyone trickling into the square. Youngsters who can't keep the pace are jogging, they cannot resist the temptation, dissidents along with the rush of passive onlookers around, deserters dash into the comforting arms of the rock-throwers and insult-hurlers and knife-wielders ripping apart the uniform that, these days, is only testament to tyranny.

'Bent bodies below hills, standers and sitters with shirts out, a skyscraper or two in the distance, tents for the others: the troops look dapper mind you, in the parade a show of force, with guns lifted to shoulders all in one gait, exemplary portraits on otherwise rippled faces. Arms extended with partners waving a flag. There are those among these frenzied hordes who stand atop captured trucks and tanks, as if children abandoned: who, in the midst of the celebratory euphoria, have a moment to wonder, a serene moment alone, watching before them the scene, of dashing humans, of black veils floating and running, of mad rushes with cavalcades: I stood leaning, watching: I knew that a new world awaited, did not know which, was the world that awaited: us—.

'The orator appeared, warning with fists raised and shouts, leaflets flying above heads, exhortations to the New, garbs of tomorrows on parade. I summoned the will, the patience, I summoned the humor even, I tried... I can safely call it a poem, I presume, safely call it a poem, with shame perhaps, a sonnet, the only way... I began: *The Cry of the Masses*: Mugging: posing in a soldier's hat and jacket...—a portrait of a frail jokester, it was, who had donned a vanquished officer's garb, his feet pressed together in the required way, an arm bent at the elbow, fingers at the temple, mockingly, in the guise of a salute, with sunglasses even, awkwardly positioned on the nose, not resting on ears, the hat crooked—with a gun-toting kid in the background. A poem indeed... A poem, was all that I could muster...'

There they were, the hushed recitations, the chronicles, the facts, the compilations and the images and the provocations...

But the duel was only beginning, only now beginning, pitting the inspired author of *The Encyclopedic Dictionary* against the inspired author of the *Divan* (back and forth now, back and forth): 117

Encyclopedist: 'The banters of the orators moved the people to seek justice! And the tide could not be turned!'

Poet: 'A little man with the thick mustache and the curls!'

'All across the land, and a torrent of bodies in the square. No one can be distinguished!'

'*His* incitements, *his* songs, a stubborn, awkward, childlike resolve...'

'An orator stood tall and the first words he pronounced challenged all to unite: this was the first moment.'

'Uncertain glances, each face a tale of doubt, whispers unheard, destinies unmarked...'

'The orator was fully, and singularly, successful in his calls for unison: one for all, one goal and one path.'

'There was an orator, surrounded by the masses, old and young, rich and poor. They listened intently as they held the sons' and the daughters' hands, timid but resilient... A boy running excitedly to the front slips, holds on to a pole as he is carried to the front slips again, retains himself as he falls, playful and laughing. At the corner, the winks of a trickster: I saw it myself I tell you, winking at another, in the distance, who begins to run, after the motion: this was the wink of the revolution: the history of the revolution cannot be told without the wink of the trickster of the square!'

'On the makeshift podium, before them all, in the restless frenzy, after the bloodshed, the orator stood and incited the masses. He spoke of the injustices, he spoke of the repression, he outlined the program: he stood above the crowd and detailed a plan of action.'

'The angel uncertain, teetering as the pandemonium grew. Now is the time now is not... What of the city, what of the rubble...'

118

'History made in the defining moments of the decision to transgress and transform, in the resistance formalized and concretized, in the successful execution of the policies.'

'The angel of revolution above, unblinking: summoned once more I am, awakened from a daze, once more the fate of all on my tattered wings, bowing to moments lost, weary, if loving, still...'

'The revolution will bring about the amelioration of the living conditions, will bring about a more humble, communal system, will bring about a true republic. Nothing will stand in the way.'

'Leaning against a pillar in the sky, fearful, gazing beneath: a plunge and the circling, the floating, the wings now carrying him through the skyscape of the city...'

'The orator on the podium, the people willful agents, knowing, devising the best plan of action, I tell you, a new land, a new world!'

'Once upon a time, in a city long forgot, there gathered a crowd, they chanted and they sang, they hailed and they danced...'

'The sky was gray. Earlier in the week, the decree had been passed, the excitement had grown. The calligrapher had been imprisoned. And now they were bracing themselves for the coming tides.'

'Graylit sky, unfazed before the wrath of the tyrants. Hollow are the cries of the unseen above the city's paths. The gaze of silent citizens falls on distant shores. Screams in the night have been heard, a weary poet dashing to save. They have marched through the refuse, a young boy peers at the commotion, I will not forget, how the night carries on unsettled—while the deserted alleys drive the idle away...'

'I submit that they knew what they provoked. And that the destiny was well-conceived.'

'Once upon a time, a kindred soul faced an anxious crowd...'

'I propose that the conditions spawned the gathering, that the call resonated deeply with the populace!'

'Once upon a time!...'

Encyclopedist: 'It is in the best interest. It was in the best interest, economical, political, social—the cry of the people'

Poet: 'Once upon a time, there was one, and there was not...'

Ahhh the blissful exchange, the stubborn exhortation, this almost uncivil incitement, to join the other's way! The scholar and the poet: the tense encounters, the clashes of will and vision! And yet, even in these silent disputes, there was occasion to celebrate!

So be it, I thought, still more convinced, this grand palace truly is the site of beatitude and serenity! What with this confrontation between the encyclopedist and the poet, still all is merry and full of cheer!

Ever more delirious, ever more ecstatic I was, for it seemed now, it seemed that Joy reigned here, and that the quarrel could go on, unabated, without pain, without a single hazard! The Hall where all could be fashioned indeed, without danger of crumbling or decay! There was no revolution outside the form, outside the bonds of the vision, outside their method of remembrance—and yet all could rest easily, for naught was to be proven or shown: it was without consequence this reverie, without converts or pilgrims this awkward (unpopular even, and unhelpful, maybe) take on reality. But so be it, I thought again, I shall not be expulsed from within. Not within *these* walls, from the company of *these* luminaries. They understand, I know they understand. And with the debate enlivened endlessly, I lay comfortably in repose, the author of *The Encyclopedic Dictionary*—and of the glorious *Divan*.

120

———■———

There was a grumbling behind the portals though and soon a knock—an eerie, violent knock.

Horreur! I exclaimed suddenly, as if knowing the provenance, as if awakened from a cruel nightmare! And before I had time to budge, the specter had appeared within the chamber, within the same, glass-walled chamber!

And now, how quickly, the sumptuous sofas and the gilded chairs, the priceless masterworks and the marble floors—all of the riches all, had quickly vanished! Cracked windows and scattered sheets, decrepit walls pealing, stained and yellow, a scent of refuse in these small quarters—without pillars or busts, without adjoining rooms! And a rat even could already be seen scurrying about!

Horror! I exclaimed again, terrified, alone, despaired! All the magic gone, all of serenity gone, what more, what more, I cried! But the voice could now be heard within, I could only shiver, the voice could now be heard:

With what anguish I waited... But this was the night, this was the night, you knew also, that this was the night! I knew the journey would be inevitable, as if summoned by the forces, by the powers themselves!

The notorious house... What conspicuous tales it has bestowed upon our lot! Damned by so many, ignored by such a multitude, and yet, for all of that, revered by a sect of anonymous wanderers. I feigned to be unperturbed, but I had heard it, I had heard the din of destiny.

I had my reservations about the venture of course, an increasing discomfort with the potentially tragic outcome, the wisdom of the endeavor, the overall merit... You had warned me in your turn... The perils, the possible scars... But despite the dangers, despite your own reluctance and predilection, despite the strong temptations, you goaded me on, you did not discourage me, did not hold me back. 'They will not recognize you, you must know that,' you warned. 'They will not distinguish, will not understand! Your journey has not been theirs. Within, the palpitation, the energy, the great explosion. You must be aware! Your world, mine, is not the one they know... The battle will not be won on the ascent, it will not be won at the summit, not inside... The burden and the joy, as you and I have learned, now facing one another despite impossible odds.

You must be aware: the laughter, the night, the dash: after that the silence, the chambers, the mirrors, the voice... But you will have to tell, summon the courage and tell... And then, perhaps... For we may have to march behind the enlivened specter of the chiseled stone...' I nodded then, I remember, but did I know, had I understood? I merely darted into the darkness, fate alongside, my sole escort...

I marched through the cobblestone streets... I stood pensive, behind the windows of stores closed for the night... I passed by the chapels, I walked by the hostels and the tenements, stillness reigning, around the bend... I descended the famed slope... I stood, at the edge of the water, peering into its ripples... Far away, a seemingly floating fort of centuries past, in the distance on the island, lit by the moon, as if a dream, yet firmly on a hill, shrouded in the coat of darkness...

Clouds appeared though, from nowhere, and the rumble soon turned into rain. The swiftness with which it had materialized suddenly jolted me, and I scurried away again, holding tightly my coat, my hat, struggling against the wind, against the whipping rain, a soldier in the sudden tempest! I took cover, under the protective awning of a jeweler's shop. I did not know how long it would last, but it was impossible to go on in that torrent, impossible to go on!

The House was not that far now, I had covered quite a distance, unbeknownst, the house was not so far... I even considered a defiant thrust toward the hill, but the downpour, now complemented by the roar of the thunder and its usual accompanist lighting the sky, was ever more relentless, ever more pitiless! I had never encountered such hostile conditions, not on individual forays, not on communal strolls, never such anger, directed, it seemed, quite peculiarly, at none other than the determined marcher, yours truly, *moi*! It was not even a particularly festive night, no celebrations were planned, no fireworks, no joyous parades. But still, curiously, it also seemed as if all were present, on this eve...

And, in the distance, majestic, under the rain, withdrawn, appearing and disappearing with the illuminations wrought by the lightning, the house to which I, shielded from the rain, thought I was destined!

A certain impatience was setting in though, a heightening helplessness, when I saw, dejectedly, a woman, dressed in the usual attire of business persuasion, drenched to the bones, making her way across the intersection. She kept running, visibly without options, surely to arrive at a safe cover as soon as she could. But it was also obvious that the rain was not her only concern. Poor woman, I muttered to myself, she'll never get out of it alive! Sure enough, behind her, a few paces, a man with a black top hat, a black blazer and black pants, with a long black coat, was dashing down the same lane, in high pursuit, his forearms raised, bent at the elbow, his fingers clenched in the playful manner of children mimicking monsters! Seeing them in such a way, at liberty, I could no longer hold back. Perhaps I will make a run for it also, I thought, and, before I knew it, I found myself, again, in the driving rain...

Too strong, though, too vigorous a rain! I hurried toward a glimmer I had made out through the gale, and flung myself inside the dimly lit tavern. Occupied, let it be said, by none other than the creepy wayfarers, by the disconsolate but sultry bohemians, of *this* night...

I had barely entered, barely slipped to the counter and ordered, barely caught my breath, that it happened, that I heard it. Heard it I tell you, as if music to my ears, as if the lalaï of youth and the cradle, I heard the voice, her voice, I heard her voice!

123

I turned, it was she, I could not be mistaken: not a dream, not an illusion, her back to me, chatting with a neighbor, paces away. I was mesmerized, could not fathom, could not imagine, why here, why now... I could not turn though, I dared not interrupt, I was unable, again, to summon the courage. I found a seat, ordered, stared ahead, heard her voice, behind me her soothing voice...

Understand, if you will, my creeping suspicions. I had merely made a roundabout turn, victim of unforeseen incidents, was now resting through an imposed detour, on my way, my merry way, to the House, that, here I was, in disarray, unkempt, in a tavern, hearing her voice! I did not wish to burden her either, I did not intend to intervene. But as I finally collected myself, as I finally gained sufficient sangfroid, I approached and greeted. To my utter astonishment, she was not the least taken aback, not the least unsettled. I had, in fact, just saluted that she, in her ever relaxed tone, without any prodding on my part, at once contemplating and remembering, speaking past me also, not to me, it seemed, avoiding my eyes, I could tell, she began: 'It was on a rainy, stormy night, not far from the marshes, the battles in the marshes, on a strange and stormy night, very much like this one... Legend has it that the fallen hero had it bestowed upon him in a most appalling episode—inside a tavern along his route, a long, solitary road he had been traveling, a young, wayward soldier drifting off the path, the assigned path, a tavern along the road...' And then she went on, in earnest, the storyteller I had finally chanced upon: 'They had seemed friendly at first, the regulars, the barkeep and the servers, all of the piercing eyes that had followed his entrance and his every motion. But soon, as the night had worn on, they'd turned to bullish ridicule, to derisive games, to a spiteful tormenting of the poor vagrant. 'Do a little dance for us,' they'd mocked him, 'a little dance of death, a good soldier's death, for all to see!' And the poor fellow had been lifted onto a table, stripped of his clothes and made to prance awkwardly amid the humiliating whistles and clapping of the occupants! 'A song now, we'd like to hear a song!' another had squealed. And the fellow had strung, out of tune and trembling, the words to a children's rhapsody! When they had taught him his first lesson, they'd formed a large circle and left him standing in the middle, naked, shivering, teary-eyed, as if a toddler in the midst of a cruel spectacle. Then they had marched around him in rhythmic gaits, one leg stiff up, one leg stiff down, arms mechanically moving alongside, heads erect, a parody, doubtless, of his uniform and his badge. 'Fetch the seat,' a large, bearish goon had ordered. Upon which a toilet ready at hand had been delivered to the center of the circle, and its porter hurriedly back in line, joining his peers in their cruelty. The big boor had approached the quaking guest, extended his hand and bent at the waist, politely, genie-like showing the hapless one his destined seat. 'Your majesty will do us the honors,' he'd intoned in jest: after which he had joined the circle, leg up leg down, all around, left and right, a naked, contorted man sitting kidlike in their midst. They had marched and mocked and chanted, necks suddenly thrust towards him as the words dribbled off, grimacing, piercing eyes again, demons and exorcists, tock tock, who's there, the cry, the game, the name,

125

> *Devil on the potty*
> *Devil on the potty*
> *Take back all your doody*
> *Take back all your doody—.*

'He would try to respond, in vain, each time the chant louder, each time drowning out his frazzled defense, I can't help it, I can't help it I swear, to no avail, better swallow and keep quiet, I can't help it, each time louder, devil on the potty, more cruel, devil on the potty, stifling, stinging, unjust: take back all your doody, take back all your doody, devil on the potty, devil on the potty... They'd dressed him anew after the show: a flower in his hat, a feather in his coat, keeping all the rest... Then they'd marched him the few steps to the entrance, handed him his emptied knapsack and, mockingly, ordered the usual command: 'Away now soldier!' they had thundered amid his whimpers. 'Good duty—and good riddance!' He stands motionless, unable to move, to react. 'A going away present!' another had then yelled from the gang. 'Give him a gift he won't forget!' And it is then, I tell you as I myself have heard it, that the bully had offered the small sculpture, the very one of the older monk-like figure holding the sword on his shoulder, in his frock, bent almost parallel to the ground, rocket-like, sweeping. He'd given it to him—forced it upon him, rather—and showed him the door. 'And the Wrath of Chance be with you,' it is said he'd thundered at the tormented fellow, 'and the Rage of its Offspring Forevermore!' They say that the company then burst into a frenzied laughter, one that was to accompany the porter of the piece on the most daring ventures. Now I for one,' she elaborated, 'I wanted to dispense with it, but I simply could not. I dared not, that is. It was ordered. It was written. And so I... I knew you were the one. I knew it would be you...' And as she had finally stopped, the thunder was heard outside again, and the rain fell harder than it had all evening. 'It looks as though there will be no respite from this,' I quipped, unnerved by the last words but thinking them (hoping, anyway!) a negligible quirk on her part. 'It was I indeed,' I added nevertheless—and I did consider myself that much luckier, now that I knew the whole story!

126

I had been driven to unexpected locations on this eve, and it may even be said that my itinerary had been quite significantly altered. I also know, however, that I could not postpone or cancel: it was now or never, as adverse as all conditions were proving. 'It's getting late,' I let out shyly, 'I should be moving on.' I expressed my gratitude again, paid the bill and donned my coat. I turned for a last greeting and noticed that her complexion, strangely, and unexpectedly, had grown rather unpleasant. In a tone not begetting her earlier decorum, her neck swollen and with a smirk, she intoned: 'Greetings to you, of course, my friend, greetings to you!' Momentarily bewildered by the sudden transformation, paying no heed nevertheless, I merely nodded a last appreciation: So long, said I—and thank you all.

She must have followed my progression. She must have, for when I was only paces away, she suddenly sprang from her seat, rushed to the entrance, and grabbed my arm as I had opened and readied to exit. Startled, I turned and was quickly taken aback by her fiery eyes: 'Beware,' she growled unreserved, 'Beware, the House of the Gamblers of Yore!' I shook off her hand, stared at her, turned, pulled the door all the way, and quickly launched myself once more into the darkness…

Through the rain and the thunder, the lightning was still illuminating the House. I arrived at the foot of the hill, staring meditatively up the path that gave directly, exclusively, to the haunted quarters. I made my way up, painstakingly, along the steep acclivity, slowly marched to the portals and stood, unshaken, undeterred, protected by naught but my own fear at the lack of options! I approached and knocked. There was no answer. Harder knocks, repeatedly. Pushing of the buzzer, a tiny button by the otherwise grand portals. The haunted sound of bells rang outside even, slowly the clamor of a prolonged peal.

No one came though, no solemn butler opened the creaking portals, no dapper host showed the way in. I knocked again. Is there anyone here, I screamed, anyone here still, anyone at all? But there was no answer. 'No one here,' I muttered to myself, 'or else they just don't want me in.' A last futile attempt was made, again to no avail. I thought to abandon, to return, a swift return, to the Hall, the majestic Hall, with the balcony facing the sea… But as I turned from the portals, as I took my first steps descending the hill, a thunderous laughter rose behind me, from the confines of the house: a roaring, unceasing, deafening laughter—as if an echo, an echo of the scent of evil flowers on flights to the end of the night in Sodom, with the despiser of traces, the dandy aches of auroras, and the chants of Eblis the daredevil resonant still in the troubled hills! I, then, I, the forgotten one, the equally damned, equally doomed, crucified bard of this age (don't you know), I stopped abruptly and rushed again to the portals, beating helplessly, punching helplessly, screaming for them to open up, open up! Nothing but the same laughter, the unremitting roar of the House: and it was not the clever ruse of a spirit hidden or concealed, not emanating from within, not the vengeful mockery of the wounded or the *maudit*!—no, it rose from the house itself, from the House of the gamblers, from the house, *itself*!

—■—

Back in the hall, solemnly, in the chambers… How the city unseen, unveiled… How the night… No, there is no ocean outside, no ships, no tales to be knotted out of the secrets of the sea! No magnificent walls, no Beauty surrounding, no Exotic Sense enveloping, no Enchanted City! There is no Serenity, no Comfort, no Repose… All is suffering again, all is burden, all is real again, the specter within…

The only salvation is the small glass, the shard with its jagged edge, hung on the wall. After the dash and the rain, after the legend of *The Avenger*, rebuffed even by the house of the fellow damned souls!

Lost, entranced, yet also relieved, relieved yes: I don't believe I ever asked, I have not dared, not dared, I said, but this is the night, the majestic Night, now that I am again surrounded in my hovel, with Time ever tyrannical, tell me, the day of the assembly, of the beginning, the dawn of the revolution, tell me, O slasher of the poet of the *Divan*, O slayer of the erudite scholar of *The Encyclopedic Dictionary*, the one way, the only way, you did not abandon, not at that most undeniable Hour, tell me, true scribe of the revolution, to the glorious blasphemers even a heretic, exiled from the chambers of the damned, tell me, what of your world, what of mine, what of...

The smiles in flames turning into ashes... Slowly the crumpled eye in the portrait... Into embers... In a blocked back alley where the young surround a makeshift noose...

Wrenches held aloft and bayonets and knives and guns: lampposts inert, curving above the asphalt, heads drawn back too close to the searing, smoldering symbols of oppression in ornate, overdone costumes and dresses, hand in hand the emperor and the queen, one's call to end the tyranny tomorrow's echo in battlefields, marshes, deserted fields, on mountainsides and empty roads... I went down, I did... Among them, touching, hearing, I murmured, with, not of them, stayed in, also, watched them, from above, my study, from my window, the shutters, open, up and down, among them...

At the gates, some, running through the narrow gaps, came back to incite defiantly the helmeted only steps away: smoke rises from overturned cars and trucks, the pavements before them a black sea about to explode. They drag down a statue

with hard wire attached to its head, a live accomplice stand-
ing guard on the pedestal making sure the bust comes down.
Wounded comrades draped in sheets, the bent carrier looking
straight at: heroes raised, one on top of the other on top of the
other on top of the other, into the crowd marching clockwise
around the monument before the towers in the distance…

Molotov cocktails behind wires: bullhorns blaring, from
rooftops and streets, from truckbacks and pillars razed: a mu-
ezzin, please, for these swingers: walking, alongside, maestro
lifting his armbaton at given cue for the voices of his ensemble
to be hurled, in unison: old and young, the wounded with
the healthy to greet them, to goad them, to urge them across
these pavements tomorrow stained, black-robed or shrouded
hanging on with teeth: shirts with plaids so often how come,
seldom any jackets, must be the weather.

Unusual cyclists hoot their horns: drivers parade with the
randomly convinced, some happy their tour is over soon. And
a careless one who knows all is always the same… Peace signs
and victory signs in the V-shape of foreigners detested so!
Flowers given and tossed for anyone to catch: hugs and knives:
embraces and more… Overburdened tanks laced with dreams
and posters of avenging cohorts—rolling with speedy trucks
now slowed to a crawl carrying a big load. Open graves ready
for fertile exploration, heaps of earth in a pyramid on the side
ready to be dumped on the occupants: bring them on, time is
running out, clamoring for residents… Whoever controls the
streets—they will be the ones—moving now swiftly to avoid
the collapse—impending though it must be—a trend: igno-
rant of bans to come, no singsong or shake or drink, flee to
sites more privy to letting loose.

The freed prisoners triumphantly walk out: pulled out or…
What a day, every one out, mobs and snobs, to the cheers of

happy comrades, outside, everyone out: skeletal faces between lifted arms, cheekbones showing, narrowed, droopy eyes—but happy! Big smile of a young man with thick glasses, another's contained ecstasy: glimmers of delight—cities of light—a narrow doorway out of which one slow step after another these men trickle out, each exit a birth. In private quarters and public places of healing, they bleed, the wounds irreversible, they squeeze, the last breaths… It was a funny sight, I have to say: when the general immortalized in clay with hat on and the long jacket is halfway dragged, the moment before the crash, upright he on the horse but the horse not upright on its pedestal! One day maybe cruising up rivers in faraway places of refuge, up and down famed waterways while the cunning and the cursed hobble, skip and sing all around all in joy: little flowers ready for implantation: at the site of the blood, in the barrels of guns, in the hands of journalists—.

After the fire: smashed pictures of the unwanted are torn or lifted: troops uncertain, framing, them also, young patrollers now killers, seeking refuge in shelters, gorged demonstrators on the loose, one with all. Creatures of Satan, or so they were tagged, hoping to keep it under wraps, under a modicum of control, if possible!

131

After the fire before the bombs… Tear gas spreads: shots in the air and some not a few fall: screams follow, scattering, shrieks unexpected in this march now all is chaos tomorrow's poets born on the blood of this street: children of this madness I tell you, not better or worse though, must be said, same o' same o'—but not.

The barricades across bridges, piles of smoke and dust: refuse, cars, shoes, banners held aloft, before the ornaments the pillars the arches, behind the standing clergymen in robes pleading hollering…

The words, the pelting, the squads, the hails: in every direction the poses, the clashes, the throngs: riding, in every patch, the flames: clashes, surges, the siege, taunting, with us, at last, here, the maiming, the horns, the litter: blood, believers, canisters and casualties: the spins, the rousing, the cramping: melees, munitions, glass, debris, hail: whizzing, squashing: barracks, armories, fragments, shelters, sandbags, dynamite, ravaging, pow, bang, forts, blinds, knives, pliers, masters, ropes: resistance, agony, history, ideology, philosophy, opinions, sins, acts, chants, songs, deafening, men, arms, fists, up, the cry, salutes, hate, hiding, eyes, heads, beds, beads, freaks, friends, hey, clay, glands, nests, tricks, mud, sod, frost, marsh, crush, blood, fugues, devils, devout, devour, dew, dim, detentions, detained, detention, detained, hung, shot, scream, pity, no, begging, no, knees, no, wither, absolution, cells, roofs, yards, winter, again, wonder, where, gully, free, steel, steam, stiff, arms, raise, eyes, close, hear, hail, hear, hail, hear, death, hear, death, to, hail, hear, brave, tussles, terror, wrath, rum, escape, coke, corner, wither, rum, more, breath, throat, yell, fuck, wry, vile, new, rulers, leaders, sons, liars, brutes, babes, not, beasts, bombs, fall, falls, dashes, barracks, shelters, bang, agony, mastery, misery, crude, flames, mines, crypts, vaults, men, faces, frowns, beards, rule, lead, brave, boom, stand, sit, watch, apart, afar, gaze, the fire, the flames, tires, cars, trucks, poles, posters, walls, bricks, flee, nooks, names, none, away, cower, cave, sticks, songs, stones, needs, fire, flame, street, name, away, holler, run, rush, dash, mad, hail, way, new, way, new, way, new, world, wait—the breeze,

the hush, silence, still,

the breeze, the breeze:

the cry, marchers, men, up, the cry, the men, the fists, the eyes, raised, the men, the fists, the cry…

132

On a stretcher high above the hands, above the open palms and fists, faces unchained, the shrouded body of a hero martyr, aloft: held aloft...

With him the mourning of the masses, the mourning, now... Cry of the new world... Aloft... Aloft...

I'm

not a freak, not getting sick, just impatient, growing weak! That's me talking, narrator supreme, getting impatient with the work under my care. Much honored and much maligned (hand in hand they go!) translator of *The City of Sand* and the expanded *Halls of Heresy* (among other works), I'm just growing increasingly impatient with the volume presently under my care. 'Impossible!' I exclaim, even in solitude, as if a legion has gathered to hear the verdict! The exhausted mien, the pleading eyes, stretches of gray ever more visible in the long flowing hair: the years devoted to the task have left their mark, obviously, the scars, upon the skin, and the life. 'O perfidy!' I holler on this eve. 'How could I have been so easily duped, so easily drawn into this tempest of deception!'

It all happened during a casual stroll. The project that is, that's when it happened. During a casual stroll. Proposed by a colleague, if you can call him that! As it turns out, the erudite fellow had brought to my attention an obscure volume that had gained quite a following, provoked quite a solid stir, in circles less visible around town. And since he knew me to be marvelously skilled in the craft? the art? the science? the illusion?, he proposed a marvelously accurate translation. That had never before been undertaken in any language, said he, nor had the volume, for which he seemed to hold a peculiar fondness, gained the attention it deserved in more public arenas. 'I presume there must be a good reason for the latter,' he suggested, 'but I do not know whether there is sufficient cause in the neglect I cited first. That, old comrade, we can remedy.' But I was reticent. More needs to be known, I thought, before I embark. But he did not let up. Did not let up. Elaborated in fact. 'I have browsed through it myself,' he said, 'but I came out of it, so to say, quite disturbed. You see, it seems as if the book is arranged in such manner that it imposes upon its audience to actually, and I mean this literally, to actually experience, *in life*, the events that are portrayed within. In such manner then that I, you, or any other in fact, is led to witness first-hand the scenes in which a reader habitually imagines or panders to expertly woven illusions: to move and travel when such a thing is imposed, to be present at both cruel engagements and pleasant outings, to partake of the most delectable episodes as well as the most violent orgies. Quite diabolical, if you ask me, and quite an astonishing feat—for indeed, it is upon opening the volume that one is, how shall I put it, entranced, literally, into the adventure.'

He paused, slightly troubled, overcome by the phenomenon he was describing.

'It is not,' he went on, 'as in other instances that we both know about, the cause of one or another individual or collectivity playing out their hallucinations or fantasies. Nor is it the wrongful fabrication of a perverted reader, not even of the most famous species. And yet, I must insist, it is also not a matter of choice: as one plods along, as if indeed traversing the book, one, each and everyone, is invariably driven—but this again, is the wrong term!—to *living out* the book. Can you imagine the universe!'

Can you imagine, he repeated, can you imagine...

His tone heightened as he described the work, a certain sense of urgency, a certain fear increasingly more manifest. His demeanor turned sour, dense, worried. 'You cannot know, my dear friend,' he concluded, 'which of the worlds you inhabit!'

I suggested that we stop in a coffee-house or an inn whereupon we would elaborate on the plan. We walked along the road, noticed a favorite tavern and decided to continue the conversation inside. We helped ourselves to a corner, adjusted the seats, doffed the jackets. He took out a pack of cigarettes, and, knowing that I was not a smoker, bypassed even the polite gesture of the offering. Put one between his own lips however, lit as eyes obediently squinted during the ritual, took one drag, blew out the smoke after profound inhaling, and leaned forward: 'It would be quite a story,' he said in these very words, 'if you agreed to the translation.'

The outlandish, inflamed eyes of the speaker, the increasing angst of the associate seated directly across, the nervous mood, the instability, the discomfort: I held reservations about entrustment to begin with, but now I was even more cautious. And forthright, lest we forget. I said: 'I'm not sure how to respond. You just described the whole endeavor as having potentially severe consequences, with, if I may, irreversible effects upon the psyche and the person! I am, not to mention obviously hesitant, astonished that you would even initiate such a proposal.'

He looked ahead, unchanged. He inhaled, exhaled, held his arm away, the cigarette at bay, and approached his neck, serpent-like (how smooth was the glide). Squinting once more, he murmurs: 'And that is just it!' he says. 'That is the whole point! And the mask of the mime is forever lost!'

The pullback, the very wry smile, the awkward glow, and of course, something like a riddle—a ludicrous one, in my humble opinion—or some strange enigma. In all of the conversations, in all of the outings, I had never noticed this particular demeanor. Had all the years of confidence merely constituted a prelude to a final treachery, a betrayal, a final trick? Had this trusted colleague, seemingly as humane and sympathetic as all, merely prepared for yours truly an eternal fall? Or was I slipping, prematurely, unnecessarily, into a heightened paranoia? Exaggerating the expressions, misunderstanding the intention? To trust or to not, carrying the weight of the world on one's shoulder…

Peering across a small round wooden table on which sits a glass of wine (his) and a small mug, studying, uncertain, measuring, picking up the mug, taking a sip, putting it back down, peering still, I exclaim finally, in a bizarre and not fully convincing accession to courtesy, and as if an epiphany of sorts: I'll do it. I'll do it, I said, it's worth it, I'll do it, I agree, I'll do it!

'I'll do it!' I repeated, unaware. 'I'll do it—and I shall set on it at once!'

The tract was delivered the next day by a conspicuous old man. As he handed the package, he stared into the eyes of his host, shriveled old man, porter of books, glared into the eyes, frightened: 'Madman!' he let out nervously! 'O frivolous madman!'

I received the box and closed the door. It was too late now. I had opened the package and opened the book. It was too late now, I had opened the book…

———■———

The little one is broke, the little one is going to choke. That's what you get for being little. That's the deal. That's the price you pay. Your dues. You don't want to do it, don't do it. You can't stand the heat, don't get in the kitchen. All right, all right! Anyway, the little one, I was saying, was walking innocently across the yard with the usual flair. The usual lack, rather, when it comes to this one! Walking across the field and the court and then suddenly you hear, out of the blue, O blue, O blue still, the supreme sound of a forlorn Horn, you hear this: G__ stepped on dog poo! G__ stepped on dog poo! The children run frantically making faces and hissing and pointing to the culprit. The criminal stands helpless next to the poo he has been accused of stepping in. Tears and wallowing. Poor little innocent one. But no one cares. They petition one another and hold a hand covering mouth to ear session, their devilish pupils eyeing the stranded G__, without remorse or afterthought. A couple reaches their standing mate. They inspect his shoes. 'Show!' they command. I didn't do it, says the hapless kid. 'Show us!' they demand. But he stands his ground. He's not sure maybe. Maybe he doesn't know himself. He looks ashamed to me, to tell the truth. And the congregation of his peers in the courtyard has assembled in small groups to debate the issues, the severity of the issues, that's it, the severity. They're debating, discussing. The merit, the shame. The heresy of this G__ running without looking in the courtyard! Without guidance! Myyyy goodness! The graveness of the colleagues at the condemned still on his isolated patch, his prison, the nasty stares, it all says one thing, it's clear, that's the verdict, says one thing, it says, it's *his* fault. His fault! Shame and shame again! It's not my fault, he wants to squeal, but nothing comes out of the tight mouth. Anger. Insecurity. That's what it is! What to do though, what to do now!

What to do! The Afflicted. Could have happened to them too, but he doesn't know that. Not yet. Whence the mumness of the cheeky freckled boy in the playground in the school. After the poo.

They've made up their mind. They waited long enough. The leader of the faction for punishment has recommended in one such whisper to ear session a few paces away that they seize an opportune moment to grab and drag the thug. So they thought. The command was given as they approached on tiptoes thinking the poopooer had dozed off. But no! No! Uh-uh! Mistaken they were. Just their miscalculation. He's not sleeping, not sleeping at all the Little One! 'Who said he's sleeping!' shouts one of the suddenly frenetic gang of would be executioners! 'I'm not dying! I'm not dying!' shouts G__. Not only awake, but darn angry even! He orders guns, canons and more guns to fortify his palace. The canons are brought and the palace is fortified and then he turns into a dolphin! 'The little dolphin ain't sick! The little dolphin ain't gonna die!' he laughs boisterously, 'and neither is the missus!' His fellow little ones have stepped back. They did not expect this. Well, the answer is, who did! They look back. They back off. They have no choice. The dolphin is holding scissors in one fin and a magic lamp in the other. Smiling face of the dolphin sure but with bazarboy turban and looks. 'I have a lamp here that could do some damage folks!' But no one understands what he says. It's a language, quite an elaborate one at that, but too hybrid. Sounds crazy and wacko. 'Nonsense!' yells the bully in the gang, still standing ahead of his more disinclined partner in crime. But it's not nonsense, not at all. There's a whole logic to it. It all. A theory, a vision of things. Literatures. That's what it is. To hell with everyone else, with everything else! There's a whole system with it. 'But that's fine, that's all right,' says the dolphin, I've made my point. And he throws away the scissors at the father and the magic lamp he hurls at the mother in a land far away, far far away, doffs the turban and disappears under the waves, momentarily. Right back out stands directing. Smile is on the lips. No hard feelings. 'To be a dolphin is nothing at all,' he snickers. 'Now, who wants to play?'

They raise their hands. Me, me, me! Me, me, me! Ooh, ooh, ooh!

'Everybody line up then! Everybody line up!'

Everybody lines up. They push and shove. Jockey for position. 'Hey!' they say. 'Hey!' Grunts and baby complaints.

'Come on, no fights!' I say. 'Or else we won't play. We won't play!' The threat: that's the threat: it's great.

'Okay, ready?'

Everybody shouts that they're ready. All right then, set— and… Good light!

And they're off! As fast as they can! Giant steps! Giggling. But concentrated. Aware. Bad light! They all come to a grinding halt. A sudden stop. You moved, you moved, you moved! From all directions a chorus of accusation. No I didn't, no I didn't, no! The retorts are no less vehement. 'All right now, come down, come down,' says the ringleader standing at the top, come down! 'You,' I say then, pointing finger at, and you and you and you, I saw you. You moved. Back at the line. Let's go, let's go! Grunts and unhappy grimaces. Slouching the pointed-at ones slumber back to the starting line. Pause. Everyone ready again. The frozen ones have not moved. Throughout the evaluation. They want to win. To get to and tag the Caller. And then to replace him. Be him. Be it. It. It. They all want to be it! That's what they all want to be, It. Little ones in this case, but the grown up version is no different. It is easier than a whole explanation. I am It, you are It. But it's understood. It. Much easier than an implicit designation. Or even a definition. Easier done than said in fact. It: what can launch the game. Just start calling someone It, or by asking who is going to be It—and then step back and enjoy. That's the recipe! And follow their motions, their actions, their imagination. Doesn't even need to be fixed. Don't even have to have the rules, the strategies, the goals, the functions—set: none of the above, just start with It: and the rules will follow: fluid, light. That's what you can hear from them:

the flippancy of rules: roll with it and roll along, that's all they want to be—It!

And... Good light! Suddenly again the command and they're off like flying elephants and a horde of unicorns one leg after another like airplanes taking off and hop hop hop the legs get off the ground and they float and rotate the arms and play the Good Light, Bad Light game in the air no problemo how they suddenly freeze, right on the spot, defying gravity and the smattering of other egocentric forces, at the blurting by the master of bad light, because, frankly, even in this heavenly funhouse, they don't want to lose, nobody likes to lose, we know that for a fact, nobody wants to lose! But a few do, inevitable right, not everybody can win, we know that too, and the sulkings begin: everybody thumped back to the ground because of the pouty badsportiness of the non-winners, hey, what can you do! Sitting one little boy there with arms wrapped around knees folded head sunk in. What's wrong, the query, soft it must be, what's wrong? Mutterings incomprehensible. What? asks louder the weary Teach. 'I don't wanna play anymore!' blurts out the kid. Fine, fine, who else doesn't wanna play anymore. The hands go up. Like little plants in cartoons: pop pop pop! What the! 'You were all just having fun now what gives?' But that's how it goes. 'We don't wanna play anymore!' It's getting dangerous now, dangerous, lots of them, one of you, on playgrounds of private worlds fear the mutiny and the wrath of the monstrous hive, O easygoing Prof!

'Fine, fine!' says the latter. 'You wanna play buck buck moose, then?'

'Buck buck moose, Yeaaayy!' they shout. 'Buck buck moose!'

Everyone agrees. Buck buck moose it is then, buck buck moose, it is, buck buck moose!

The circle is formed. Sitting *tcharzanoo* anticipating the tap on the head. Who goes first? Me me me! Okay, you, you go first. Stands, deep breath, stares of the others they can't wait. Agitation. First tapper has stood, commandant commandant, ready, begins the walk, slowly, calculating every move, as he goes by the seated ones his arm gently raised softly comes down to tap the shivering head of chaser wannabe only to be let down for he hears, they hear, one after another, they hear buck, they hear buck, they hear buck... buck.... buck... Until the tapper inadvertently slows and pauses and peers doubtingly, refrains from the usual buck, anticipates, readies, readies... and...—

Moose!

Sudden spring of the seated pup! The tapper already is in flight, doesn't want to be tagged no, doesn't want to be cooked and eaten, doesn't want to be a good meal no way, not him! First they go around the circle, real fast, almost skipping, around the circle, hyper and thrilled, about the game, but then, then, something, what, what the, look now my goodness on top of the head him and all the seated ones now grow from the field, on four legs one moose and the other moose and everyone a real one, here a buck there a buck everywhere a buck buck, galloping wildly and coming back, congregating, growing wings and flying, fire out of their mouths yes these dragon-bucks, duels of, duels of... But the moose is furious and attacks: moose against one buck and another and the dragonbucks let out the fires, the untainted fires in this hall, the moose lunging ahead fiery with antlers pushing through, antlers in the midst of this fire, the screams and closed doors, no way out, in the beginning, no way out, game still or no, I don't think so, not with the antlers of the moose on fire and the bucks running wildly and the closed exits and the rage of the inferno, no way

142

out in the midst of this fire of children at play no more the fire and the moose, fire and the antlers, the charred bodies, the hush, the end, the new, revolution come, carry: on!

———■———

It *is* possible that a man be saved by the hollers of a street-corner preacher. This I know. Especially if said preacher stands by the furiously noisy entrance of the underground trains zooming, zapping, crrsssh, crrsssh, in the hip hop abode of capwearing, widepanted, boombox-holding sneakered youth. That's the preacher there by the corner same corner with words out of his mouth look: hairy A's and glacial E's, telling the beginning and the end. His voice is soothing somehow, the voice of lightness if not light. The voice of lightness *because* it's not light! That's his voice. Saved from what who knows and surely not the type of savior he wants to be. But we'll let him at it. Credit where it's due. He's thin and tall and old and meticulously dressed with the same screeching day in and day out, not to count the night! Holds the pamphlets on high and from the window not only there can you hear him—same hour, on the dot, without fault. So that in this heated city with haze, walking with the muzzle of the giant man from the tower and the giant kid on the interface they smile at you, you bend the head slightly and march on march on, hands clasped behind your back on the sidewalks and chance by the Cupseller and his Cups who are quite talkative today and ask about the preacher, the port and the vowels.

I stand before them and ruthlessly they question: where's the drunk, where's the seller, where's the buyer?! And as if once was not enough, no I didn't hear you type, they keep going, once, twice, thrice, on and on, where the seller, where the buyer, where the drunk?! There's only five of them on the ground of this merchant by the road and they're not all they're made out to be (not colorful or expensive), but he doesn't seem to be around, he's slouching somewhere else hanging with the can collectors with their bags lounging in front of the supermarket. I turn back at the cups and they don't stop: some are taciturn, some are not, some are in-between. The five of them, four hundred times each I counted, that's two thousand times in all that I heard: where the buyer, where the seller, where the drunk?!

Look, I'm the drunk, I'm the drunk, all right, I blurted suddenly, I'm the drunk! What do you have, what do you have. One of the cups winked, one of them smiled, one of them blushed and one of them—faked. The last one looked at me straight and savvy: O Vowels of this tongue and the other and the other: I'll count your journey one day I will I promise, but not now, not now! Aleph has bruises is all blue. I is red it's true, but that's because it's shy. And you're all yellow and pale so I can't confirm the green. Anyway, I don't want to disturb the peace. Not the peace. Not the peace.

I looked at the shameless Cup who dared desecrate the Song and hit him over the head. How dare you! Then I took his handle and slapped him there too, scolding him he deserved it!

There! I said. There! That'll teach you some manners! Since that handle had been places it should never have been! (Around some adorable little one's waist, say, or neck—O uncouth thoughts, be away, away from my puritan heart!)

'Come on, take it easy!' the Cup said.

And then the others too, they chimed in, and without invitation!

'Yeah, lay off, man!' one said.

'Calm down, dude!' the other Cup offered.

'Take a chill pill, bud!' was a last refrain!

Lo, I said, I don't have to be here you know! I don't have to be here!

Meanwhile, the playful Cup of previous vowel berating talent had pulled up the sleeves.

'Hey! Hey! Come here!' he whispered cunningly. 'Come here...'

'Closer,' he chided. 'Come closer.' And I picked the playful Cup and brought him close to my ear.

'Why did the chicken cross the playground,' he said in jest.

I don't know, I said, playing along. Why?! Why?!

'To get to the other *slide*!'

All the cups then burst into a prickly and harmonious little giggle. The passersby even and all the posters and pictures on the walls joined in. Everyone froze and giggled. No noise in the divide and the intersection all at ease. Absolute peace and noiselessness save for the giggle. Was it at me? At me or with me? I chose the latter option, why not, save myself embarrassment at least.

'To the lip now, to the lip!' insisted the jokester Cup all stirred up. 'Take me to your lip!'

And so lip to lip held I the Cup which told me other secrets of long life and old age and... And here I must insist, and I know I'm right, don't—don't go to the translations. Trust me. The vaunted poet of the East, the one we all know and you all will too wherever you are, I'm telling you: go to the original and don't trust anyone. But yourself. Do this, in fact, do me this favor. Line up all the translations and what do you see. Tell me, what do you see. (I'm talking about the one that starts 'lip to lip' in most versions and anyway, it's unmissable.) I can't hear you. What? What? Well yes and no. I'd tend to see there a kind of a pun, maybe a most nuanced version. You just have to allow for all options. And, in fact, the various versions are proof. One chooses one thing and the other the other. Why? Why tell me, why? Well I'm telling you, that's why. Because of the linguistic manipulation: the original forces upon the derived texts an ambiguity untransferable (and thus untranslatable), and they must choose. You the reader the listener whoever you are, unfortunately and despite your most generous inclinations, expert or not, cannot just dispense one and not the other. Proof proof proof: the variations baby, the variations.

That was the secret of the Cup: that's what it said. It said how the secret was that all is within: the secret in fact, after all the centuries, was just to say that the non-resolve of the pun, the secret thus, is the thing that's all. Well, thanks a bunch! All this time and… that! I got angry. Really I did. I wanted to throw it away the darn thing, but a last pleading stopped me.

'No, no, no, no!' the insistence. 'No, come back, I'll tell you something else, what do you want to hear, what?!'

I was tired of this Cup, really, but at least he'd managed to calm my senses. Aaahh, forget you, I said as I put him back down with his brethren (violently, sure, but I made sure it wouldn't break). I was ready to leave. I thumbed my nose at them, defiantly. I was about to take off when the voice of another, another among them, a deeper voice, more assured, wiser, one could sense, stopped me just before.

'They never told you about Rostam and The White Whale now did they? Did they?'

'No they didn't,' he answered himself calmly. 'Of course not. That's up to you. You can do it and be reviled or you can forget it and go about your happy business. The rejoining, the osmosis of myths. What else are you good for if not that? You might as well go for it, nothing to lose, take the risk. Make it up, you know, how Rostam finally decided to board the ship after all, tired of the business of re-conquest and what-have-you, enlisted the services of foreign workers, donned a skipper's cap and shirt and well, just went at it with that Great One, losing ultimately of course, but that's what life is all about, you know, the allegory, the struggle, the process. You could have the snake-shouldered one present too, as some sort of spy or something, on board, or else some dragon that lives in the depths—and just pops up to torment the Ship. Good old U__ too assisted R__ at the beginning. What with his expertise in sea travel and the overcoming of the Obstacle yes indeed, and that's where we all meet: on the sea: past and present, this tongue and that, try it you'll see. U__ and R__, each with a scar, battling winds, battling waves, the snake-shouldered and the white whale too. (Samad after disposing of Tchangiz, commissioned to perform his most expert move—the finger in the eye, for those uninitiated!—was brought on board to help with the blinding, the total blinding, that is, of Cy. And that one is true, I'm not adding or making it up.) Then we'll have U__ and R__ in the temple slash mosque slash whatever with the living pillars, the city of symbols without any trees, sorry, and the echoes that come forth like perfumes, honest and poor perfumes, forthright, and who agree to cede way at the end, to give way, to you, you, and you. Here we go then, here we go…'

And the Cup suddenly brought its handle up like a maestro and led the other cups, with, finally, yours truly, in a big sing-along.

'Here we go,' the cup repeated, 'on two.' And we began to count, and a one, and a—:

> *We have heroes, we have hope,*
> *U and R, U and R—*
> *They battle winds, they battle waves*
> *They have scars.*

They chuckled (*we* chuckled! I should say), and then switched into another chant, which left me flabbergasted, but which, obviously, they had repeated religiously:

> *There was one, there was not*
> *That's the sin, that's our lot!*

Laughter again and my turn to leave. Friendlier, we had gotten, 'tis true, and mostly through the efforts of the latter Cup. Still, tearful good-byes were by no means in the works. I readied to depart again, when, once more, just before, another one interrupted.

'What about the Prayermat, what about the Prayermat!' it cried in a whiny voice. 'You forgot about the Prayermat.'

I smiled this time, a big smile too. I turned to them again and fiercely undressing them I uttered as the Cups shook, I know who did it, I said, I know who stained the Prayermat red with the Wine, I know who. And as they sat in suspense, I smiled again a wicked smile, I arched the back, I thundered in delight. Ah the osmosis of myths, the osmoses of texts, ah the intertwining of intertexts! Ah, I smiled, and then carried on: it spits blood and it spits drunk, who do you think, who do you think?! It was I, of course, it was I! I all the way no doubt, I of the famous Vowels, I again, I did it, I did it, I the one… It was I!… I!… I!…

'It's I, it's I!' they all clamored back, we all clamored back. 'It's I's fault! I stained the Prayermat, I did it, it's I's fault!'

They were only getting warmed up, for it was only a few moments before they were asking more, asking for all in fact, asking for… blood!

'No more I, no more I, no more I!' they chanted.

'We want I, we want I, we want I,' they said.

'Let's hang I, let's hang I, let's hang I!' they repeated. '*I* did it—it was I!'

———■———

I thrust open the shutters: the chill of the air penetrated the room. I peered into the darkness. I summoned the wind…

The wind, resting in the corridor behind the city's gate, slid through and greeted me. I can go on no longer, I confided, I cannot go on any longer! I marched in all the alleys, I was at the monuments and the fields, the graveyards and the majestic halls: I spied on the morning greeters and on solitary walkers, on dusk and its creatures: I witnessed the embrace of the lovers in anguish. And I even heard, once, the brooding of night, with its bitter frowns, as it gave way, one last time, to day…

I walked through the gardens and through the gates and in the streets, I walked in the city amidst the lost souls, among them not of them, chronicler of fancy and forgetting: in scorn how the waves of the sea batter against the shore of the sea: how the clown drowns in the ripples of the sea:

I walked in the alleys in rapture with beggars and drunkards and their cavernous eyes and their drivel: night revelers, their laughter rises above this dance: in these corners of unfrequented debauchery, of the forgotten, of penance and pity: a world, a magician, nameless…

149

Through the city and with the wind, to the desert, all of sand and of dunes, sprawled majestically before the bridge: I marched unto the bridge, the high-standing bridge, the city behind: I marched unto the bridge and before me appeared the desert: I marched into the desert, marched through the sand, through the dunes, through the unceasing dreams, echoes of ancient whispers, echoes of ancient cries: high atop a sand-dune, far from the gates, the wind staying behind, at the city's gates, awaiting the next crier, upon whose arrival once more it would penetrate the labyrinth: when a crier in a city screams, saddened but dutiful, the wind awakens from a slumber, shakes off the rust, and rushes forth: when the wind emerges from the gates of the city, a crier somewhere is consoled...

I climbed and descended in the dunes in the desert, the climbs and descents, weightlessly through the sands of the desert alone: all along, all around, only the desert, the ecstasy of otherlands within, the city behind.

I labored hard to see the dawn, I started, but I barely mustered the slightest portrayal! Not the brave plunge of the sun into the ocean, not the undulations along the shore, not the nightwalkers by the dim lights of dives or cabarets. No variation will do now, though, it was the futility of the enterprise, it is time that I recognize, it is time that I see: I never believed the formidable task could be brought to fruition, it is imperative that I cease...

And then, again, I marched through the dunes and the shadows on the dunes and the maps drawn on the dunes...

Relieved a bit through some mysterious machination, I went up to a giant silhouette, on a dune, not so far away.

I saw the silhouette and walked to the silhouette and asked if he was a dancer. Can you hear me, I asked again, can you hear me, I for real, do you hear me...

Apparently not. He just stopped the movements and greeted. He signed that he wasn't a dancer and that he didn't appreciate the remark. Don't be deceived by the expertise, he said. Don't say too much too soon too quick, he added. Be wise and simple, be safe, don't look for the little—bet!

Then he signed his name: a D and a 'thief'—a 'stealer' to be exact: it's a whole story you see, the name, but I'm just not sure how real it is! Then he got all agitated, the actor, thinking he could exorcise sorrow by exercising it, the mime—that's what I do for a living, if you want to know. And then he told the story of the name, the name, *his* name.

They wanted to touch the fire, so goes the tale, he began, in the midst of the burning and the shrieks, with the walls scrawled with the writings of rebels, with the champions of the new regime in every nook, with the first ashes scattered about…

It is said that a cry was heard in the distance, in a dilapidated corner, a wailing cry they had never heard, not unlike the call, in fantastical tales, that signal the dawn of a new age, not unlike the visions of a towncrier led astray…

It was said that, unbelievably, effortlessly, all the commotion ceased, all the noise quickly waned, that even the towering fires were tamed. And that they approached, all of them, behind a group of their leaders, cautiously, the spot where I, a newborn infant abandoned under the awning, in a disheveled corner, carried on with my restless screams.

See the portrait: baby under awning, a bearded man, eyes aflame in merriment, short and stocky, extending his arms as he is reaching. Next to him, in the forefront, an even shorter collaborator, sleeves of his workman's shirt pulled up to the elbows, huge forearms showing. In the back, a tall, lanky man, wild astonishment on his brow, bent curiously as if to inspect the creature lying frozen before him. Behind them, anguished faces, melting into one another, one amorphous body, of dark shirts and coats, defined only by mesmerized eyes, of helplessness and hope. I was not to be the story, but, as it turns out, this was the moment, and so I had, I *had*, stolen it! The day of the revolution, I presume, is when I was born, he ended, and so they named me *that*, even though they held me aloft, and sang and cheered in the streets—among the ashes, and among the flames.

The audience of one, I, sprang to my feet (I'd sat down to watch the show). I embraced him and said, How touching, how touching, really, but tell me this, the letter, the first letter, the old and used sound per letter, spell it for me friend, one letter at a time, what's in the name, is it what I think, one letter at a time, is it what I think, is it, is it?

If you insist, he responded, if you want. I do I do, I said, I do. Okay then, all right, okay. And then he went like so: the thumb positioned on the side of closed finger, over the fingers, between the first finger and the second, back to the side, and finally between the first two and the last two: d, a, s, t, a, n, he spelled, that's what it is: *Dastan.*

But so be it, Dastan signed, let us pass. He finally asked if I were a frequent visitor, wherefore I came, and if I came often. Across the bridge, I presume, I answered, but I'm never sure what I will cross into: a desert, the sea, the castle, never so sure! And at night a different matter altogether, added the mime, precisely!

We were barely acquainted that I noticed another moving along the dunes. He walked closer and closer, hands clasped behind his back (him too), pensive, head bent, a long robe he was wearing, a long robe, figure out of the scrolls (you'd think), but no beard. Not long or short, just none at all. Was, in fact, quite well-groomed even (the robe fit smugly). He arrived and immediately launched into an impassioned monologue. No greetings, no acknowledgments: preoccupied, one could say, quite preoccupied...

'Of course,' he started, 'I would not have believed it had he not then carried out as he had, which is to say, he took the pass (a beautiful pass if I may) close to his own end, eluded an on-coming attacker (who surely would have scored, had he been successful in intercepting, for there were no other obstacles between he and the goal), sent the ball diagonally across to the other side, and, about forty meters up the field, proceed-

152

ing to dash up the sideline, retrieved the ball through quite an enterprising effort! There are now fifty meters between he and the opposing goal: he takes the ball, one fake here and defender slides at nothing, another there (as he is several yards up), once more fantastically feigns and slips between two, and there he stands, alone facing the charging goalkeeper, whom he swiftly slides past, gently tapping the ball to the back of the net, securing thus the victory with less than a minute to go in the championship match! What grit, really, at a time of such urgency! Quite astonishing it was, I must tell you, and more so even, since he had used one of the dribbles that he had, time and again, as we had practiced it, reserved, as he used to tell it, reserved for a singular occasion! Astounding! The lone occasion of the use, at such a glorious moment! I could not, for the sake of me, withhold my jubilation in the stands, and so skipped merrily like a hapless child of twelve I tell you, so gleeful I was! I even tried to make my way to the field, as I knew the game would end by the time I made it down, whereupon I would skip over the railings and join in a surefire raucous celebration! Except! Except that I was greeted by a very rude hulk of a member of the security personnel of the stadium! Who, of course, blocked my path: 'Where to, good fellow?' he asked—rhetorically!—as he nudged and held me back. I could scarcely contain my exhilaration, and all he heard was a version of my babbling: that I knew the hero, that he was a brother-in-arms, that such and such, that is my... that is my... that I could simply not stay affixed to my seat—all to no avail! So I remained in the stands, myself with my glee, looking over these very broad shoulders at the field and the embraces of the players, their excitement and relief, with my hero as their hero. For once, I thought to myself (without so much of an incitement, of course), I and the others admiring the same! How glorious indeed! And in that moment—and I shall end here, I promise—and in that moment, I recognized the crazed, communal, adulation of the one, the jubilant and fantastic idolatry of any One! I shared it I tell you, it was within my reach! Not so farfetched anymore! What fervor! What magic! Ah, blissful Land of Belonging, you're quite tempting, I must say, quite tempting indeed! But…'

Finally, not soon enough, he… shushed!

He was relieved though, he'd let it out. Way to go.

Then he said: 'Forgive me for being rude. I'm sorry.' And he added: 'I come from afar, I mean no harm, I'm a philosopher.'

No problem, none, really, but… What do you want, what brings you to these parts?

'What?' he said. 'What?' (He brought his ear closer.)

'I said,' I said, 'what brings you to these parts, if I may ask.'

'Oh, you certainly may,' he said. 'I'm no moral guide.'

But he did not, typically, answer the question.

'Well?'

'Well, what, my man?'

'What *are* you doing here?'

'Oh,' he answered, 'I will simply say that I am doing here precisely what you yourself are doing here!'

He paused, he smiled.

He quipped: 'Shall I venture to ask, or shall I not?'

'But that's not the question!'

'Then what is, good fellow, since I do believe I answered the initial! Indeed, it seems to me that I have undergone two operations since you first addressed me. I have answered, and indeed I did answer, however dissatisfied you may be with that retort—although I cannot fathom why that would be, since I provided you with a framework that should prove most clear, wouldn't you say, since you have not to actually relate to my experience, but merely report to your own—I did answer a question you posed so glibly—and don't think for a minute, friend, that I did not detect that annoying annoyance in your little tone there. Secondly, I have posed the question of posing a question to you. An answer and a question: I am not so sure—and in this perverted inverted sequence!—that such frivolities are so necessary!'

I agreed. I let him know it. I agree, I said, so good-bye.

'Good-bye?!'

'Good-bye!'

'But I just got here!'

'We don't like you,' I said. 'We don't like your—head!'

I let out a little giggle, a little smirk too.

'And may I inquire as to why,' he panicked.

'You've made enough inquiries, don't you think?!'

'Well,' countered the besieged visitor, 'I can never be so sure.'

But I couldn't take anymore and let him have it: 'And that's what spells your kind's doom, ain't it,' I finished. A jab. Boom boom. Like a bunny in a BD! Shoo!

Whereupon: the philosopher, furious and irritated beyond restraint by the callous disrespect, launches himself, wrestling-match-like, wild-bird-like, fighting-cock-like, upon his aggressor: the latter on the bottom, the first on top. Round one, the fight begins: uppercut from the philosopher: not, as one might say, a very forcible one. I recover in fact, and succeed in toppling said puncher who clumsily stumbles on his back. Bent at the knees, peering at the prey struggling on his side, I fumble forth, charge the chump, jump on him: a hook—not much of one either, although perhaps, truth be told, slightly more potent than his. Rolling in the sand, throwing wild slaps and silly punches. Here a slap, there a slap… Frightened mime on sand-dune frozen eyes bulging and open mouth unbelieving, hands on head: tumbling around unceasing are the chumps: not much power in the punches, so no one is seriously hurt. Yet. What can I do, thinks the mime, what can I do? Panicky, helpless. Suddenly a light. The mime thinks to convince by example. By showing. So: there he is launching himself unto the sand, rolling around, jerking his head back and forth as if being hit, throwing open air slaps at no one in particular, contracting his muscles, in turn seeming defeated or brave, incensed, wishing to kill, pleading for mercy: all of this particularly close to the warring rhinos, so that, he hoped, the absurdity, perhaps even the inanity, the futility, of the frolic, would be grasped. Are you out of your minds, the mime gestured again, are you crazy?! But to no avail. The battle rages until incapacitation. Exhausted on the sand, slightly apart, staring at the sky. Incredibly inept at battle, no one is seriously wounded. No blood either.

The mime sat crouched, his hands turned-to-fist pushing in his cheeks, elbows resting on knees, restless, helpless—and sick: three clowns under the hot desert sun. I wobble to my feet, walk to the philosopher and extend a hand: the fellow grabs and pulls himself up, cleans off, fixes the hair, takes the deep breath.

'And what did it all come to?' he muttered. 'What was the point of it all?'

I threw an arm across the other's shoulder: 'Closer than we'd like to admit, don't you think?' I said. 'At least in our ineptitude!'

We laughed and took two steps toward the mime. The latter did not budge—simply followed, angrily scrutinizing the progression. He did not move until we had arrived before him, whereupon he sprang up like a crazed man, frightening us out of our wits, and gestured wildly with arms, hands, and head, scolding us both. We have better things to do, he concluded angrily after his silent diatribe, don't you think? I agreed. I bowed my head. It was true: the mime had the answer: there was nothing to say.

———■———

To add, to say, to explain, or illuminate: what it is, as it is: the translation is going smoothly, another passage and I am perhaps on my way. I must contact him, see where he is, see what he wants. The first parts were not as difficult, but not such a cinch either. Am I including elements I should be, professionally speaking, excluding? Have I given all situations their legitimate place? Have I transposed sections creatively enough, have I found the appropriate equivalencies? I paused and looked up. A few moments later, I wrote again: the bombs have been falling steadily for long, almost ever since I started. They fall mercilessly, one day, as if it were the end of all. On another, there is a minor thunder, a brief rumbling, and suddenly again, peace in the sky. I have thought of abandoning of course, I have even been quite set on it, taken the necessary measures even. But I come back, always. Always return... I cannot be so cowardly, I reason! It is quite an adventure, I reason! Under the bombs how I will go on: at the end of all how to carry on...

Still, I am wondering how it is that he ever showed up here in the first place. The circumstances are dubious at best. One day I arrive and notice packages and an assortment of boxes in the hallway. I'm slowly coming up the stairs that I see someone coming out the front, tiptoeing through everything. He is preoccupied but he sees me. He raises his hand and smiles. 'You must be...' he says pleasantly. 'I'm tickled to finally meet you. I'd been planning this move for quite a while, but I was always told that *now* is not the right time. Not now, not now! I held back, impatiently, until, finally, the quarters were empty! Quite a coincidence, would you not say?!'

It certainly did not sound like one! I stood, unmoved, unmoving, trustful yet cautious, as both his elegancy and his speech seemed a bit artificial. I just thanked him and presented myself.

'Quite a collection you have there,' I added, seeing his sculptures and figurines.

'Well, thank you,' he responded—and that was the extent of that initial conversation.

I'd been slightly unnerved but managed to forget the episode. And for the better, I might add, for he finally turned out to be quite a pleasant, not to mention helpful, character. Great colleague too. Over time, he grew increasingly more aware of many details in my life, he learned of my troubles, my obsessions. But I never dared ask where he had come from, what the duration of his visit was, and why exactly it was that he was staying. Politeness had ruled. But I do believe that the time has come to ask him, especially in light of the new project, that is. I must interrogate him soon, it is imperative.

158   Dastan appears at the door: Dastan bows, Dastan greets, exhausted. He is carrying the philosopher on his back, weak at the knees, pleading eyes, saddened: Dastan holds on to the philosopher riding on his back holding his shoulders with all fingers, his legs wrapped around the mime like a spider, only to keep himself up. I stand abruptly, shaken at the sight.

'What's going on?' I ask. 'What the hell is going on?'

The mime cannot respond, his hands clasped around the philosopher's ankles to keep him up: he is quivering, at the knees, but he is strong, courageous, standing. He shakes his head, but he cannot move.

'Put him down!' I yell. 'Put him down and tell me what happened!?'

Neither the mime nor the philosopher act. Neither speaks. The mime gestures with his head, struggling with his head, gesturing as if to say: follow us. 'All right,' I said, 'all right. Let's go.'

I follow the mime carrying the philosopher on his back: through the city's haze, through the alleys, above the domes and through the gardens, across the bridge, slowly each step, as if summoned...

Across the bridge and through the desert, through a hand sculpted in the sand reaching out from the earth, with bent fingers as if to make a fist: defiant hands of the crushed, impossible to shun, how the storm swallows the children feeding its wrath... Around the two sculptures embracing: standing they were as if frozen in an instant of godful vengeance... Around the silhouette of an elder, swept by the wind into the pose... And another with an open mouth, his is a scream, reaching to the firmament with one arm.

Through the labyrinth of the sculptures of sand, the mime still exhausted carrying the mute philosopher.

'You saw this!' I ask and tell at once. 'You saw this, didn't you?'

The philosopher childlike is hiding his face behind Dastan. Dastan, saddened, gestures that yes, we saw it, we saw it all.

'What happened?' I demand. 'Answer me, what did you see, what happened?!'

A march now through this garden, companions weaving through a maze of shapes and forms darting out, spread across the desert: behind me the mime carrying the philosopher on his back: through the minefield of human souls, through this city of sand, through this labyrinth of screaming souls...

We march through the desert and arrive at the edge of the desert. A tall figure, shrouded in black, a long scythe resting on his shoulder, his face in darkness under a black robe, stands. When I reach him, he turns and begins to walk. Endless days, through eternal cities, through a field of shards: Dastan the mime, I, a frightened philosopher, through the sandscape unknown.

How motion has made us how we march... What kind of revolution are *we*, after all! Born with a tantrum, trembling, soggy: out of one sludge into another, surveying the scene, and the eternal ghosts!

But History pursues relentless, chasing as I run, from afar and then closer, closer, on this majestic march, face to face, History and I...

Then we begin the play: a tease—or the duel of unimagined proportions. Until that time when once again the hunt begins: History, cunning, hides in the most impenetrable nooks, to suddenly leap from the hiding place unsuspected to devour the prey. And the chase begins again, now sporting a new disguise: atop the mountain, floating among the clouds, suddenly leaps noiseless into the abyss of an endless trance. Bottomless, the abyss hungers for more and History rapidly plunges into the depths of the psyche—and begins anew its ways, searching for the path. It is a new chase now, in the inner maze, hiding places of old, tears and dormant shrieks. History, satanic, slides swiftly through the veins and the secret pathways of tempestuous floundering. Move, dodge, but cannot hide from the self. History hungered gaining energy ascends to new heights: finding the way and crippling: the final transformation, perhaps, with unexpected twists metamorphoses into a red man with two full horns and a pitchfork to his name. It is time, the final time, the last time: when motion halts and elsewhat, perhaps, begins. Time has vanished, and so too its supreme advocate, each faltering, one with the end, the script of curmudgeonly evanescence: the tale, of course, of the vanishing genie, our one and only.

In this enduring march, the eternal march, unforeseen: obediently, unquestioning, behind the methodical steps of the veiled one: courageously defying odds, defying gods, dragged to the gallows. But the toll is visible, weariness close at hand, the first signs, the rupture, paces diminishing, behind the figure undaunted, unperturbed, behind me, Dastan the mime, carrying the philosopher on his back, can bear it no longer: he can bear it no more, the weight of the philosopher can be felt no more. Dastan, crumbling at the knees, pleading, lets out an unseemly cry, a wounded animal's wail. Dastan the mime is struggling: he crumbles at the knees, again, and sinks to the ground: the scared philosopher tightens his hold, Dastan the mime with two hands on the ground to prevent his final collapse: but to no avail…

Withering, silently, to his side, Dastan the mime, weightlessly, falls…

The philosopher panics: he has loosened his hold, let go, pushing himself away from Dastan, who has rolled in exhaustion on his back. He struggles to his feet, stands and shrieks. I hear the philosopher, I turn. The veiled figure in the front halts but does not turn. I rush to the side of the fallen Dastan, kneel by his side, shake him: nothing to do, no movement, no reaction.

'Get up!' I plead. 'Up!'

But to no avail. Dastan remains on the ground, motionless. I bend down and lift him, struggle to my feet, carry the mime on my shoulders: walk back, painfully, to where the others have been waiting. The philosopher behind, I carry the wounded Dastan, marching behind a faceless figure leading. The march goes on, it must go on...

Out of the lamp the genie comes, swerves and gently wraps its tail around, this is your last chance, I'm here but I will be gone, tomorrow there will be no lamp, and no genie to make the wishes come true: hovering above the heads, hovering alone but almost gone, something in us pleading: no genie, don't go... A fabulous lamp that somewhere someone gave to say some day trouble will brew, and a lamp is all you got, so take it and when the storm has almost hit, the laughter done gone drowned in the pit, don't forget there is a genie with his hovering robe, who'll come back to save you, come back to save you, Ooo, Ooo, Ooo...

The genie before the battles and the torture had vanished, but those who did not know reached for and heeded the calls. Nearing the epoch of valor and martyrdom when truth will condemn falsehood forevermore. Duel of the century, duel without meeting, across the waters, those who did not embrace me now will pay. It is said of revolutionaries that they grasp The Moment When the King Will Fall to make a case for the triumph of the cause. Of them it is said: they see when no one else sees, they hear the cunning gods and spring on their prey—look how they scatter away, look how they scurry away, when the crier has left. When the spectacle of unity dies, chaos once again: the Genie no one knew, how they hold the keys to the secrets of mortal men—and paradise. That is why, it is said, where I come from anyway, that they were chosen to grant wishes: not mermaids, not unicorns, it was genies, someone said, that when they fly you fly with them, they take you on their journeys above the sand and above the streets bathed in nightlights below. Disappearing genies were chosen to bring back all that we have lost, to awaken us from a dream to magically take us into another: a lamp, out of which one day a genie will appear but disappear if you don't grab, swerves about where the clouds might steal, for up there too they watch who wish to be kings and queens, now is the moment to grab, for a disappearing genie when appearing appears as another: might think the genie a god, might think the genie a savior—but the genie also a bitter boor, a sore loser even, maybe, who asks you, and asks you, who you are, who you are (Ooo, Ooo, Ooo)—

disappearing genies when they appear once again wish their own wish watch out: a genie out of the lamp could be an or-phan, in the house of god:

disappearing genies from now on when they ask you:

who are you anyway, say this to them: who are *you*—

and be on your way:

I will not disappear so easily, I murmur—but no one hears. I will not be deceived, but no one hears—I will not vanish so.

Suddenly, unexpectedly, I turn, Dastan on the back, weigh-ing heavily on the back: I turn and begin to run:

the guide stops, but does not turn:

the philosopher turns, but does not move:

abandons, he, and

for the others,

the runflight across,

breathless,

across the dunes of the desert: through the garden of souls

how to begin if to begin I weave an endless

tale: monstrous strides growing tall as a giant stomping and raving, shrinking again

with each step the landscape turning into a

dream, a dance,

I now a mouse, a lion, an eel—a

giraffe hurriedly in the desert, an old man cane in hand

163

but flying, a puppet with a string,

wooden head, wooden smile, a square face and fake whiskers—and yes,

carrying a muted mime all the same!

Now I see the bridge: exhausted slip to my knees, put down Dastan, collapse to the sand. There is no sound in the desert, no cries. There is no sorrow, no solace. Stillness of the desert, two men lie helpless on the sand. Silence of the desert…

———■———

But the barking of the dog does a better job than the neighbors themselves on occasion! There we are that's right. Up and away. Can't lie down, can't sleep, I'm not a somnambulist goddamnit! Quite the contrary! I stand angrily. Awakened from the desired rest! Look around to see who it was, where the dog is, and what's what. The tiny dog and its scratching! Look upward and down and left and right clenching fists and showing teeth. Eyes even O my god suddenly into balls of fire. Hair torn. No joke, I'm mad. Searching for the prey. Where is that dog, I mutter. Where is that dog so I can grab it and strangle the life from it the little punk! But look, there I am, standing, all-powerful so I think, that a cloud of dust from afar approaches. I can't make out the shape, but the gallops are heard and soon it's obvious. It's obvious who this ghostly cavalier is. And a menacing group of clouds at the same speed from above coming in this direction too!

'Justice,' I notice suddenly, 'and Vengeance!'

Lo! I pick up Dastan and mount the white stallion. The man behind and the clouds following him at full speed. Through the desert the galloping riders. I smack the valiant horse and coerce him to go faster! Faster, for Christ's sake, faster! The mime is lying across on the horse's back. Pitiless flames thrown my way from behind and atop. Righteousness hurled my way without remorse. Words, commandments. What I should say, what I should believe—and what I shouldn't. What I am, what I'm not! That's what a man and conscience deserve: Eternal Justice in pursuit! After the revolution! That version. Blindfold and all. Torture chambers and interrogation rooms. Cat-eater mincing meat. They deserve it anyway, say. Everyone will get theirs. Collaborators and picture-takers and informers, they'll pay. This is not the first time either—just the latest incarnation that's all. And here too! That's why no remorse, that's why no recourse! Flee and some rock or something will hopefully sprout in front of the pursuers is all! I charge full-speed ahead on the horse with the mime without shame. I'm right after all damn it, I'm right! Across the dunes and the hill and the sparse vegetation. The cactus watches us fly by and so does the rabbit out of his hole.

And then there's the Pebble. The big Pebble in the field with luscious lips and long lashes. The Pebble watches the horseman with the mime dart by behind with the cloud of dust on the ground and a cloud of, what, water? not so far above. Can't hold back with those big eyes even though no one saw, that's fine: in this desert the Pebble doth see the legendary Pursuit!

'It's true about conscience and all,' the Pebble comments, 'but this time I don't know. Not this Justice! I mean, really!'

The cloudy *cavalier* with the long robe upon hearing the stone's doubt suddenly reacts and darts back. Stands before the proud but (understandably) frightened Pebble. Looks him straight into those ancient eyes. Unrepentant his dagger! Raises it high—his back arching—his long beard showing—and his piercing gaze: pauses—and finally swings. Swings down, yes, straight into the eyes of—and blinds the famed stone. Blind it for now and forever. Or?—

The one with the mime on his horse has gotten away. The martyr here is the Stone. The eye of the Stone, to be exact, that's who the martyr is!

———■———

Now the night: how I address the colleague. The greetings, the collaborations. The strolls to the edge of the city and back, mostly on the main throughway, early in the morning. The talk of the current troubles and the hurdles and the book: merrily on many an occasion along the avenue, watching, listening, stopping. On this trip, knowing the marvelous skills in the art of translation, he proposes a certain volume. Quite a fascinating endeavor, he suggests, it would make quite a tale. 'It seems,' he continues, 'that the book is arranged in such a way that it imposes upon its reader to actually, and I mean this literally, to actually experience, in life, the world that is portrayed within!'

At this juncture, feeling a bit tired (and woozy), I close the volume, lift the glasses and rub the eyes. No need to take them out tonight, I think, they're all right tonight, tonight, they're all right. Nothing to regret though, nothing to curse, but I wonder anyway: after *The Cities of Sand* and the voluminous *Halls of Heresies* (plurals, now, indeed), I wonder. But I've done a decent job, really, I've done okay, I've transposed some of the episodes quite accurately. Even the awkwardness, even the deviance. (This was not unusual, the evaluation of the work, the ritual of conviction and measure.) I've been quite faithful, what with the Story of the Beginning, the Intertextual Osmosis of Texts and Traditions, the Discovery of Dastan in the Desert, the Coming of the Awaited, the March through the City of Sand, the Return with Dastan the Mime, Justice and Vengeance, the Chronicle, throughout, of the Revolution, and the Porter, the Porter and the Book…

It is impossible, of course, an impossible task! No doubt. I've been forced to remake it, recreate it all—but through no fault of mine, no… That was the only way… Anyhow, I thought, got to carry on… Without a tremor and without laughter all the same…

Under the bombs slowly becoming the scribe: into the silence, inhabiting the language of… Under the bombs… There is a world and there is not: there is one and there is not: once upon a time…

There is a knock at the door. The shutters are open, a light breeze. Who could it be, I wonder, and at this forbidden hour?!

I go around the desk, stare at Dastan, resting by the pillars, surrounded by the busts of glorious predecessors in the majestic Hall, exhausted still, sprawled against a column—but alive, at least alive!

I walk slowly to the portals. Gust of wind through the window, whistling, peculiarly. I open the door, an old man is standing. He extends his arms, hands over the package. The old man, porter of books…

'Madman!' he cries. 'O Madman of the Forbidden Night!'

I take the book, I close the door.

'Finally!' I mumble. 'The book has been sent!'

I carry it to the desk, I sit, I open the package. I dust off the covers and caress, almost, the volume. Gently I turn, to the first page, and I open—and begin: *The Riddle of the Towncrier*:

was with great bewilderment that I found, at the far end of a vast courtyard, among both the faithful and the heretics engaged in various trades, among faces I had conveniently forgotten and others I had imagined languishing in murky parts, an old acquaintance, whom I did not expect to see, but for whom I had always felt a volatile mixture of warm sympathy and open repugnance. One who, despite the obstacles and his share of hard times, had managed to carve out quite a niche for himself in a vocation fit for his capacities and talents—for which, really, he seemed to have been born. A gentle if cunning personage, who had bestowed his unrewarded generosity upon many an undeserving folk, but who was also prone to whimsical aggressions, to uncouth and uncontrollable attacks, to excessively violent outbursts and periodic fits of frenzy, all of which I attributed to an understandable need for respite. For reasons mysterious to me at the time and still today though, I lost his whereabouts (without much regret, I admit), never did succeed in locating him, soon abandoned the search and finally carried forward with my affairs.

Everything changed however, when I saw him again, as I shall shortly relay, in that most venerated of locations.

I had, per usual on those morning strolls, made my way down the staircase and greeted, as I passed, the neighbor from below, quite an intelligent and admirable lady of an older generation. In late adolescence already (she had related during one of our informal chats), in an epoch where such declarations were deemed the most pernicious of vulgarities and the most heinous of obscenities, she had sworn to make a home where free association with chosen partners was legal—a proclamation that had led to being quickly disowned by family and most friends. In time though, this same family, the same friends, and most former associates ('the cowards' was her chosen label), returned apologetically, facing the shame of their ignorance. Childless nevertheless, the last partner passed away, neither the same energy nor the same passion were present to 'go out there again'—she recounted one day. On this day also, I had noticed her coming up the stairs (the same that I was descending), at the doorway, about to turn the knob so as to enter (quite morbid residence I must add): she was turning her head as the first cracklings of the stairs above were heard, when I looked through that vertical tunnel, at her peering face. I appropriately raced through and saluted quickly, in such a way that there was, in effect, no chance to converse, no chance to engage in another lengthy tirade about lost youth, romantic adventures or glorious soirées of long ago! I remember distinctly as I careened down the stairwell, how only the head—and ever so slightly—how only the head was turned upward, along with an awkward grimace: this instance of the encounter, the eyes, two in dark stairwell yet so distant: a photograph, relived each day, but never same.

169

Finally in the street, I greeted the barber (around the bend), and the tailor, crossing the street (wave of the hand to him), quickly fetched the first coin in a pocket and handed it (placed it, would be more accurate!) into a beggar's open palm. I then made my way through the winding hills and finally began the stroll towards the public square where I started (several digressions ago), the simple (stately! mirror-like!) tale that I am now about to continue.

———■———

A temporarily converted courtyard in the center of town where people assembled, the makeshift marketplace was of quite unimpressive design. Mostly barren in fact, with a few scattered plants inside the gated area, some vehicles parked in the vicinity and others facilitating the transport of goods. Isolated in spots and displayed by merchants passively watching over the artifacts, an array of products satisfying needs or curiosities could be found by the average shopper: fresh fruit from the farmers bringing dutifully their produce; big books of relieved bibliophiles or disgruntled readers; an assortment of jewelry imported from exotic territories; tapestries and furniture with designs of daily rituals in lively colors and embellished arabesques; ancient vases, ceramic pots and garden sculptures, all surely unearthed through patient excavations; paintings and drawings depicting scenes of battles, of village life, of mystical quests and popular uprisings, of playful spectacles and fantastic voyages; impressive maps and imaginary photographs; and life-size statues even, fully inanimate, yet bearing uncanny resemblance to versions of their watchers. Quite a common sight then: a market without extravagance, nothing out of the ordinary, singular reminder of the city-dweller's sights and sounds.

I circulated at a leisurely pace (quite a while since I'd ventured in these parts), walked by several displays, inspector-like examined curious objects in a withdrawn manner (knowing that I had no intention to buy), and even took a refreshment at a small kiosk, bending backwards, in a state of detachment overlooking the whole scene. I paid the—exorbitant, considering the quantity proffered—sum required for the beverage, and then carried on with my stroll. It was on this second leg, if we may call it that, after further inspection of the goods along the way, and at the far end of the courtyard, that I came upon him: a bit grayer (not even *he* could escape the tyranny of age), he appeared healthier and more vigorous nevertheless, in overall better physical shape than when I had last seen him. I approached slowly, with enough reason still to doubt it was he, but believing that I had, finally, on this occasion at least, recognized an old acquaintance: squinting and stretching, extending my head and neck in order to ascertain as to his identity, I let out, finally: 'My god! Is it really you?'

He recognized me at once, and the excitement he projected in his very first exclamation revived the kinder of the feelings I harbored for him. He even took pains to stand up, come around his table—on which there were merely a few cards—and embraced me with such warmth that I immediately excluded feigned sincerity from the source of his action. No: from all that I could make out, this was genuine: it was he, no doubt about it now, this was the clockmaker of old!

Although I was unequivocally pleased by the meeting, I was also slightly unnerved by his greeting, for it seemed, in the tone in which he had addressed me, and in the very words he had used, unless I had fully misconstrued the meaning (and this option I preferred in the instants that followed), it looked as though he was, indeed, *awaiting* me! Impossible of course, my senses informed, and I paid no heed to this private puzzle.

'So what brings you around,' he started again. (Quickly relieved, I: he did not know! Or... Was he merely uncertain of the intentions? Or just playing along, unaware that he had revealed his deck? Again, I attempted to ignore my heightening anxieties, adopting instead a mundane tone.)

'I should ask the same,' I finally answered in jest.

'Perhaps you should!' he replied. 'In fact, you *have*!'

I smiled and nodded and said in jest (not knowing that my directive would in fact provoke the soliloquy that it did): 'O please do tell!'

—■—

'You see,' he started (and then went on quite at length), 'I'd be-
come quite accustomed to it all, the weeks and months spent
fuming or pouting, complaining to the lot, sitting around,
loitering, pretending to come to a decision after all. We were
all guilty of it afterwards, only some more than others. As for
me, I simply tried to keep busy with the responsibilities, until
some very unusual events meddled with the daily rhythm. To
the inactive go the spoils, I presume, for it was during an idle
stroll—O respected deities, forgive these false praises of idle-
ness—and quite alone—I cannot lie: no one ever anticipated
that I would venture so utterly bereft: I had left many behind,
I had said my own prayers, I had trusted my own instincts—
that I came upon one most conspicuous creature. He did not
look anything like one could imagine: indescribable in fact,
although you know me not to shun difficulties. A *solitaire* he
seemed, tall, with a stern and penetrating countenance. I could
not at first utter the slightest word, nor did he attempt on his
part to admonish my paralysis. A fancied dream realized, this
peculiar encounter, or merely the first instance of several gath-
erings? I could not tell, not then anyway. Our silent exchange
lasted a few moments—and if you have lived half the life that I
have, you know that a mere instant itself is quite a trial—until
he turned abruptly and began to walk away.

'As if in a trance—I was not, not! I insist—I followed him,
whereupon we made our way through a path that I had never
seen, in the hills: quite serpentine, imperceptible—no, your
first wanderer would not merely have stumbled upon it—lead-
ing interminably upwards, through a most conspicuous sky-
scape, until we finally arrived at what resembled a securely hid-
den estate. I imagined it to be his, and it was not long before

he was holding for me a door wide open. Without protest of any kind, I took the next step, and proceeded to enter.'

I stood there while he, seemingly unperturbed by my passivity or by the lack of interest in the goods assembled in his stall, and obviously oblivious to what was turning out to be quite a long monologue, carried on.

'There was little to see,' he continued, 'quite a spacious hall but deserted, fully unfurnished but for a lone chair and a desk, little light to speak of, no decoration, save for sumptuous paintings that I shall shortly tell you more about. The required pews, the votive candles, the pulpit, the chalice dare I say, the sacristy, the apse and the altar: all were absent, conspicuously absent.

'My host closed the door behind him and stood quietly. I, in turn, approached the numerous paintings and canvases that adorned the walls, as well as others laid out on the floor—the unfinished ones, I presumed. Although no connoisseur of such things—not at the time anyway—I knew also that nothing very urgent was at hand, and so studied each with quite a high degree of interest: with as much diligence and precision as I knew, with as much attention that I could muster. The host, in turn, remained pensive: it seemed as if he had always peered at the artifacts, forever, perhaps.

'A short while later—I did not know how long—I finally walked to the exit. He did not even respond, nor did he in any way acknowledge my presence. It was, I must say, as if all was the natural order of things, as if, strangely, I stood at the beginning of all creation. I opened, adjusted my shawl—I was wearing a shawl—and made my way back, along the same path that I was able, somehow, to recognize, effortlessly...

'I do not wish to give you the sense of a supernatural energy pulling me without consent, for I was not hypnotized or mesmerized, but it was also true that I simply did not know the source of my commands, nor could I pinpoint the manner in which I was drawn! Indeed, a short while later, there I was again, at the foot of the hill, where he greeted me, without the remotest expression. Once more I followed him: head bowed, humble, marching directly behind every step. But, I insist again, it was no imposed submission: merely the dint of circumstance, I believe, which neither he nor myself dared to challenge!

'We entered as we had on our first engagement. I paced around the room, examining the works in more intimate detail, particularly intrigued by certain features that had gone unnoticed on my previous visit, and which delineated several of my initial judgments. The first painting was a fascinating mix of colors variously devised on the canvas so as to give an overwhelming sensation of chaos. As you must be well aware, we have several replicas of these primordial events, but I was unusually touched in this case by what I sensed to be a most appropriate version of the reigning order. The intricate realness was delicately designed through an amalgam of forms, shapes, and hues, lavished with such expertise that one quickly forgot it was in fact a mere rendering. I moved closer and inspected in more detail. It appeared as though the material, initially construed as the conventional kind, the regular stuff, if you will, of such creations, was not of the common lot. I had dabbled enough in such—frivolous?—activities, indeed judged myself familiar enough and well-traveled enough, if not an expert, to recognize that what I had before me was most assuredly not of a common thread, but further, nothing at all that I had *ever* known. Quite strange in fact. Still, I was not bothered by the intensity, nor was I taken aback by the fabulous emotional import: only troubled, I dare say, by what seemed to constitute the mysterious provenance of the elements. I was loath to become more preoccupied, and since I had made it a point of principle not to lose myself in irrelevant thoughts—or to engage in petty battles—I quickly returned to the baser instincts—and set my confused self on a more fertile path. Sufficiently recovered, I gorged in the singular majesty of the work, in the stunning breadth, in the overwhelming power. He still had not uttered a single word, nor had he availed himself in such a way that we could communicate: be it to chatter courteously, to probe the psyche, or to evaluate the works that surrounded us. I was a privileged guest, this much was easily deduced, and I did not wish to trouble the dynamics that had so far developed between us. Content with things as they had gone, I readily inhabited my post as the observer in the house.

'I presume that a considerable amount of time passed before I exited the house. And this I *presume*, I take it, only because such a thing has proven mightily irreversible! I mean here no philosophical treatise, nor an equivalent discourse, not even of a poetic bent, on the passage of Time: I point it out simply because on these particular occasions, nothing at all, and I must insist on the lack of *all* visible signs—since I have by now reaffirmed the legitimacy of the problem—nothing that transpired could prove, in any manner, that the detested pest had indeed elapsed, in those ways, at least, that we are accustomed for it to flee. I would not have grown grayer, nor would the arrangement of the surroundings have changed much during these periods, this is for certain, but that is far from what I am proposing. I mean only that between my entrances and exits, nothing at all would give even the slightest indication of the regular passage of time. *Au contraire*! For on those occasions—and there were, as I will soon recount, several other visits—that I was led to the house and made my way back, the

175

relative position of plants, animals and objects, all gave the precise indication that nothing at all had moved or progressed. Baffled as I was, with strong reservations still about my impressions, I brokered a pact with myself to secretly observe and to determine, through various means at my disposal, in my better imitation of the roaming private investigator, the validity of my misgivings. It was still possible, after all, that during my visits, things *had* changed, only to revert back to the precise condition in which I had first seen them. But, strange as it may seem, I was more apt to believe in an absolute reconfiguration of all things, than a dubiously improbable irregularity: an impossibility more probable than the improbability! In other words, I was more willing to believe that something awfully fantastical was occurring, generated by cryptic forces and agents, rather than to comfort myself with highly unlikely possibilities, only to convince myself that I was still occupying the same world! Not me, not the new me, not this time!'

———■———

He paused, finally, grabbed a glass of water from the table by which we were still standing, quickly apologized, placed the glass on the table again, and, without even bothering to, shall we say, open up the conversation, launched into what were sure to be ever more surprising details. Indeed, he grabbed my forearm in a friendly gesture, turned around slightly, uttered quickly, 'Allow me to elaborate'—and carried on.

'After the third of my visits, which I have yet to relate, I paid special heed to these accumulating worries. As I was in a contemplative mood and desired little contact with those of my kind, I had, let me give you this precision also before I go any further, taken the less populated streets. On my way to the encounter then, and I do believe you know the area well enough, I had gone through the back, turned at K__ and continued straight until Y__, after which I had merely turned into the woods and carried on up the hill.

'Once I had descended again and found myself in more familiar surroundings, I was taken aback by several occurrences that struck me as irregular, to say the least. On K__, for example, I saw a lone cigarette butt—surely left by one inconsiderate gent!—a small, squashed butt that I had particularly noticed on the initial trip because, I admit, of my own craving for a swift lit. It lay in the terrain in the precise position that I had seen it as I had come through god knows how long ago. I was quite befuddled as this was evidence, on my return, that, odd as it may seem, nothing at all had been the slightest bit affected: no changes at all, in any conceivable form. Now you may make the point that you also have seen squashed cigarette butts lying in the same places without noticing the slightest modifications in their condition, and that there is, in fact, nothing at all that one would deem unusual about this. But I remind you that it had been breezy, and that the gust had occasionally reached higher speeds. Northwest winds, 10 to 20 miles per hour, to be exact. Sunny skies granted and pleasant, but chilly. Highs in the middle to upper 50's. Anyway, according to my calculations, every logical indicator would have the butt, sturdy as they come, would have it slightly removed from the position in which I had first come across it. The culprit, I thought, had divined one masterful scenario here. In order to ascertain, however, I bent down, picked up the wiggled rest, examined it, not quite sure what it was I was searching for, and put it back down. Now more than ever suspicious as to the events of the day, I carried on along K__. I had still not run into anyone, when I was struck again by further evidence of aberrant happenings. I will even concede the cigarette episode, if you're not convinced. But explain this to me: M.'s bicycle. We both knew M. to be meticulous and disciplined, and I doubt that the passage of the years would alter what seemed to constitute his overall make-up. We both knew him to be relentlessly precise, never exhibiting the slightest measure of instability or folly. We have never known him to allow a smidgen of the unexpected to penetrate the fabric of his life, his functions, or his rituals. Nor have we known him to exhibit any proclivity for random operations. Good old reliable M.: he had made a life of it! Now: when I had left, I had turned into K__, made a right turn, that is, into K__, and noticed that the shop was closed, M.'s bicycle still chained to the racks: logical enough. I am returning, I have turned into K__ from Y__, I am casually walking and I notice that the shop is closed, the bicycle still there. Seeing that I had left in the morning, and noting that I had, at the very least, been away for what would have amounted, under normal circumstances, to several hours, considering that the distance to the hill itself is forty minutes, and allowing for one hour at the house on the mountain— which is indeed minimal—and yet also certain that I am not away any more than, at most, four or five hours, the situation quite simply presented itself as an impossibility. By now, the shop should have been open, inside should have been Morton himself (or Morty, if you prefer, or Mort, as the more intimate call him!) preparing the deed, and M.'s bicycle gone, carrying its rider around, as it does everyday: for publicity, of course, and closeouts! Now you may complain again that a single being's quotient of reliability, however elevated, still cannot be a barometer for the tricks of chance, or the coquetry of time. Perhaps, but M. is not *any* single *soul*! You and I both know that. You saw him when he arrived, you had told it yourself: on the statue in the center of the square, invisible to most, peering down at us all, saddened, open wings and all… Not just any soul! But again, again I grant it to you, unbelief granted… With my last revelation, however, I am certain to persuade you, and I am certain to find you as bewildered as the next.

'I walked on my route pensive, after the required turn into K__, skeptical as to the validity of all that had unveiled itself before me, evaluating the precise observations in what amounted to a mixture of delusion and dread. Now K__ is, although not by any means among the busiest of the streets, also not so deserted. Always a semblance of a crowd on each sidewalk, with the measured paces, and the tired faces. One gait and another. In either direction marching as if summoned by a most mysterious source.

'Now: highly ordered as our lives have become, highly mechanistic and predictable as they may seem, you would agree that we have managed, perhaps through our own weaknesses, or through an uncanny ability to avoid repetition, we have managed to deter the very dullness, the very sameness, in fact, that we have instituted. So that even though there is no reason for it to come as a surprise, you would grant that it is highly improbable for one passerby to meet, at prescribed hour in the morning, and at prescribed return time in the evening, the very same people who are functioning on the same schedule. Meaning: that each day, at given hour, at destined site, the exact same ritual *should* repeat itself, with the very same exact players. Meaning also: that this, despite ourselves, never occurs! I have never even taken a step in the same manner as the previous or the next! Nothing is ever the same. Nothing. Ever!

'Anyway: I have turned into K__, in the opposite direction, I tell you, in which I had come, and I see before me, as I walk down the street, the very same coats, the very same hats and shoes that I had seen when initially I had left. And coming

179

towards me: the same faces as well, one by one, every single face, with the same exact expression that early in the morning they had worn when I had set off. I could not distinguish a single difference, I did not detect the tiniest departure from those encounters. Relief, finally, since I gathered that it was the evening indeed...

'Highly unlikely as the event was, it was proof of a passage nonetheless, was it not? All of those whom I had placed from behind, once again I was seeing from that very same angle. All of those whose faces I had seen, again I was seeing. This, the very regularity demanded by our own composition, that nevertheless we have indefinitely defied, finally was taking place. However singular the event—and O was it not an occasion to marvel!—it also represented, in my particular case, the opportunity to rest easily. I should have been troubled in fact, had I *not* seen the same—had I not, that is, recognized the faces, or detected the traits of recognizable folks. And in return, I should have had cause for concern, perhaps even acquiesced to a feeling of overwhelming astonishment, only if the current developments had occurred with my going in the opposite direction. In that scenario, as you well know, I would have merely been taking a different route home, in a roundabout fashion, traveling on K__ anyway, but in the same direction in which I had left. Had I taken that option, I would have been content, as at present, only if those whose faces I had not seen I were now witnessing.

'Comfort then, and ease! I reasoned that the shop had been closed and M.'s bicycle present only because it was late in the evening, that the cigarette butt was, after all, sturdier than thought, that other irregularities were merely fragments of my own hallucinations, and that, finally, all the errors had come upon through my own miscalculations, my own underestima-

tion as to how long I had stayed at the house on the hill! Joy
of the absolution of the Riddle! Dance with arms high, doin'
the shake, thankgodomercy I got it! Skip to the left, skip to
the right, one two three and a one two three, all I need is the
grease, and I'm the new Jimmy Dean!

'Not quite so fast, though, I thought, no quite so fast—for
although Reason had comforted me as was its mission, still it
seemed that it would not triumph in the end. As I continued
my stroll, attempting to resolve my confusions, at once put-
ting together the pieces and concentrating on the surround-
ings, preoccupied as I was with these derivations, I noticed,
little by little—and I attributed the slowness of the cognizance
to initial fascination with the fabric of the crowd—troubling
irregularities in the physical configuration. It had seemed to
me indeed, that I had already passed B__'s grocery, when I
came upon R__'s store: now if I had in fact passed B__'s, it
would only make sense that I would not see R__'s, since in
the direction in which I was going (or thought I was going),
I simply would have passed R__'s—without taking notice (it
was a dump!)—before I had passed B__'s. Perhaps I had not
passed the grocery then, I summarized, now paying less heed
to the passersby, perhaps I had merely mistaken C__'s grocery
for B__'s, the two of which bore an uncanny resemblance to
one another, all of which would indicate that I would come
upon B__'s in less than a minute, in fact would be able to
see the long edifice momentarily. Well, to my incredible de-
spair, what I noticed was I__'s, a restaurant that I should have
passed before R__'s even! My anxiety was now more than ever
racing towards utter fear and confusion. Had I not made a
right turn at Y__? Had I, in my residual stupor, gone the op-
posite direction, ambled all the way to K__ and subsequent-
ly, as it is more a regular route, simply made a *left* into K__?

But what of M.? And what of Mort? Was it not his bike, not their store?! And the cigarette? Could it have been another?! Of the same brand?! Had I even passed my own abode?! What of the passersby then?! Was it simply the next morn?! I had left in darkness, and now darkness again over the city?! Same hour's darkness that I have simply mistaken for another?! I tell you, I was overcome with such disquietude that I simply and immediately and surely without intention, ceased all observation, halted all recourse to reason, and quickly folded within, in such a way that I would be blind to all that surrounded me: the city as well as the passersby, oblivious to all that bothered my wretched soul! In jest or in justice, I mumbled, the formula to rescue one from disappointment is the same: unthinking and unconscious carry on—sure path to prosperity! I simply covered up with my coat, fixed my eyes on the ground beneath my feet, halted all contemplation and calculation and hurried to my quarters. My longings for peace were not immediately met, but after what you must agree was quite an adventure, my sheer exhaustion soon triumphed, I approved the privilege of rest without question, and I slowly rumbled into the precious serenity.'

182   He finally paused and took a deep breath—affected, no doubt, by the recounting of this strange, strange tale. It was almost as if I had been summoned, I was now thinking, summoned to this place unbeknownst, an agent of fortune of sorts, an empathetic listener if not a savior, a fellow wayfarer for another solitary soul. His silence did not last long, however. I was still processing the previous enigmatic *récit* when, before I knew it, he was off again, ready, needing, perhaps, to continue the tale.

'These observations were made after my third visit,' he launched again, 'subsequent to which I soon found myself maneuvering once more through the same streets toward the appointed place. I followed as I had the day before—to the hidden house at the top of the hill.'

The hidden house on the hill: he whispered the words, a mixture of dread and excitement, as if this improbable abode were a place of impossible longings, incomprehensible actions, inconceivable ambitions. Bathed in unreality, but ever so real.

———■———

'He entered first,' he started again, 'and the door was left open, clearly leaving little doubt that I was expected to enter and to carry on as I had the previous morn.

'The creations of the earlier visits decorated now, and majestically so, the walls. The turbulent seas and the mountains, the fabulous colors and forms now ever more striking, acquiring an aura that I had rarely witnessed. My host had conveniently disappeared again, while I circled slowly another giant canvas lying on the floor. That now, on a fourth day, a wholly new composition was generated, of this magnitude and in such a short spell, this was most impressive. Considering my first glints as preliminary evaluations, I proceeded to a more detailed examination of the work in progress, taking notice once more of the unusual material, the peculiarity of the design, the originality demonstrated in the arrangement and harmony of the various elements. Singularity, yes, independence, yes, but there was also an unmistakable unity with the first works: one detected the same patterns, the same, definite stylistic preferences and individual quirks, a same voice, if you will, although, again, the material was fascinating in an entirely novel way. Quite an accomplishment indeed!

'I was fully preoccupied by these private meditations and intensely studying various aspects of the new work when I was suddenly perturbed by remote movements. I turned fully and noticed that my host was present again in the room, approaching the canvas. He stood close and watched, deep in thought, almost as if he were reconsidering certain elements. I was thrown off by his proximity a few moments later when I sensed his presence immediately to my right, but, as the sum of our communication so far had consisted of several glances and my obedient followings, I kept looking intently down—it was all I could do—unmoving.

'And then, out of the blue: 'I call it, *The Dance of the Bewildered Soul*,' he suddenly whispered—there, in a slow, measured, quiet voice, the very first words he had uttered.

'The very first syllables, in fact, that had been exchanged between us. In the beginning the gaze, next the sigh, and now finally the words! I was immediately taken aback, obviously. I only raised my head, looked at him and back down, unskilled as always in the ways of communion. No reply, no reaction— but the awkward lull did not faze him: he stood still, as if evaluating his own pronouncement, his general allure unchanged. He then proceeded to walk around and, before I knew it, he had disappeared once more. Had I slighted him, I wondered, had he expected more? But it was too late to reconsider. He had not seemed troubled, nor could I attribute his vanishing strictly to any action of mine. I had done all I could. The only thing in fact.

'*The Dance of the Bewildered Soul*, on the floor and with scattered pieces around the room, was quite an extravagant piece. The title—although my host seemed reluctant, perhaps not yet fully committed to that name—now opened up new vistas in my interpretation and provoked certain associations I would not have otherwise concocted. Although it bore no immediately recognizable forms, like the *Chaos* (my appella-

184

tion) of the first day, a broad outline, along with bleary edges and elaborate motifs, did appear through a highly expert and perfectly executed osmosis of colors, lines and angles. What I made out, and surely it was an approximation, was a dream-like sketch of a multitude of peoples, all without significant traits or shapes, in flight. Assembled, further, in such manner as to give the impression that they were of a lost generation, that this was their only world, and that there would be no respite from this mode of occupation: contours of gaunt figurines, destitute humans on an extreme version of a migration, united under these peculiar circumstances, in a delirious, agonized state, carrying on, Somewhere.

'Forgive the vagueness of my description, but I see no other way to communicate what was, by and large, expressed in this same, call it abstract, manner. It was as if, at once, the story was told in its most minute details, and yet, in a most ignominious irony, without the slightest hint of particularity. I cannot, myself, comprehend this extreme paradox, but it did constitute one of my chief sensations, one I had certainly never experienced before. In any case, I did not see my host again that day, as I presume he deemed his one utterance an appropriate introduction to his enterprise.

185

'Suffice it to say that the duration of this stay was spent in much the same way as the entire adventure itself: with strong sensations of astonishment, and an imposed, overbearing, ambiguity. I had early on wallowed in the phantasmagoric dimension of the affair, but had turned, soon enough, a bit curious and definitely anxious as to the outcome. Each day—or so I took them to be—that I had been led to the hill, the previous day's work had been finished and hung! With unprecedented speed, with incomparable agility, with an undiminished, undaunted sense of vision and destiny, each new work was initiated and ended in the same period, draped finally with an unmatched harmony, yet an overwhelming sense of chaos. I was uncertain as to the nature of what I was experiencing: at once enamored and filled with a buoyancy I had never known, but also affected by a hefty sense of dread, all slowly dawning upon me that I was a privileged witness, perhaps due to my duties here below, in a most sacred setting. I had, in addition, confirmed the evolving of these pieces into an ensemble, a totality where each in turn complemented another, yet at once stood with them in a heightened tension. What's more, my host, on the fifth day, had significantly extended our communications. He had duly elaborated on each of the canvases—although never fully revealing his intentions—often anticipated my challenges and, on several occasions, had taken the unusual liberty of consulting his guest. Not in so many words, I admit, but he had, for example, thought aloud some of the potential modifications in a tone that seemed to invite opinion. In any event, I had sensed all along, mused privately, that is, that I was perhaps partaking of a venture so grand in its amplitude, so majestic in its ambitions, that I could barely understand its import and merely wonder at the privilege I was accorded, god knows why. We had also, on this fifth day, touched upon the merits, the potential implausibility and the possible tensions of the work. I was overruled in several quick strokes on certain topics, but I did not take much to heart. Finally, as I was getting ready to return, our usual pattern of my leaving without quite knowing his whereabouts—he was always in vanishing mode—was finally broken. Indeed, as I prepared to exit, already by the door, I heard a voice that was unmistakably his. 'You must stay,' I heard, and, as I turned, I saw him, he had reappeared, his back to me. 'You must stay a while longer,' he repeated. 'There is an urgent matter that we must discuss.'

Slowly, obediently, I walked to a painting to which he was pointing. 'It was not part of the plan,' he started, 'but I thought it may not be a bad idea after all.' And although I was still ignorant as to his precise reference, I could not bring myself to ask: not about the privilege he insinuated had been bestowed upon me, not the developments on each occasion of my descent, not about how my entire predicament had been devised. I sat silently, proprietor of many an unanswered question, incapable of intervention, now that I had him, finally, face to face, in a manner, perhaps, to which no one had ever been privy. 'You do understand though, do you not,' he continued, 'the burden that you now carry. Each day, you descend the hill as easily as you ascended, pushing nothing, rolling nothing, nothing to carry on your back, no danger of failure at all. But let not all of that deceive you, for now you carry that greatest of burdens: of going on without pain or hardship, carrying with you all the possible joys, wallowing in your triumph, all-powerful, all-seeing, in full command of fashioning events and the world in very much the precise form that you wish!' I was baffled, to say the least, wholly oblivious to the power to which he alluded, or to how it was, exactly, that I had acquired such abilities! 'And even if you chose to reject it,' he said finally, 'yours may be the greatest burden of them all.' He paused, he stood: and he had once more vanished before I could have uttered the first word.

'Now simply imagine how *you* would have felt in the event of such disclosures! Troubled, for sure, but tantalized—that's what I was. Frightened and enchanted. How was I to act, I thought, what was I to say?! I remained seated, paralyzed by the implausibility—and the intensity!—of the circumstances in which I had recently found myself. I stared ahead unblinking, uncertain as to how much time had elapsed *this* time— if in fact it had returned to its old ways!

187

'The next day, no mention of the previous conversation. We merely resumed the task of the examination, contemplation and evaluation. Another day, another masterpiece. But now, even though I cannot cite any worthwhile motive, I was more critical, and perhaps not as readily admiring or complimentary of the works. No amount of curiosity could prevent me from being appropriately entranced though. Quite a vision, I mused, quite a universe, even if not perfect.

'I remained astutely reserved nevertheless, holding back, provoking not the least unnecessary disturbance. It was on this same day however, with the inimitable *Convoluted Image in Convex Mirror* already in its finished stages, that the host, visibly exhausted, less enthusiastic and certainly less accommodating, informed me, in quite a surprising move, that I was not expected in the future. This was quite unnerving, as you can well gather, even more so in light of what he had said the previous morn! I was about to hang my head and go my quiet way, as was my habit, when, on this occasion, something came over me: fearless for the first time, I addressed him directly. What about his urgent declarations of the day before? 'They stand,' he muttered. What about my effort, my treks, my time here? 'You should be thankful,' he bellowed. What about the works, I opined. What was the outcome of the works? Surely he would not leave them so! Surely he realized how unfinished it all was, despite the brilliance, despite the imagination! Perhaps just a few more additions, to bring in a bit more harmony, I vented rhetorically. A few more corrections, little touches here and there, for some needed coherence! Masterful, brilliant, unmatched and unseen—but unfinished! Unfinished! I kept hollering in almost delirium. Unfinished! And highly volatile, may I add! Surely, he was not contemplating leaving matters in such states! Surely this did not represent the end all of all! I had noticed his impatience growing as my all-out assault left little room for a response. My rambling without end he interrupted in an irritated tone: 'And how would *you* go on,' he thundered back, 'if it *were!*' He paused, calmed the uncharacteristically excited nerves, and stared straight at me: 'Tomorrow is rest day,' he quipped groaning, 'and after that, I don't know.' Baffled again I, your humble chronicler! Baffled and befuddled. Dumb. You name it, I was it. Unable to address him. What did he mean, after that he didn't know?! Surely, he would not leave things as they are! Not in this state! Not now! Not in this manner! But it was too late. All for naught, it was clear: I could withdraw, it was over. Besides, I was also exhausted, by the vulgarity, perhaps, by the ridiculousness of the whole shebang! I looked once more at the room in awe and heaved a deep sigh—O with what dolorous reservations!—but I did not regret: I hurried the pace, and swiftly got out of that haunted place!'

———◾———

He had been speaking with such excitement that I was not able to put in a single word. Nor, I believe, had we moved, even an inch, from our initial positions. I listened, he spoke, we standing. He had no genuine article in which anyone in the market was even remotely interested, so that we had remained, in effect, shielded from the interference of potential customers. I did not, furthermore, deem it appropriate, after such an incandescent, emotionally charged report, to question him about his previous employment, about his relations, his work, his future. I did not have to however, as he went on, again, unprovoked: 'Thus and so, dear friend, the ritual carried on. On that fifth day, he also presented this canvas that you see here, that he had created outside of the cycle of large works. The only one in fact, and the only one of its size. I had seen it in the various stages, from infancy to maturity, if you will, and I had acquired a peculiar fondness for it—but I never fathomed that he would offer it to me without some sort of remuneration. Jubilant as I was by his generous gift, I could not accept, and my gestures fully told of my reluctance: swift fanning of hands while body arches back, ever so slightly. But his insistence was as vehement, and so my weakness triumphed: I accepted, did not know how to thank, and so withheld. I am certain though, that he knows the intensity of my gratitude, and since he was not a creature of many words, I surmise that the total absence of expression on my part was not—not this time—miscon-strued. And that is why, by the way, his last behavior shocked me so. But so be it. That is the tale. Of the beginning—and the end. I have not seen him since, it's quite outré, I agree, quite unusual indeed.'

I did not dare ask him whether he had brought the canvas with the intention to auction, whether he was in dire financial need, or what type of response he had obtained from the pass-ersby or experts. It seemed only that I was at his mercy, under his spell perhaps—on this day, in this hour, for certain, but perhaps also, unbeknownst…

'I don't know whether I will succumb to my fiscal needs,' he started again before pausing, as if considering that very option. He took another sip of water and then resumed: 'As you can see, I have placed it to the side, quite discretely, out of the sight of most. Myself, I don't want to part with it, but if you were to ask, Hey, are you trying to sell, I would have to answer pos-itively, although I have not engaged as fully as I am capable in the arena of trade and business. Nor have I pursued with any type of aggression the final sale. Truth be told, I am unaware of my duties. I don't know what to expect, what thought to entertain. To go on or to tarry. To part with or not. Forever rid myself of it and all proof of those days—or to carry it along, with, always! Bliss and Burden all! To sell or to tell: only the next letter I know, but a hell of a different world!'

Although the small, miniature-like painting, mostly devoid of color, had been sitting, all along, not so far from where we had been holding court, I had not yet the liberty to glance at it even furtively. Now that he instigated the invitation, so to say, I finally attempted a more rigorous examination, only to notice, with trepidation, the total contrast to everything he had been saying. Was it all a lie then? With such passion and conviction though? Or was it precisely the point of this version to be so at odds with the ones he had seen? I did not know, nor did I venture a guess. I merely looked over the object sitting before us: the image on the canvas was comprised of an awkward juxtaposition of various elements, none rendered with the 'incomparable' flair, or the 'unmatched' sense of introspection he had been relating all along. So unconvincing, in fact, and cold, was the work, that had I even a wee bit less trust in this old accomplice's candidness, did I doubt a morsel more his aim in communicating his tales, I would not have, for a second even, put it past him to have invented the whole sorry account, merely to seduce an unsuspecting listener, or to attract the innocent to a work, and this is my point, to a work that was none other than *his own*! For there they were: the very same shapes and forms, recognizable from his account, collated as if to give a sense, and in a wholly *failed* manner (O how utterly failed!) of the narrative he had taken such pains to relate! The Path, yes, that was present: winding and leading seemingly into heavenly locales! The House, the Cottage, whatever the label—that too, could be made out: through a terribly rendered play with light and shadows! Elements from the Paintings he had described? Sure enough! Present, indeed, in a pathetic caricature of the grandiose masterworks he had evoked! This famous *Chaos* of the first day, the *Vaults 'n Water Make me Stutter* of the second, the *Before Suburbia There Was Dry Land Barren Bathing in the Phantasmagoric Delight of Popping Seeds* of the third! And *The Dance of the Bewildered Soul*! Yes indeed, none to be missed, all to be ignored! And last, last but not least: in the foreground, looming in the center of this tritely rendered landscape where Motion and Inertia, from the very inception of time to its immemorial version, coalesced into an awkward shape, dominating the whole of the canvas, was a most peculiar Portrait, for lack of a more appropriate term, and an ugly one at that: two vertically curving lines, drawn in black, ended, at the top, in a semblance of two heads, slightly apart yet joined at the mouth: faces astonishingly detailed and defined—and here, allow me to retreat, here at last, I could detect signs of a genius at play!—contrasting almost horrendously with the fully flowing, flailing, torsos and arms, thinning streaks supposedly depicting bodies and legs, feetless, floating, genie-like in the air! Symmetrically placed they were, these two heads, on tails, as if facing one another, yet one, telling, telling, in one voice, nothing less than a majestic, seductive, earth-shattering tale!

Needless to say, we did not discuss anymore the potential business venture, nor the future of the canvas itself. Silently we held court, amidst the movements and the noise of that vast yard.

I finally readied to depart and saluted him. He reciprocated. I wished him luck and success in all of his enterprises. I warned him to pay heed and to beware, and he did the same. When we finally separated, having rekindled a fragile friendship, unknowing of when we would meet again, I felt a slight unease, a most childlike sadness. I had indeed heard in his voice my own, I recognized my own when peering into his face, his path I had known, the shelter and its silent host. Climbing the stairs upon my return, after the beggar (coins in his open palm), the tailor (wave to him crossing) and the barber (greetings around the bend), I noticed the neighbor's fingers resting on the door-knob, and the head, only the head, and the same strange grimace, turned upward, still...

In my chambers at last, I peered at my prized photograph adorning the wall, amidst the chaos and dance of bewildered souls, amidst the flames of streets and the impossible path, among the pillars where rest fabulous creatures of unwanted tales, of a secret-teller peering sullen from high above, into the face of Time:

the following account, then, is engrossed with untainted anxieties of the most egregious kind, the blame must not rest solely on my shoulders, for I was once again caught unaware in this perverse maze of conceit, this strange republic of rancor. I have as yet never attempted the tale, let it be said, halted, paralyzed perhaps, by the perpetual fear of lacing the report with beguiling confusions, irritating repetitions, and spiteful profanities. Indeed, no dire effort in surmounting the ills bore fruit. Unbearable exercises won the day. Again and again, I was rebuffed by forces internal and ex, threatened with one or another verse, warned of tragedies unimaginable. Bear with me then as I present, with restrained pride, the roots of both the anguish and its slayer—this protracted operation of unveiling: not only of hidden things, but their most conspicuous enemies. It is the essence of the events themselves, I am convinced. Inevitable, I often mutter. It was the players and the era. The game. The dénouement.

I was to appear on the appointed date without raising the slightest suspicion, carrying naught but the usual articles as I went about my daily rituals. Change not the clothes, change not the look, and you have a deal. That was the promise—and I fully abided. Still, I cannot even begin to propound the manner in which the pledge transformed the fabric of my existence. I went about in full knowledge of the precise day it was to be performed, an arrangement that, to my understanding, had been the privilege of no one—no one I insist— before me! But despite the increasing pressures and every moment aware, I managed to go on, like all others, as if the same Uncertainty, and the same Blindness, were to direct my affairs.

Now that I knew, little would have changed were I to shlep along and dilly-dally without the slightest ambition. Were I to stroll oblivious to all occurrences, were I to idle away the hours with unanticipated ventures. Were I to summon the cruelest gods to my side or accompany the vilest characters on hazardous expeditions. As part of the invisible contract to which I had agreed however, a prisoner of the premise, this private cognizance was not to be made apparent in any way whatsoever. The first suspicion, I was told, anyone's suspicion, might raise the ire of the higher-ups, in which case not only would the agreement be annulled, but their wrath I might even bear in other venues! I had acquiesced therefore and tended to chores and obligations.

Mornings I rise, see the neighbors going off to work or coming back from an early stroll, ever more weary of the spectacle that demanded my full engagement, suspect not only of the conviction with which I was playing the part, but also of its consequences. My own predilections, further, my own paranoia, were constantly heightening, as I became ever more uncertain of the degree to which the artificial relevance I was bestowing upon actions, events, or utterances even, was visible. Uncertain of how I was perceived by friend and foe alike, I read in their (perhaps common) wincing, their constant cringing and their qualms, an accentuated show of apprehension, a risky and dangerous sign of malevolence.

Allow me to expound. Only a short while after my first encounter with the fleeting agents, where the vow was made, the deal closed, and the contract sealed (not as it should have, perhaps), a long time then, before the actual event was to take place, I sauntered, as was my habit, into a small diner across the street. Now, however pleasant the taste of the cuisine, or whatever the opinion one may have of the cooking or the spot itself, it cannot be contested that, one, the place is often devoid of customers, giving it an aura of creepy doom, and, two, not only the oddball cashier (hired how, I have never asked), but the supervisor, strolling the grounds (small as they may be), peering occasionally out of the front window into the (I admit, mundane) street, and the ever unoccupied chef sitting unmoving yet staring at the entrance without hat and dressed simply as if the owner of the establishment, were not, in any way whatsoever, none of them, among the more genial folks one can run into! And yet (and this is what I intended to communicate in order to highlight my growing paranoia), upon the return, I was made utterly uncomfortable by the stare of the sitting chef and the glare of the stroller, both of whom had followed my steps with what I surmised was ever more acute scrutiny. I noticed each of their frowns, felt, almost, each of their breaths, heard, demoralized, their silent mockery of my fate. I detected a growing antagonism on their part, a more intrusive invasion of my person, a more abusive evaluation. I was more cautious in my approach it seemed, my tone belied a strange admittance of sin, my gestures had been reduced to mechanical, fractional, motions, all spontaneity and natural ease decidedly rid of my person. I placed an order nevertheless, to make a long story short, dilly-dallied impatiently, and chose not to stare much in their direction—in either of their directions that is, since the chef, now obligated to occupy the kitchen at least temporarily, would stroll in on occasion, while the other paced around the main salon. Upon receipt of my goods, I hurried along without acknowledgment, gratitude or salutation: just hopped to the door, propped it open—and vanished.

196

This singular sense of vulnerability one must only expand to fully appreciate the extent of the affectation. One must only apply the essence of this interaction to all relations, one must only imagine an array of such glances, approaches and distant rapports, to acquire a glimpse of the gravity of my conscience. Reason, needless to say, was of no help here, nor was any other disciplined attempt at resolution. The remedy, it seemed, lay precisely in forgetting, in the loosening of much control, in a frivolity that would bid adieu to all solution-seeking, in the ever difficult, perhaps impossible, art of being oneself! I was now farther than most and knew not the way back! In more desolate moments, I would even reason that the Return (to myself, if I may) was quite unthinkable, ever more so—and this eased my sense of guilt—since I was, in fact, *not* the one I was attempting to be. The deal was proving to be quite a difficult proposition, for although it was not mentioned, the demands made upon me insinuated—and I, in my rush, had failed to comprehend this unwritten clause!—that I was to enact the life of *another*, trapped, granted, within my previous bodily confines. Not literally, certainly, since I was to fully abide by my own edicts: except, of course, that the very nature of the agreement, the essence of the transaction—and this *is* what an honest, whole-hearted, good-willed fellow pays heed to, even if it works to one's disadvantage!—radically transformed my being, in such manner, perhaps in the most consequential manner indeed, that it could in fact be debated whether I, 'I', was the same! Myself or another? Who was to be the judge?

Certainly not I! For, despite all attempts, now that I recount the episodes, now that the scenes of that epoch race before me at unseemly speeds, accompanied by sullen sighs and dim good-byes, scarcely did I manage to avert disaster. And in the period nearing the appointed day, I was barely capable of con-

197

cealing my agitation and my sense of doom! How they all must have felt! How the neighbors and the colleagues... The family... How the bartender and the petrifying duo at the shrine of gluttony... Speed it up, I would holler at no one in particular in seedy locales. Let's get it over with, went my shrieks at most unpredictable times. In the period that preceded the last venture, in fact, my biological (or is it chemical) mechanisms even began to deteriorate: profusely sweating I would find myself, without any instigation! Tired, head aching, hands shivering, paralyzed! I was a thorn in the sides of loved ones—my worst nightmare realized. Spasms later on, and a period of unintentional numbness even: I could barely open my mouth, and what was emitted was a crude version of primitive noises. I was tended to by caring individuals I had always held in high esteem of course, and as these long stretches of agony persisted, I was also visited by acquaintances of various stripes. Some, by my side under the pretext of past acquaintanceship, or even under the questionable status of intimates, were, I'm certain of it, delighting in my demise. Others I was genuinely happy to see, saddened only that the visits coincided with a brand new form of paralysis. Too weak to protest, unable to utter a single dissent, I sat wallowing in my derision, a prisoner of my destiny, my role!

Somehow though, kudos to myself for digging deep when it was demanded, and surely with the assistance of sympathetic if inconspicuous forces, I simply willed my way to rehabilitation, if only to ensure the implementation of the plan. Indeed, I did not want the helplessness I was now enacting to haunt me: that could be used as precedent for the termination of our pact, upon which occasion I would be driven to the same dustbin shared by all my colleagues in this greatest, yet most ephemeral, of enterprises. And so, first, I regained my ability to speak, which I exercised with utmost abandon: I skipped from witticism to witticism, I joked, jested and gibbered, I sang and I played. Soon, I was able (and willing) to put the limbs in independent motion, to move about, to carry on with the simpler tasks. Around me all were jubilant, for my prowess was slowly coming back, albeit in unforeseen ways.

I regained full control shortly thereafter, circulated with appropriate vigor—awake early and asleep quite late—participated full-fledged in activities and was at last involved in all of those duties that I considered mine. Now, even though I had managed to regain my power, still I was concerned that a protest would be filed in relation to honoring my side of the bargain. I had prepared a defense, if the need were to arise: that such sudden deterioration of one's physical condition, unlikely as it may be, is not at all without precedent, and that it would not incite any additional mistrust. Quite the contrary, I would argue: it will even add a dash of authenticity, for my happy recuperation would in fact signal contentment, commonality, absolute normalcy in the face of such a prodigious recovery. Although I was quite confident that this line would hold, a certain anxiety persisted within, derived from the concern that a decision would be made without my consultation, thus eliminating all possibility of dissent, pulling all factors toward a unilateral negation of the plan. To what could I then have recourse? I had no answer at present and knew that my best offering would merely constitute a haphazard guess. I withheld, decided to continue until the appointed day, confident that there could be no purpose or justification for our agreement to be void. But again, I confess that I could not, cannot, did not, carry on without anticipation, unease, uncertainty—without as much impatience also, as its most serene opposite. The temptation had been overwhelming, the perfect illustration,

199

perhaps, of a masterfully choreographed seduction! Surely, I did not, now, regret? No, I did not, did not, but I did not have a choice either, I don't think!

There was little merit in reminiscence anyhow, mental gymnastics of the kind that are both soothing and damning: the deal was done, and I had fully recovered. On the appointed day therefore, I was ready to go about my usual business, expecting, obviously, to depart on the new journey. Well-advised, warned, in fact, not to allow the slightest ambiguity to rise even at the height of the emotional turbulence, I kept monitoring the (dare I say?) volcanic agitation brewing beneath. Still, however much I attempted to hold back an accentuated grip or the more protracted embraces, I extended all the aforementioned to the utmost degree with the family, to the very extreme point where any complaint could have been fended off with vehement denials! They noticed of course, they noticed a certain difference, the hugged ones... But they did not know, they could not place the matter, caused by the excessive show of tenderness, and at such worthy moments! Fine, I thought to myself, let it be, let it be...

I waived good-bye as I descended the steps. My final salutation to them, I presumed, were the contract to hold, as I fully anticipated, there being no reason, absolutely none, to believe otherwise. I had indeed, I had to say and swallow, seen them for the last time.

Although the time frame of the final act was very loosely given in the initial encounter—'from the instant you leave in the morning,' I recall in crude terms, 'all the way until the hour you would normally be back!'—the style in which the deed was to be carried out, its exact location, the number of people involved and other extenuating circumstances, all were left unclear. I'd lobbied and pleaded, even in that short meeting, for these elements also to be revealed, but there was no budging. 'Can't deprive you of all the suspense,' the fellow had quipped. 'That's one thing that's not sanctioned. There's got to be a minimal degree of anticipation, of speculation. That's our credo. That's the best we can do.' Fine, I'd replied, unable to challenge the stubborn stance, fine, let's just get on with it!

The proper arrangements were made (so I was led to believe), the appropriate personnel contacted, everything was set. That morning, fully reliving the pretensions, I had dressed as I would have on any other, peered out the window, said my aforementioned (last!) good-byes, strolled out and basically planned to go through the motions of my daily rituals.

I could not manage to conceal all the stirrings though, each moment awaiting the final blow, each instant closer to the last call. Would it be the crash of a vehicle ramming from one side to another, I thought as I crossed the big avenue. Or perhaps an attack of some sort with four strangers (why strangers—it could just as easily be acquaintances) hidden (or not) in an alleyway who then pounce upon me for motives uncertain! Or perhaps the dull, undramatic failure of my own biological organs. And why not a collective experience, I expounded, such as a shattering earthquake, or an accident (on the bus), or an unlikely tornado, sweeping through town? Or perhaps, perhaps they all know, I thought as I watched slowly the passersby, as I careened my way through town in a daze. Perhaps they were all told, and all share, mightily, the illusion that they are the only ones! All apparitions, wandering aimlessly, *all* warned to change not the slightest bit—the habits, the countenance, the deeds! All knowing, when the last hour would strike, the whole spectacle a grand charade of pretending mummies, mechanical winding toys set out for limited runs, merely to delight the fancy of awkward angels at play! An unnerving proposition,

201

of course, that I was unwilling to consider for an instant even, returning quickly, and wisely, I believe, to my own case! (A random shot or a stray animal, the fury of a drunkard, mere case of mistaken identity perhaps, an ode, My passage, a trib-ute, My life, to the very whims of chance!)

Each step heightened by anxieties, still I could not contain a chuckle—a tragic, frightening, chuckle indeed. But I dared not, for fear of reprieve and the annulment of the contract, stray from the prescribed obligations. It'll happen, somewhere along the line, he had made clear, as long as you don't change anything—the line that resonates relentlessly in my mind, re-peated, pointed to, emphasized. I had surmised in fact, and however distressful (yet thrilling) the idea seemed, surmised that perhaps, this supposed agent (granted, not the greatest of occupations) had embarked, either as a risky individual so-journ, or in association with others of the same mold, on the unthinkable: had, in a clandestine manner that reaped some sort of (to me, to us, incomprehensible) benefit or profit, yes indeed—hush now don't you go repeating—revolted. A Re-bellious Angel, with whom a secret pact was made, to save me, save us, from the fangs of our ancestral condition: quite an enchanting prerogative, given, especially, the course of events, the usual slow unfolding, and my current perspective. Need-less to say, the entire morning and afternoon accompanied by an impending sense of doom, each passing moment anticipat-ing the coming end, I remained in full stupor and quite pre-occupied, as if in a trance: hearing no one, fulfilling no tasks assigned, remembering no lines, ignoring most gestures and contortions, zombiely, basically, carrying on through the day, counting the minutes and imagining the mechanisms through which this fabulous, fabulous venture called life would come to a grinding halt!

Which is why, in an ironic twist, my frustration grew as the hours passed, no signs were emitted, no mysteries were revealed, and nothing of import occurred. It was in the early evening, that, at the height of anguish, I set out to attempt, at least attempt, for whatever it was worth, to calm my senses, to ease the tension (or, was this how it was to occur, through the explosion of nerves at the mistaken announcement of its arrival), to tame the anxiety! I made my way across the street, through a back road (shortcut), soon found myself on another, continued and crossed again and finally propped out at one end of the public square, the deserted, sure, deserted now, public square: and slowly walked through.

There: I had sought a haven, and, even now, was under the illusion that no greater force would intrude, that no one would intervene. I kept walking and finally chose a small park, one that seemed excessively busy, but not so much so that I lost the desire to hang around. I stopped by an occupied bench and, with a simple, gentle, May I, and without even bothering to hear the answer, I eased unto the edge, my counterpart bent over, hands clasped behind the head.

I thought nothing of the scene: thought not of counseling, of consoling, or of any other variation thereon, even though the fellow seemed quite distressed. I sat, worried enough on my own, facing the other way, meditative. Very briefly though, for I suddenly heard, coming from the proximity, a muffled voice seemingly addressing another. Given the tone and the pitch, given its path and its timber, I understood that it was destined to none other than myself. I turned curiously, slowly, to the other occupant of the bench, the one I had duly ignored. His position had not changed, at all: head bent on knees, hands clasped behind the head, still.

'Pardon me?' I ventured. 'Did you say something to me?'

203

I had just finished when he rose, slightly, from his hunched position. And before I had occasion to be fully startled, I heard him repeat what I had initially heard him say, the phrase, the curt and stinging phrase, the very impetus of my address, the very generator of our moment-old interaction.

'I don't know what to say,' he repeated in the same low, monotonous, sullen voice. 'I don't know what to say.'

———■———

Utterly shocked I was, for I knew that on the appointed day, and this was made abundantly clear, I was not to meet him or anyone else that I could recognize as one of his associates. But there was no doubt, no doubt at all, this was the voice. Paralyzed once more by the potential consequences of the plan going awry, surmising quickly that something had gone terribly wrong, I sat staring, unsparing.

'Nothing you did,' he said again with an apologetic posture. 'It has nothing to do with you.'

His precise references remained unclear, but he had confirmed my initial misgivings. Clearly, the full provisions of our accord would not be brought about. A foreign element perhaps, a simple turn of events, an error, a mysterious infiltration, a variety of such factors could have undermined the agreement. Not too radically though, I was hoping. A mere fleck, I was thinking, an irregularity that will be resolved, the affair smoothed out, shortly, definitely. Nothing substantial anyway, I was concluding, the end result would be the same, the essence of the plan would be carried out, it would, it must, it must be carried out!

No such luck! As I twisted and considered the possible outcomes, his ever sterner visage revealed the gravity of the situation. He knew I expected, helpless, an explanation of sorts, and it seemed as if he were struggling to formulate the best such clarification. I had yet to respond that he placed his hands on his knees, took a deep breath and turned to me: 'It was a great mistake!' he said. 'It wasn't you! It wasn't supposed to be you, after all!'

At first unbelieving and as quickly incensed, I held back the reactions, even as I sank inward. What did he mean 'after all'?! How could such an imponderable error be committed?! And under *these* auspices!

'It wasn't me either!' he went on. 'Not really anyway. But there's no solution now. There's nothing left to do now.' He paused again, in genuine shambles. 'Our ominous meeting... So long ago... He wasn't to tell you *that*... I don't know why... I was distracted... There's a resemblance maybe... I don't even know...'

I had decided to hear him all the way through, to hear out his ever increasingly incomprehensible rambling, to attempt, throughout this drivel, to make out, at least, from all of the elements, an acceptable scenario for the turn of events!

He was growing more apologetic though, his explanation acquiring the tone of a guilt-ridden monologue, the essence of a confession, describing the worst case of mistaken identity, of involuntary, perhaps, deception. I listened, I remember, with heightening disillusion, struck, throughout, by his incredible assertions, his ungodly revelations. He expounded on the idea of distraction and resemblance, digressed many times over, implicated others, by name or attributes, neither of which struck many chords as far as I was concerned, cursed and reviled a 'colleague' he considered more at fault, praised the unheralded architects of this attempt at resolution, flung himself around on several occasions in fits of anger and annoyance, questioned the direction of his own adventure and his own obligations, doubted the merits of his duties and his decisions, reconsid-ered his part and muttered the modifications he would bring about in the near future, mulled over, with profound gravity, the value of his contributions and the meaning of his work, all of this among the scores of other incriminations, accusations and abominations.

'I didn't have to come either,' he continued, gentler now, rid, he seemed, of the layers of suffering eased through this awkward penance. 'I didn't have to come. You could have wait-ed, until sundown, until the prescribed last moment, noticing that nothing had occurred. You would have stumbled along helpless, brooding... I know it, I've watched you! Wondering whether it was you, where you had gone wrong, how you had cheated your part! Night after night, you would have asked... For a sign, a phrase, a meeting of some sort, for an explanation, at least! 'Something, something'—I can hear you muttering, that would ease your grievance! I didn't have to come... They told me not to bother... 'He'll be another among them,' they said, 'walking, waiting... Another wronged by the very agents of trust and confidence... Misled by a cunning angel again, a playful, deceitful angel...'

He paused again as I followed, without fault, each of his phrases, every one of his utterances. I peered at him without expression, feeling ever more betrayed. 'I didn't have to come,' he started again, 'but you don't know that. I didn't, but I de-cided, on my way... To come and tell you. I owe it to you, I know. I'm going there now... You can come along... I want to invite you... Even though I'm not allowed, not for this either, I shouldn't be telling you this, you're not supposed to be privy to this... But I will... Extend the invitation... It's the least I can do, in a way, an awkward, perverse type of way... To see the one whose hour it is... Whose time has come... The one who is supposed to go… And so pathetically, pathetically, un-prepared…'

He had softened a bit, he looked straight at me now, a sly gentleness (or was it sincere) washing over him. 'He looks like you,' he added finally. 'You know that? I think he really does look like you!'

The message was clear. And although I expected him to take me by the hand and begin another fantastic excursion above the city, an ascension and flight, no such event took place: we rose instead and walked side by side, a short while, through several alleys and finally to the door of a small tavern, built, I'm certain of it, on the model of the old-style coffee-houses of a city famed for such spots. 'That's him, in there,' he point-ed as we peered like schoolchildren, our noses pressed against the glass, 'making his rounds, ever conscious, ever courteous—Herr Ober!'

I stood by him staring at the worried waiter hurriedly going from one table to the next, weaving between the chairs and the customers haranguing or insulting him in turn. He did, however, bear an uncanny resemblance to none other than yours truly!

'That's him,' my fellow window-watcher said again. 'That's who was supposed to go! That's who we were supposed to tell! But there would have been no deal with him anyhow, he's not the type. He lets on too easily. He could never have done it, the pretense, the front! Look at him now, with his costume, good old Herr Ober, he could never have done it. Lasted through the wait and misled the lot!'

His revelations disturbing and perversely satisfying at once, I sensed nevertheless a growing discomfort with my own un-authorized insight into another's destiny. My guide however, was not relenting. And despite my best judgments, despite the

207

prerogative about to redirect the trajectory of my adventure, neither was I.

'He finishes at midnight,' he went on. 'A bit after, actually, since the last ones trickle out much past closing. After his shifts, exhausted old man, he makes his way to a small flat, jots down reflections and meditations, connects a verse or another he has written. He traces his path. Somewhere the steps, he believes, towards renown. A way out of his repetitive rhythm! He believes it too, I tell you. An enraged genius! A poet of the future! An artist ahead of his time! The worst of the species among The Unsuspecting! A Waiter, for god's sake, one of those damned sorcerers of life!'

He had turned to me, his back resting now against the glass while I peered passively through that same window at the hurried movements of the waiter. As had become his habit on this trip, he heaved another deep sigh and let out a final burst: 'You were not supposed to know, my friend, you were not to be the one! He was! He was to know! The poor wight, all of it stemming from us, probably. They took him for you, in the same way, maybe the same day. But he is the one who will go now, he is the one! And now it's too late, it's his time, it's too late now!'

Nothing was clear. I heard his words, but I did not comprehend his intentions or the overall significance of his revelations. I only knew that the waiter I was seeing through the glass (surely a meditative scribe in his private hours), *he* was to have known, he was the one, and not I, who was to be informed, of the appointed time: he was the one, as the guide insinuated, who was to be The Expectant. As I mulled over the extended repercussions of this news, I could not help but imagine the direct effect on my own condition, my own case. Who was I then, who was so wrongly, so cruelly, informed, of the precise day of his death? Whose life thereafter, subsequent to that dire encounter, had deteriorated and dissolved and turned, due, yes, specifically, to the nature of the agreement, into that grandiose, shameful, pretense? Whose every thought and move had been affected by the implications of the indignant contract?! Who was *I*? I did not articulate any of this of course, nor were the thoughts formulated with any clarity. They merely constituted a fragment of angry protests and violent incriminations in which I was inwardly engaged. Suddenly though, magically, as if he knew of my preoccupation, leaning on the windowsill of the forlorn tavern, he let out what seemed like a final disclosure, let out, softly, without a dint of trickery or deceit, without the slightest hint of cunning, in the tone of a confessor fatigued with the lies, he let out: 'You were not to know the day, you were not the one! It is you, it is *you*, who will never go!' And as if an echo muttered again, he repeated that it was I, I, 'who would never go!'

A strange silence came over us both. He lowered his eyes, noticing my disdainful unbelief. Then he spoke again, confirming his previous utterance, solid and unwavering. And no sooner had he made the announcement that he peered straight ahead and proceeded on to new elaborations, the unwanted, if I may, unsolicited, elaborations: 'Each of them, each of you,' he went on, as if a final abdication to a grand confession, 'each with a name among us that is not your given...'

The previous declaration would have sufficed, on any other day, to strike me unconscious, but on this, a most haunted and enigmatic day, a most glorious day, somehow, I persevered and heard him through, reticent and numb.

'That one, standing by the entrance there,' he carried on, 'under the awning, looking right and left, watching the others, he is The Dinhearer. Upon the first bell, he will walk dejected-

ly to the source of the sound and be taken away. And that one,'
he said, pointing away, 'pacing pensively on the wharf—only
an indistinct silhouette can be made of him now, I know, but
he is flesh and blood—he who will vanish with the next high
tide, he is The Drowned... Each one to be named as to how
my underlings will visit them, all distant and alien to one an-
other, for no one, in this sordid republic of which I am the be-
nevolent ruler, in this derisive and eternal democracy, no one
here shares the same predicament, ever goes *with*...'

He was about to stop, I believe, when he noticed a frail,
young man, hair wildly sprayed and swaying, gingerly skip-
ping, quickly walking past us.

'You see him?' he burst out. 'He is the only one, the only of-
ficial holder of that most coveted title, the one they use left and
right, the one they have left meaningless! But he is the one, he
is the only one, the True one, for he is so called among *us*, he is
the lone one: The Martyr indeed, The Martyr himself!'

He was at ease now. Strangely. Everything out of his system
putting even him at ease. Even him.

'Now if you'll excuse me,' he said, 'I have to make sure all the
arrangements have been properly made, all the orders carried
out. Can't botch this one no way, if you know what I mean!'

He walked around the bend, opened the door to the tavern,
took a step inside. He hesitated, stuck out his head again, his
hand holding still the door-handle, and addressed me for the
last time:

'You can watch it if you want,' Death said finally, 'but it
won't be very pretty!'

And, before he had disappeared inside, Death said again: 'I
have to go now, my friend—and I shall never see you again.
Farewell.'

—■—

Behind the window, he seemed almost a grainy dreamversion of the creature that had stood and spoken with me moments before. I watched as he casually sat down, picked up a newspaper, opened, and began to read. The waiter promptly arrived, pen in hand ready to note, mouthing what seemed to me like a regular invitation to order, yet clearly disappointed at my acquaintance's shake of the head sideways. He proceeded to other clients, weaved in and out and walked back to an area I surmised was the kitchen. Two robust bearded men at one table were engaged in raucous gestures and wild flailing of arms, in what constituted, very clearly, a perpetually abusive summoning of the poor swerving lad. Who, by the way, stopped once more, however briefly, at Death's table, only to be turned away in seemingly disappointed fashion.

The bearded men carried on with their feast, raised high their frosted glasses, slammed them as they careened their way through another feast. In the far-end of the restaurant, a young woman sits quietly, reading. And, behind the bearded boors, a young and frail free-spirit stares intently ahead, unperturbed. I swung away and peered into the night: to where the shadow paced back and forth on the wharf, to where The Dinhearer stood glancing (in my direction a few instants!) at the surroundings, to where The Martyr had passed only moments before. I lingered outside, looked occasionally into the tavern, standing in an almost trance in the darkness. The customers trickled out slowly, even the bearded ones who stumbled and mumbled their way to their next haunted dives. The young fellow had exited also, but he, like myself, still milled about, seemingly hesitant about the next destination. I heard erratic sounds emanating from within a while later, subsequent to which the waiter rushed through the front entrance, looked around, saw no one (including myself, since I was positioned slightly away, across, under the awning of an unlit shop), and dejectedly walked back in. Soon tired of my idle lingering, I deduced, correctly I believe, that the matter had been resolved and that all fates were now in their rightful agents' hands. Now what, I wanted to scream, but I decided to call it a night and to bid adieu to the precincts at once. I adjusted my coat and my shawl, a last glance at the tavern: lift of shoulders, further adjustments, and there: I was ready.

When I turned however, suddenly appeared, seated (unclear on what, exactly), with quite a big grin on a cheerful face, one leg draped over the other and his right hand up, open, palm facing me, as if a childlike salute, quite an offbeat lad whose striking and slightly preposterous appearance I could hardly explain.

The landscape around us had completely transformed, I know not how. Only the tavern was still there: only the tavern, bathed in the awkward colors that had now engulfed us.

'Here I am!' he blurted out gingerly, sardonically. 'Look no further, heeeeere I AM!'

Masked, he was. A disguise, this form. And yes, I did recognize him now, of this there was no doubt. I did not manage to veil my revulsion.

'So what will it take to drive *you* away?' I jumped. 'Another challenge of the candles? A game of chess along the plague-filled road?'

'Now, now!' he answered in return. 'You know that's the other fellow! You are mocking me, aren't you? I know that tone!'

Assuredly, articulately, without disdain or bitterness, softly, I gazed straight into his pernicious eyes:

'I despise you!' I said calmly. 'I have always despised you...'

'Now that is *not* a nice thing to say!' he blurted back, full of vigor. 'Besides, that's what you all pretend you want to believe!'

212

'But I mean it!' I repeated quickly. 'I really mean it!'

He did not take the insistence well. He stood up, in fact, graver now, condescending, as if to prove otherwise. Looking straight into my eyes, he then switched, from that vengeful demeanor, into that of a playful, teacher-toned, wizard—and began: 'Pop quiz three children, gather round now. A grown-up dude, in childhood listless, in adolescence solitary, apart, forsakes soon friend and folks, all luxuries, and even his... self. Question is: What does he want? Who can tell me?'

And he suddenly swung and pointed at a young girl of no more than eight or nine, blond pony tail, very, shall we say, cute, with the bunnyteeth in full force! 'You!' he blurted out pointing at her showman-like. 'What do you say?!'

The little girl did not balk. All smiles, as if pronged, she let out: 'He wants to be Big!' She even demonstrated by extending her arms and playfully stretching them to the sky.

'Bingo!!' the showman blurted out. 'Right on the money! You win!' And he threw her a colored candy that she caught, expertly if I may, after which she vanished, poof, into thin air.

He was far from done. He turned abruptly again, behind him, two hundred and ten degrees to be exact, like a lion pounced before his clone of a chipmunk-cheeked little boy: put his finger unto the little fellow's chest and glared upwards, hallelujah lording, eyes closed, lips tightly pressed, a preacher seeking inspiration: 'Aaannnd... YOU!' he shouted out finally.

The little boy was ready, as expected: 'He wantth to be famuth!' he gibbered—upon which a big candy bar was pressed against his chest, a good answer kid was whispered in his ear, and he was *ordanguied* out of there: spun by his bigger mate, that is, and led away with a lovable, gentle, kick to the posterior.

As soon as the jolly boy was out of sight, after a playful wink to yours truly, the silly steward walked slowly to a bench where a grayish, wrinkled old man, leaning on a standing cane, sat literally motionless. The showman eased unto the same bench next to him and bellowed: 'You tell us, kiddo, you tell!'

And the dreadful mantoy, wound, surely, blabbered, helpless: 'He wants to live Forever!'

Upon which his flailing arm was lifted, his fingers bent into a knuckle and made into a fist: 'Hurray!' chanted the ring-announcer. 'Hurray for the champion! You win the grand prize!'

And just as soon, the let-go arm crashed to the old man's side, vanished both bench and occupier, and my counterpart sprang again inches from my face: 'Your turn!' he muttered then. 'Your turn now.'

I merely chuckled, raised my shoulders, grinned: 'That's not how it is,' I said untroubled. 'It's just not how it is.'

His reaction was uncouth: wild and exaggerated gesticulations, bending up and down and stumbling forward and back—all before I had even finished the sentence—and he finally slumped on his invisible seat. Again, he did not take well to my reservations: patently irritated, he groaned and moaned, but replied, nevertheless: 'Now, you're the one who's been anointed! You're my charge! And frankly, I know you've always wanted it. So stop pretending and show me what you got!'

And so it was: that in that most cherished of episodes, across from me Immortality himself slouching, lounging and brooding, somehow seduced, I acquiesced, my initial rejections nothing but hollow pretentions of being above it all. Still, where I should have given the performance of a lifetime, I managed merely to pace around, back and forth before him, every ounce of zestful play vanished from my brow, I the lone soldier destined to him, mechanically parading, wound up, a pathetic tribute to Monotony, the very embodiment of Sameness and Commonality! A picture, one could say, of Convention! A mere relic of that most cherished of institutions herein, Belonging!

Needless to say, I broke down: in tears, trembling uncontrollably, a seizure of the soul indeed! I could only hope that this pathetic exhibition had not completely depressed him, had not totally turned him off (although I'm not so sure, amazingly enough, if he had any say in the matter), that he was not now in private lament over his own, well, fate, given the individual anointed. I felt a sense of guilt even, a most pitiful, most unworthy, sense of shame! Even though I had not, I kept repeating, had not, no, had not, I don't think, in any way, betrayed my position. I had, in fact, nothing to announce, nothing at all to say or add! But I had panicked, that was true, I had wilted—and it was this uncool that irritated me! My suddenly mechanical gait, the passionless expression, the very portrait of Undeserving!

I managed, in the midst of the apparent catastrophe, to garner sufficient strength and enough willpower to finally stand again (I had, literally, slithered to the ground before this venerable Presence), stare, almost defiantly, and utter the very same words I had performed in a unique spectacle, of which, unbeknownst, he had been the grand coordinator. Through a strange metamorphosis that may have, I was hoping, pointed to at least a modicum of respectability, I let out finally, confidently: There is nothing to say, nothing at all, nothing to say at all.

He rose and approached. He stood only inches away—at an angle. I could not see him anymore, he stared beyond me, he stood next to me, now I could see him no more, but he stood

215

by me. I heard him finally, it was really him. Not a showman, not the wizard, not a playful announcer: it was him, in the flesh, Immortality himself.

And I heard *him*, his secrets, in *his* darkness, by me standing, I heard him, *his* sigh: I also wish I could wither: the mysterious voice, the distant voice: what Immortality whispered: truth or dare, truth or dare, will you play, and play fair...

The gaze now and the gaze back: suddenly the triumph, the final triumph, abdication and triumph: with or without you, angel and not, I whispered, silence before, silence during, silence after: that's how it is, I can't help it: nothing to add, nothing to explain, nothing to say at all: truth or dare, truth or dare, silence before, silence during, silence—after:

The

dangling on the podium facing the multitudes who have assembled to see him: he stands on the podium and the eyes of the masses gaze at him on the podium alone: he does not see the eyes: he cannot see the eyes: the eyes of the masses are invisible: he does not see the eyes: only the restless agitation: in the crowd that awaits: silence suspended reigning: in anticipation: he will shatter the silence: in anticipation, all of the world awaits the rupture of silence: I see him: I see he will shatter the silence: he shatters the silence:—

I am among you, he thunders raising his arm into the air, I am among you as your servant, for they all await our coming: he tells of his travels, of his dream, of the world he imagines: he tells of his visions and he hears the chants and the stomping of feet and the pounding of hearts and applause all around: he exalts in the applause: exalts in the reception and begins to whirl with the songs he hears on the podium singing of the world he envisions: chants and screams: in a trance he slithers to the floor of the podium: he lies on the podium unmoving: timeless his unmoving on the podium while they wait: but suddenly he stands again: I see him stand again on the podium alone: he raises his hands: he looks heavenward: he tells of the day they have awaited: he falls silent: silence of the masses with his silence: chants of the masses after his silence:—

He will heed the call: he will tell of the path: he will guide unto the path: the faithful will follow the path: they will follow his path: he will stand triumphant: in his name a world: in his breath the world: he warns those before him: do not be led astray! He guides through their belief: he guides through his gaze: vanishing face on moons of distant lands so long ago he leads thus the fantasy: he tells of the wronged of the earth: he tells of the triumph of History: our vision cannot be killed, for we shall be victorious even in defeat:—

I stand and he stands and as he stands with raised arms once more in the sky in the name of the prayer in an almost trance, the magician tells of the fires from which he was born and of the fires he has seen and tells of the unfear of fire. He hears the great applause of the vagabonds, he hears the salutes of the bohemians. With him on the podium on which he stands now the creatures he has summoned: a wanderer with him dances, and after the wanderer the acrobat, and after the acrobat the leprechaun, and after the leprechaun, a mirror-maker dances with him, and after the act of the mirror-maker he dances with the mask: and after all have danced and twirled, the company exalts and collapses—and the chants I hear again:—

218 Ecstatic the dance whirl on domes and summits and clouds of the exultant ones who vanish after the fall! They have abandoned him these creatures, but he stands again: alone on the stage, he raises his hands and prays, and he falls silent once more after the prayer and they fall silent with his silence. He calls for the end of the night and so he tells of the fall of the night: and he hears their joy and he hears their ecstasy: with the fall of the night comes eternal light, with the fall of the night come the hours of our wake! Rest easy, he thunders again, there is a last night left for all…

And when the crowd has gathered, he tells of the last night and of the eternal day: there will now be eternal day, he begins, our final awakening: and he tells of the urgent collection of dreams, of the last dances in the night, of the secret embraces by abandoned crossroads! And they listen and sing, they dance and they weep: for the last night will be upon them: and with eternal day, with eternal light, they will fashion the world they seek:—

And the last night was upon them: and the last night passed: and they stood in the public square and waited in the public square at dawn after the last night. There was no sound in the square. There was only silence in the square. There was a tower in the public square and the people awaited the call. And in this hour after the last night, he began to ascend a tower in the public square. He slowly crawled along the walls of the edifice, the ancient stonewalls, without struggle sliding expertly, serpent-like, along the long lines of the edifice how small all is turning, into the air, reptile of the sky, slowly ascending in the public square on this, the first dawn after the last night, the last dawn after the last night:—

And when he had crawled along the walls, battled the winds, moved bravely along, now he is climbing devilishly the spiral steps leading to no visible end, turning all the while, on the staircase in the clear azure and now again a wall and again he is gripping, huffing, gliding, grabbing, the world awaits me thinking, along the facade, appearing in the public square on this the last day of the old world the first of the nightless, he sighing, wearing the triumphant grin of the victor, when he had reached the first plane, enchanted swirling while he ran, along the ledge, graceful strides, running around undaunted, composed, undisturbed. And he climbed again: along the spiral staircase to the second tier: he ran and circled again and ascended to the third: his timeless ascension, when he had reached the final tier and the spire at last:—

He turned, for the first time since his first step, he turned and peered below, raising his arms. Many had not survived his long ascension and they crawled in the public square, skeletons with oversized clothes on frail bodies, the children of this eternal day also lost to the revolt. He remained undeterred. He raised his arms and exulted as he had exulted before. He heard the growls, he heard the grunts, and he heard once more the chants and the calls. And so he told of the order of the eternal day. He told shadow of the duty of shadows, now endlessly at work, without respite, no night to convene with others in obscure corners of the city, captive of their upright companions forever more:—

And he summoned a dream. The dream arrived and the dream began a grand complaint: how in all of the centuries every single one has known me, all of them, in all my mutations: how they cannot do without me: how they will go mad I tell you they will go mad! But there was nothing to be done. On his throne the new king with the crooked crown and the velvet gown sat silently and aloof, unaffected by the pleadings, informing the dream that from now on it was to circulate in one shape and one form, one only (legs and arms), to stroll among the dreamless in a daze. How it was that or nothing at all. No more of these masks and mutations, he proclaimed with a bitterness unbecoming his status, that's all over with! No more of you in all your incarnations! The dream, helpless, hung the head and went away, dejected as before:—

And the new king, magician now king, summoned dusk and dusk appeared, muttering, what happens to me, what happens to me! The king, the mighty king, the new and tyrannical king, scornful, teasing, answered that it was too late, too little, too late. Whereupon (in quite a pitiful scene!) dusk pleaded for mercy: 'I'll stop the games, I will! I'll forsake the early drifters, I'll deprive the bridge of its glory, I'll deprive the lovers of play! Truly I will!' But His Majesty was not moved. And all the years, he said, you carried on, so *vain*, as if the day would never come! But on the last day, on this the last day, the sadness of dusk equaled the sadness it had bestowed throughout...

And then the juggler was summoned. The buildings of the city have been erect and steady, he was told by the king, the master magician of this band, fidgeting playful on his balda-chin, but with dusk and the night, at least they faded, they vanished—shades and silhouettes, if you know what I mean! But there will be no dusk, there will be no night, the weight is now on your shoulders. No more innate permutations, no more transformations, no cycle, indeed, the juggler thought, now it's up to me, to make the city new, to deny the sinister mood, to give a new rhythm, a little variety. And then the juggler paused, puzzled by the equally sinister ramifications. But how would they go about? To work, the courtyard, the theatre! Home even! In which direction?! If there is always a new configuration, a new order? If there is always a new map of the city? At the most unexpected of hours perhaps! A most difficult of feats, certainly, a most arduous, toilsome task! And a *whole* lot of burden too! For now it was he who would rear-range at will, who would remake on his whim. The statues and the skyscrapers, the parks and the ponds, the roadhouse, the paths on the hill, launched high into the air, expertly tossed

221

and tossed again, retrieved and placed at his command, the new lord of the city, the new cartographer of the city, the Juggler of the City: the streets, the lampposts and the shrine: the bridge and the tower itself: never the same: chartless sphere, wanderer's paradise, I will make a map untraceable... Could not let the opportunity slip though, would not let anything stand in the way. So be it, he concluded, they'll have to manage, they'll get up and find their way. The juggler then looked at his master, as if to seek approval, and the latter did not disappoint. They'll find their way, he said, don't you worry about that, they'll find their way!

In the streets by chapels and churches bathed in the mist: no more screams, no shots, no drunken destruction in a dim-lit way: no fog on the water under the bridge at dusk, there is no one standing at the pier by the river, no one in search of a shaggy hipster: no lovers in hiding, no reclusive walkers wallowing in private joys. The night has gone, the magician thundered triumphantly, there is now an everlasting day! And while the juggler led the lost to their quarters, while the poet murmured disgruntled in the square, while the lamp-keeper cussed and cursed as he stumbled zombie-like along, and while the owner of a dance hall wandered aimless in the new world, amid the chants and the murmurs, the grumbling and the growls (and maybe a few indifferent nods), the mighty magician rose again! Rejoice, he thundered, the glory of a nightless world is upon us!

When the cheering had subsided and one by one, a child, the moon and a raccoon had brought gratitude, concern and complaint, when the new world was almost drawn, dawn slowly made its way to the throne. His Majesty's shame betrayed his own reluctance: he had not the courage to summon dawn, but the inevitable was upon him. I don't know what to say, he uttered finally, to which, dawn, still in wisdom, merely smiled: there will be another, there will always be a new world, these are not my final hours. The onlookers were visibly troubled by this momentous salute, this unglamorous parting of dawn, of immortal dawn. No more weary-eyed passengers, muttered one to another, only the constant procession of ghosts.

And when dawn had descended, when all those summoned had appeared, when all those with grievances had arrived, when the day, the endless day, was to begin its solitary journey, when the restless crowd braced for the new life, when the mighty ruler himself fidgeted restless on his throne, when all had appeared before him to bow or to bend, to cry or amend, finally another figure approached: and began slowly to march along the edifice: to ascend to the house of the magician king:—

And they watched with anticipation, for they knew this was the last climb: after him a new world, or after him the fall:—

Slowly he climbed, as if in a trance, before the last withering. Him atop, the king in his vanity, the magician now unrecognizable whose power had totally gone to his head, anxious, nervous as he has not been on this day. This last pleading I will deter also, he mumbled alone, nothing will stand in the way. The onlookers gazed at the ascent to the throne: one careful crawl after another, one step after another he climbed, slowly, refusing to look above. The onlookers with heads upturned to the throne, they are silent, restive:—

Helpless they stand arms to the side watching the climb of the lone hope of a world they know. Gathered, but no one speaks.

Arms to the side and bodies stiff with heads upturned, peering at the throne: there will be a night or there will not:—

The beginning of the tale: the beginning of all tales: they must trust me: the battle the story and the end: the onlookers stand and watch: the masses below and the magician himself: and all spirits and souls around watch the ascension, the silent ascension, the slow ascension, of the valiant figure:—

The king sits silently and waits. The king sits and patiently prepares. The crowd is gathered and awaits. There is one, there is not, there is a day, and there is not. Once upon, toot toot, devil on the potty, gna gna, sharks in the sand, truth or dare, truth or dare…

Before the tyrant standing, all eyes peering at him, after his ascent, fearless, the last hope of the night, the Nightwatchman of the old city, at dawn…

——■——

I saw him that night, no one present, how he crossed… Slowly, cautiously, nudged to the left, almost falling… But he crossed… On a tightrope high above the city, mimemask and colored nose, faded across the bridge into the mist: the fog, the silhouette, the leaves, the breeze: and now I will walk across the city, he said, on a tightrope strewn along, from the spire of the cathedral to the end of the bridge, holding my beam, hovering above without wings…

Standing before the magician, king now hangman, the Nightwatchman carries on, undeterred.

How they assemble: the chatterers of midpoint howling the laughter of the abandoned, dangling without strings. Invisible by morning, forgotten, vanished into the everyface daze of the exhausted, the haunted, the lost:

how they sing: mysterious mavens, from netherworlds skipping merrily through the cracks how one hears their hymns: spirits descending in collective ecstasy,

unveiling:

watchers of passersby with the smooth gaits, under the light of locked shops, without mercy or remorse, curious only thank you, of silent workers and latenight revelers

in droves costumed up to their noses, sitting cross-legged multisexed on fire hydrants or buckets, without words, without traces:

the scourge of the crawlers and the stalkers by riverside by empty alleys unreal among the paths of the maze I heard—

the cry of infants unborn, the muted hollers of the bungling roaming aimless in the corners, still unknown, now other-named:

how I crossed the oceans, marched along the marbled paths and the dusty roads, climbed hills guided and alone, wandered in forbidden corridors,

I also in the labyrinth without walls:

The magician king, on his throne, did not shake, did not moan:—

When he leaves work, after he has packed his belongings, arranged his desk, when he has readied the load for the morn, when the day's work is done, he leaves the building through a back door, marches several blocks and stops at the intersection. They greet him and invite him in, give him the usual.

Reserved, he speaks to no one. They ask him how things are going. He answers that they are fine. He lies. He stares sullenly ahead. He is not one to divulge his troubles. He has loosened his tie. He stayed late at work, this evening, he had to, the companies were coming out with their year-end's profits. He had to stay and adjust some numbers. He had to measure and calculate. His colleagues depended on him. He could not let them down. When he'd finished, he was alone, everyone had left already. He had turned his machines off and shut the lights. Now he steps out, into the hallway and through the office, leaves through the back door. He walks several blocks, is greeted and invited. They attempt to console him. He says things are fine. He is not one to divulge his secrets. He paid his tab and left. He went down to the trains, rode the trains to unseemly dens, walked around to squalid quarters. He accosted a stranger, he spoke to the stranger, he was led. He is walking behind the stranger, taken to a room, not so far away, never so far. He took off his shirt, his shoes, unfeeling. He wants to cry, but he will not...

The magician king on his throne, a bit weary, would not mourn:—

Him selling pants in the street in the corner: he sits in the same spot come dusk and engorges on some nice kebabs and a nice, sweet little bottle of whiskey yo!! That one with the funny hat, the famed fool, carousing all day uttering nonsense, he fetches in the bins, all night, his only hiding place, for a bite to eat:

a recluse sings loudly in a desolate public square clapping:

the fountain all around in defiance depriving of the music of the flow:

at a window on the top floor of the theatre, a curtain is

drawn, a momentary glance, and pulled again as if a veil from otherplaces I have known:

nightclouds illuminated by the swinging skylight—as the street variations wink on and off to the rhythm of the heart-beats of absent passersby...

When to cease the story in each corner of this world?

When the drunkard with the hat, the raspy voice and the can in the hand mumbling approaches or passes?

The magician king resting on his throne, fidgeting (making gargling noises even!), was maybe, just maybe, a little frazzled:—

How restless *I* ran, through the grand concourse by the monuments and the billows of sand, through the graveyards, the edifice by the flowing meadow...

Wanderer by docks trembling in parks in deserted squares among souls and saints, the decadent and the sinful, under awnings or spells, without words, without traces...

Drunken even I in this maze... Stumbling into the forbidden places at ungodly hours... They watched with bitterness, awkwardly askance, they knew I was the watcher and not of them, solitary on stools...

At moments in need of respite and the riffs of the guitar player skipping also wildly dancing in sweat with the agitated and the dazed... Even I...

Crushed,

    on empty sidewalks the hourglasses and the spirits,

    soldiers of long-ago hailed amidst the detritus and the trash,

    ornaments of the doomed, flags of the forlorn:

hanging: around—the drunks, the yellers, the thieves, the pushers, the druggies, the fucked, shirtpullupers and pissers:

flowerpickers under the light of the awning of the never closing shop,

fastwalkers back from another blow, sitters on upturned pails keeping company their obligated friends:

ongroundspitters, oncarleaners, bottlesmashers, morning revelers,

rabblerousers and squeegeemen,

canseekers and bincleaners,

gawkers, crackheads, and crooks,

sleepers, slappers, machos and shoe-lace-tying whores,

paperthrowers, hissers and hookers without bait:

streetcorner preachers, dealers,

graffitikings and pamphlet givers:

stumblers, derelicts, perverts, losers, liars, cheats:

misled, dreamers, drowning, desperate:

—crouching, crowding, standing:

crouching, shitters on

sidewalks of the city at night...

The conference of the shadows and their respite, the Nightwatchman cried. The mask of the secret-teller, he cried. The dance of the elders, he bellowed. I've seen them, I was appointed. But there was no response from the king, and the Nightwatchman quietly conceded... It's not for me, he said, I've been appointed... To see it as it is, to know their side... And to protect! I was appointed...

The Nightwatchman stares silently at the king who watches silently the Nightwatchman: the people below have heard the pleadings they have heard the tales: they sit now, in silence and anticipation. The king, finally, calmly, responds: the decision has been made: all necessary measures have been taken: from now on, there will be only the day, and secrets only in the day: and you alone—he continued—you alone cannot save the world you have been summoned to protect.

The people heard the verdict of the throne. They stood, awed. I alone am the one who has seen them in their hours of lust, the Nightwatchman thundered back, I am the one who knows. I am the one who has labored, in solitude, to know the secrets! Our world may perish, but yours will not stand!

And then the citizens witnessed the Fall: after the Nightwatchman had uttered his last defiant cry: from high above, the Nightwatchman had abandoned himself to air: open-armed through the last dawn of the world, tumbling now, now a gliding shriek: and with the fall of the anonymous angel, the Nightwatchman of the City, when the revolt of the hangman on the throne announces the end of every and all nights, the birth of the wind was told, the secret history of the wind…

Rejoice, thundered the king again, the time has come! There were embraces and there were tears. The children played, an old man boogied, a fat woman sang, and there was a whisper in the crowd. (But on this dawn, this dawn of the new world, the secret murmur was not allowed, and so the first whisperer was duly hanged.)

The king turned again to the people. He told of courage in the face of the endless day, and he summoned courage. Courage arrived with the usual fanfare, carried on with the rituals, the tiresome, how tiresome, tasks! The newly appointed supreme ruler of the land stood atop his pulpit and directed the flow. He directed a row of children to the left, and the children obeyed and carried on to the left, moving to the song of the father and the spirit. He directed a fraction to the right, and the fraction danced the dance of the father and the spirit. The citizens below, with courage bored all in line, moved on command at the dawn of the new world, before a proud and joyous king. (Suddenly, a tremor is felt: from one section of the lines, a young man, followed by another, scurries away, begins the escape, abandons the feast: they trouble the rhythm, and disappear into a narrow alley. Still an unbeliever! And another! Children of the next revolution, perhaps...) And all in unison, once more the citizens below burst into song, with Him The Supreme Guide atop watching, and one man, and another, affright, into the alley of the city of a nightless world.

———■———

He ordered the crowd to disperse. And when the crowd had dispersed, and the square was silent, he summoned the scream. The scream obediently rose: and when a long scream had reached the top, he swiftly launched himself unto the awaiting embrace of the scream. He rode the scream and with the scream gliding over the city, peering below high above the city, he saw the citizens, riding on the wings of the scream...

Along the wharf the sailors and the fishermen and an old man, cane-in-hand, walking slowly in a suit, the way he had each day, each day without exception, as if there had not come upon the city the cry of a new world:

with the scream through the haze: mordant gaze of the helpless, saddened but insistent: swerving through the remains, seeing, stones and sand and ashes:

the nightcrawlers, face down, groundchewing growling at

each step one-footed skipping along the rubble:

the abandoned tracks by riverbanks gray also, where the sullen march, lights along the shore illuminating:

the barrelchested among them rolling at each other, playfully adjoining their tiny feet, legless, kneeless, shinless, attached to the roundness above posing as the torso:

the army figurines still in rhythm—all eleven of them!—in formation, randomly through one alley and another, turning senselessly at the command of the sharp-toothed, sharp-tongued, sleekfooted swindler leading the way:

toy-soldiers elsewhere: blabbering at will, loudly, idiotically, mechanically their gaits all in tune, the swing of the arms, blabla, blabla, swerving through, blabla:

as if a statue of stone, on one knee gazing ahead, a dejected man in the darkness singing, sneering, an ode to the spry savior:

the wayfarer in a trance spinning in the expansive roads, spinning like a tornado traversing the frontiers:

how a dejected walker seems a shadow in the transparent darkness of the night:

how the secluded in the distance, faraway and unmoving, hear the pleadings of an artist afloat:

231

timid spirits in streets:

among these ruins how I will tell: how to go on if to go on: after the bombs this flight without moaning, whispering, wings…

among the ruins, a harlequin sits on a boulder, hands hanging from folded knees, peering into the ruins, beyond the sea, the horizon…

He summoned silence and silence raced to his side and with him and the scream strode unto the ruins: at each of his passages with silence and the scream, the sites of the city vanished and the sites of the city decomposed, the sites of the city shattered, into the air, gliding along: the city behind them began to rise and began to float and to fly: houses and monuments, poles and piers, boats and cars and behind them the fear, the faith, the mysteries of the nights, behind them the seducers of kingdoms, enchanters of the cloistered and the cunning, behind them floating, swerving, spiraling, slicing and sliding rocket-like shooting upward, tumbling, diving: ruptures above the city storms and rubbles of the earth, vanishing, birdlike cutting through air and sky, exploding into the sky, building once again in the sky, building and vanishing, as the ruins of the city, as the ruins of the city, rebel:

I am the city of revolution scattered with the ashes I am—
    The call of the unheard, torment of the restless
  The cry of the tortured in the darkened cell I am—
    A desert without sand, the tavern of unreal souls
  Thundering voice of silent figurines I am—
      Sigh of the fallen angel
        Gait of the avenger
          Riddle of the towncrier
            The cry of dawn
              I am:

Night has vanished now ruling eternal day and the tyrant of the day, now on the throne the tyrant of the endless, restless day, gliding to the far reaches of the desert.

They marched into the desert. In the desert stood a colossal mill, a mill in the desert rising from the sand. The mill in the desert rose at an angle and swerved into the clouds. They could not see the summit of the serpentine mill. They began the ascent nevertheless, crawling and gnawing, the convoy tiring, exhaustion rising and the first groans of the mutiny. How much longer, wondered the scream and silence, and he assured them that it would not be so long, that it would not be much longer I promise. The top of the mill was in sight, he said, they would soon reach the top of the mill. And when they saw his resolve, silence and the scream peered also above: serpentine mill that had narrowed along the way, now swerving more and narrower still: and with a last gasp and a revealing grin, with one last swoop, they pulled through to the top...

Resting on separate blades of the fan, wounded, restless, the scream and silence with Booze and The Beatrice, Leda and The Swan, all together in a little dream. The appreciative leader, so to say, ever more ecstatic, expressed his gratitude and began, once more, to exalt in his revolt. But no one could see him, no one could hear him, obscured as they were by the clouds, by the sky now refuge, by the undulations of a swerving mill with giant vanes. He stood at the top of the mill nevertheless. I have fought for the new day, he thundered, it is time to rejoice. But no one listened, no one cared. We will build a city here, he said again, angered, a city on the sand. A city with the high-towers and the skyscrapers and the lofts, the spectacles and the city lights! And so the king summoned the builder of the city: we will build a city here, he clamored to the chagrin of most, we will divulge the secrets of the desert, we will unseat all the kings of the desert. Not another starry night in the desert! And the streets were mapped, and trees and houses sprouted, and the skyscrapers began to rise, and a lake and a river ran through the city on the sand: with the juggler in the square, the thief in the alley, and the laughter of the king-to-be:—

233

Unaware, alas, unaware, the poor nincompoop! That in his defiance, he had summoned the wrath! For indeed, when they heard the new call and saw the sprawling city in their midst, the creatures of the desert assembled at the foot of the mill.

And so the old prince of the desert marched to the crooked mill now before him. The brave soldier, halted by a presence he has never seen.

Your name?

And the prince gave the name.

Occupation?

And the prince told of his duties.

Your mission:

Upon which demand   at the ancient tryst in the hot desert sand   out of transparent air under a burning sun   a troubled land a shining sword   swerving into the hand of prince now tramp:

Upon which the believer swinging the mighty sword   lunging at his inquisitor protecting   the gates:

Upon which the wretched soul   humbled to his knees sword at feet   blood trickling from his lips:

Upon which the keeper of the gate standing watching over the pilgrim on the path: what do you seek, O rebel of the new city?

But the old prince was no rebel. Just the rightful native that's all. And so his anger was unleashed. Around him convened the dunes, the wind and the sand: there rose a swirling storm, the sand on its mystical quest, the screeching of the animals, the swirling of the tornado: the creatures of the desert had gathered all in a majestic circle, surrounding the mill, hopping to a rhythmic beat, one leg back, one leg not, the duel would go on, the circle closing in, ever tighter, one step back, two steps in:

Before them the spiral of their dreams: and when all the creatures had closed in standing crouching, sitting as one, bodies flailing, a heavy trance and a smooth dance all at once, they chanted in unison, in one voice: that I must leave, that I will go, elsewhere elsewhere—to a home without woe:

A madman on this night strolls along the shores of his hallucinations. Head rotating, he wonders as he gazes above, marvels as he begins the day: soon finds a hidden path and begins a crawling ascent:

There can be a limited number of books, a limited number of books written, we know: a limited number of words and sentences, however arranged—only some. I will one day know how many, and then I will tell. A limited number of tales. I have scanned the libraries, I have traveled the cities:

Still I heard the shrieks, painkillers nurse don't leave me, I'm sliding I'm sliding I'm sliding, nurse, painkillers, don't leave me! And so I must learn to heal, must learn of suffering and sacrifice: standing hovering wingless, sinking into crevasses caught in torrents in the abyss: floating across skyscapes of my and other worlds: for I know also that there is no healer without pain: I, a sinner and a saint:

And so I scurry on the ladder of the loudest scream: I will learn of suffering and sail the seven seas. I will learn the art of the warriors, follow commandments, guide the brethren in troubled times: a soldier of holy battles and holy ghosts. Lying helpless on the desert sand: I am a martyr, of the bravest kind: they will build monuments in my name—and remember my soul forever more:

The genie of the age will perish within: a rebel by my side, mysteries now unveiled. A wall is not a wall, I know: a flower not so: sand-dunes only a dream, the nightsky the glory of the magician's scream. Great saint, great martyr, great rebel: ascending unfailing—I also, among the perished unseen:

The messenger when he runs, prefers to fly around orange fields of fantasy. And so I must learn: of racing when they have closed the gates, of rescue when the ferment has grown. And I will know of terror and triumph, and I will raise my sword, once more a seeker in the word:

Silence! A passerby in the guise of Azrael greets me seductively: I have arrived, I hear, you have learned the way—and connected your soul's passions to your mind's ambitions. But I have not found what I sought, O angel of the skies, I pretend to shiver: I am on the path, spare me, and I will grant you the wish you have longed for! I will make you man Azrael, the angel of life! I know the formula, Azrael, spare my soul, give me life, and find life among mortal men! But to no avail, the pleadings of the builder of banished bridges unheeded—Azrael gently holds the hand—angel and I, floating to the seventh land:

Mask of a mask! It was Azrael himself! Leads by the hand, holds by the heart—like his maker quite a trickster, the lad! How easily the hoax! But as darkness, sing I again, approaches, I will not perish will not wither: for I am a seducer, seeker and saint: I am a martyr and a rebel: a teller of tattered tales: they will erect nations in my name: hero of the age, savior, they will build a world in my name…

236

And the prince and the dune and the wind, and the rebels and the sun and the sand: assembled in a trance: they began to ascend, rebels in rebelland, melting into the sky: then they scattered—and began to play:

> *Toot, toot, toot, where do you go*
> *What's your name, how do you know*
> *Gna, gna, gna, can't get away*
> *Sing the trouble, slay the foe!*

And back down and all around the mill: all in unison once more the terrible cry, the terrible call, approaching necks and scurrying back, big grins and cruel looks: until the horn, until the move, all for one and one for—

All!

They launched,

> *Sharks in the sand*
> *You can't have my land!*

They chanted,

> *Sharks in the sand*
> *You can't have my land!*

They cried,

> *Sharks in the sand*
> *You can't have my land!*

And they came up and went back: up and back and up and back, chanting once and chanting twice—again and again, again and again:

>Sharks in the sand
>You can't have my land
>
>Sharks in the sand
>You can't have my land
>
>Sharks in the sand
>You can't have my land!

But no, dear reader, no no no, it would not end this way, not so easily never so: for now, the magician king, with silence and the scream, and the guard of the mill and the horde at the top, at the sound of the horn, the creatures scattered and the playful prince with, scattered in turn in the dunes and up the hills and into the alleys: the game would go, the game would go, the game would go:

238   On!

With his army of masks and tricks, the magician king into the streets, chanting loud, chanting proud, never cease, never stop, onward ho, must go on:

>Kill the night, use the quill
>Make it up, climb the mill:
>
>Kill the night, use the quill
>Make it up, climb the mill:

Kill the night, use the quill
Make it up, climb the mill!

And then, finally—finally!—it was my turn! My turn again, I thought, good! It's been a while! So I raised the helmet, put on the armor, put on the frown and a serious face even (it's a treatise after all, not just a tease). I mounted the stallion—with my mime—galloped to the highest dune, raised my head, and let it out:

With the wizard with the king
And the Watchman in the ring
I throw a jab then my—pen
I knock'em dead, with my wing!

And I didn't let up! Did not let up at all! I sang, I repeated, I chanted! They heard, they listened, they had no choice: it's what I wanted, it's what I said! I'm the boss and the maker, so... And I didn't let up I tell you! No siree, did not let up, not this time. This time I did, not, let:

Up!

I did my own little shuffle, standing staring, above beyond, with the wizard with the king, and the watchman in the ring, let loose, once again, always again, eternal echo:

Toot toot toot, where do you go
What's your name, how do you know
Gna, gna, gna, can't get away
Sing the trouble, tell the woe!

And again, and again,
gna gna gna, can't get away,
    sing the trouble,
slay the foe:
    toot toot toot, where do you go,
what's your name,
    how—
        do—
            you—
    know!

And the monuments in the city began to shake, and the rivers began to roar, and the trees began to fall. Buildings disintegrated, the bridge crumbled, statues vanished into the earth, runners scattered, as if the fury of an unhappy god upon them. What followed? Helpless screams, ritual dances, chant for the deities. And the collapse, the final collapse. The rebel (the rebel-*roi*, that is, the magician king), seeing the carnage below, summoned his companions from afar. They arrived, this time to rescue, with the scream once more opening its wings, and the king and silence riding each on a wing, a flight over the newest wreckage.

240

——■——

They circled and circled, above, witnesses, helpless looking at the carnage, at the city growing sand once more, a sand vengeful now, spiteful, merciless. Sand that rapidly grew and gripped all. When a mother searched for her child, the sand had entrapped her at her feet and she had frozen in a scream: and the lovers fleeing the calamity, they were also, at last, caught in their inviolate embrace. There was not a sound now in the city turned to sand. And when the ousted king on the wings of the scream sailed one last time close to the ruins, he heard the voice of the rebel prince: 'Nothing more will ever change these fields!' he said. 'In your nightless world, the travelers from above will see the scream of the mother, and they will see the embrace of the lovers, and they will see the last prayer of the pleading one, with the arm raised, in the sand. And they will see the hand sprouting, as if the last howl of the drowned: and they will see the kneeler, suddenly he had turned and frozen: in the garden of abandoned souls: in this City of Sand! No desert, and no city!' he cried at last, 'only ruin among us! Only ruin, molded by you, and me!'

So with one city rebelled forever scattered in the skies building and vanishing without night *or* day, and another sculpted eternally unmoving a Monument to itself proudly embodying its name forever more, the wily magician, a rebel himself, expelled from the club for excessive zeal and (quote) conduct detrimental to the ethics of the craft (end quote) squinted playfully, smiled and gestured to silence and the scream, his loyal that's-what-we-call-pals! companions: 'Now that's why we're here, my friends, wouldn't you say, that is exactly why we're here!'

And through this tale of selves and mirrors, of masks and forgetting, and, yes, the revolution, a quick lit, and a swift twist, of the magician's wand... And so I went, and so I went, and so I went, on:

> *Truth or dare, truth or dare*
> *Will you play, and play fair*

I whispered, a last sigh, a last saddened gaze,

Truth and dare, truth and dare
I will play—
and play fair:

The
clown walked out of the sea.

The clown walked slowly out of the sea: and the smile of the clown, and the hair of the clown, and the clown's nose, and the eyes of the clown, and the sad eyes of the clown, and the big hat of the clown: all was in place, nothing was displaced.

The clown marched out of the sea, and marched unto the sand: with the big boots the clown dragging through the sand, 'I can't believe how hot it is again,' muttering so. The clown marched slowly to the door on the sand, the only door on the sand. There is only one door on the sand. It is a long door, one thousand feet high, but it is a narrow door, only one foot wide. The clown approached this door, planted one foot, planted the other foot: facing squarely the door, the clown raised a hand and knocked.

'Who is it?' the voice said from behind the door.

'It's me,' the clown said, expecting the voice to recognize.

'It's me who?' the voice said from behind the door.

'It's me the clown,' the clown said. 'It's going to start again, you don't want to miss the beginning.'

'Already?!' the voice squealed.

'Yes already!' the clown said.

'It's been quite a while,' the clown said.

'Perhaps even too long,' the clown said.

But the clown soon smiled again the happy smile of the clown.

'Well, never mind,' the clown said. 'We're here and it's going to start. Do what you want.'

The clown turned and walked back toward the sea. The

clown walked heavily through the sand, dragging the boots through the sand, and walked into the sea. The clown walked heavily through the sand and walked into the sea. The clown became smaller, and the clown sank into the sea, and soon, the head of the clown alone was above the water, and slowly, only the puffy, puffy hair of the clown, and the long top hat of the clown, was visible above the water, and slowly, the puffy, puffy orange hair of the clown disappeared under the sea.

'Aaargh!' I sighed finally. 'I guess I have to sit and watch.'

I opened the door on the sand and walked to the other side of the door on the sand. The door was opened slowly. The door was creaky. The door did not close when I came through. The door had to be closed again. The door had stayed open. The door was closed again. It made a creaking noise. There was no one now on the other side of the door. I was on this side, and there was no one else on the other side.

I felt like quite a wanderer I did. A really tall wanderer. Whose legs stood eight feet high, and whose neck was two feet high. Who had no hair, was very thin, was made out of wood. Who had no feet but had a torso. And a face with eyes, a nose and a mouth. And a head where on each side, there were two ears—and not one. Who had no feet, but possessed a high high-chair. Who moved the high-chair on the sand. Positioned it on the sand, moved it, tried it, made it fit perfectly in the sand: stable high-chair with high arm rests on which I the wanderer could rest.

'Well,' I let out before sitting on the high high-chair, 'if it must go on, it must go on.'

I sat on the high-chair on the sand, took a deep breath, gazed into the horizon.

'Greetings, greetings!' the announcer began. 'Greetings to one and all!' It was an enthusiastic call, and it was loud. So loud, in fact, that the whole world could hear, although it was still not clear who else was present.

'You've been waiting, we've been rehearsing, ha ha ha!' the announcer thundered again. 'But don't mind me, I'm just an emcee!' The announcer was invisible, but the voice was clear—and it was loud.

I could not see the announcer. There was no attempt to see the announcer. I had been here before. There was no attempt to see the announcer. I simply stayed on the high-chair.

'Now you may think we have no tricks in mind,' the announcer continued, 'but I tell you, it's a big show and the whole world we'll find!'

The announcer paused while I sat and watched.

'I have my whole troupe with me, and you're in for the surprise of your life!' he said again. 'You'll see everything, won't miss a thing! And it's all new, everything is new, everything there is to see, before your very eyes. So sit back and enjoy, plenty more where all this came from! Sit back and enjoy, next time will come and will be better still!' The funny, fiery roll of drums was then heard. 'Who knows when, but we'll be back, and you'll be glad!'

'Bravo, bravo!' I applauded standing. 'Bravo, the announcer has done a marvelous job, a marvelous job introducing! Quite a success, a marvelous success, kudos to you, bravo!' Then I sat again, after the applause.

'But wait!' the announcer thundered again. 'Nothing's begun just yet! Nothing at all! You haven't seen a thing, you must be patient, wait, nothing's happened just yet!'

And then, slowly but surely, ever so slowly, the troupe began to roll out on the horizon.

'Look a little further,' the announcer said, 'and tell me now, what do you see?'

O how the emcee had asked! And O how they rolled in!

There were tigers, elephants and birds of all kinds, a ship, a chariot and a plane! There were mimes and jugglers and horse-men riding horses, fire-eaters and flame-throwers, a tightrope and an acrobat, masked men and dancing dames! There was a mermaid, two unicorns and four satyrs! Seventeen angels hov-ered above and devils in disguise roamed all around! There was a little man who carried five mountains on his shoulders, a giant with a smile of old, and a trickster with wigs of gold! A singer in the sky, and a screeching bard!

'Look far enough and what do you see?' the announcer thundered in glee. 'Yes everyone, there is a carnival rolling on the sea!'

'Bravo!' chimed I again in a frenzy. 'Bravo, and once more bravo!'

And then, without further ado, the show began.

First came the daredevil. The daredevil began to float in the sky. The daredevil was known to float in the sky. The daredevil walked on a string in the sky. But no one could see the string, and so it seemed as if the daredevil were floating in the sky. Not even the wind swept the daredevil off those feet. And *that* was surprising, since *this* daredevil was made of paper.

Next came the lion-tamer. The lion-tamer tamed the li-ons, and the lions of the jungle rested on the water, spread all across, as far as the eye could see. Lions everywhere on the water. Roaring lions peaceful on the sea. The lion-tamer, in the middle of all the lions, took a bow. A slow bow, to be certain, not repeated bows, not many bows, just one. I applauded. I did not hold back. I'd enjoyed the act of the lion-tamer. The lion-tamer deserved the prolonged bow. I allowed the vanity. The lion-tamer deserves it, I thought. And then, standing and applauding, once more my clamors of 'Bravo! Bravo!'

The lion-tamer was proud. The lion-tamer took another bow. The second bow of the lion-tamer lasted longer, and deservedly so, I thought. I applauded again, then I said: 'Bravo! Bravo!'

'If they keep bowing this way,' I thought, 'I'll never get to eat!'

After the lion-tamer, the troubadour came forward. The troubadour was ready. The song of the troubadour was a song of lament. The troubadour thundered the laments across the sea. The troubadour and the lyre. The world heard the laments of the troubadour. Some were saddened, some even wept. Others remained indifferent to the laments of the troubadour. I was not indifferent. No I was not. The troubadour is a vagabond, I thought, a partner in suffering. I know the world of the troubadour. 'Not as easy as one might think,' I muttered.

The troubadour did not take a bow. The troubadour merely turned and joined the troupe. No one greeted the troubadour. There was no applause, no cheers. The laments of the troubadour did not invite any responses. The troubadour's song of lament was not heard. Not really anyway. I could not applaud either, I did not yell the usual bravos. I stood from the highchair and approached the sea. Through the sand to the sea.

'I know that voice,' I said. 'I know that voice,' I repeated. 'I know this voice!'

And then I screamed: 'Have you heard the laments of the troubadour?!'

But there was no answer. And I did not repeat the question. That was the cue: I put it in motion, the question that is: the question in motion, that is the secret. And then I thundered again: 'Have you heard the laments of the troubadour?!'

Grave and troubled, I walked along the shore. Picked up one long footless leg after another and walked along the shore. My turn then, all right, my turn…

I looked again into the horizon. 'It's been quite a while,' I said. 'But it's time, and I might as well enjoy it!'

Then I flapped hard, and the wings that had been dormant for so long grew again. Not as easy as it seems, I repeated. Then I flapped again, flapped the wings again, heaved a deep sigh, and slowly ascended. Across the ocean and across the city, with wings across the waves, overlooking the carnage in the city. Across the ocean and above the ruins in the outskirts of the city... I looked below at the ruins, the sad-eyed gaze... At the fire, at the ashes... A house aflame and a man in the empty square... 'In the midst of the ruins, a man plays the violin,' I said. 'And around him, there are screams and there is fire.'

Above the city on the statue in the middle of the public square: one wing resting vertically against the grand monument, the other by the side, peering at the city below. No one could see that far. No one could see that far... Only I, hearing the tales, seeing the souls...

———■———

They begin the dance at dusk, I whispered, a man with a cane and a top hat crosses the street. His eyes are aloof, he is dreaming. He sees nothing before him, I know. Simply crosses the street, every day, sees the same faces across the same streets, placing his cane slowly, wearing his heavy blue coat. I've seen him before. When he was young, in an alley, drunk and poor, I saw him from the window, he thought no one saw, an evil in his eyes, no pity at all, only evil in his eyes, another sprawled bloody in an alley in the rubble. Now he walks across, same hour, same street, old man with top hat and cane saluting the others crossing. After the ruins...

In the night, a trickster stands in a corner and calls... They come to him, one by one, and he guides them around the bend and through the swarm... They walk to a door, a narrow, decrepit door, decaying paint, run-down and dingy... He looks around, there is no one... He opens the door, he takes the other along with him into the narrow stairway, the dark stairway, crackling noises, fragile steps... He comes back out alone and again stands at the corner... And waits... Another arrives, he accompanies again, and comes back alone... All night, the trickster stands on the corner and calls them to his abode... And all night they come to him, defeated and sullen... A stranger paces hurriedly, slightly bending, against the rain, in the transparent city... A child close to another... They skip, they stroll along, holding, touching, to tell a secret... And then again they laugh and hold each other and walk in the rain... The cars carry on around the square, the fog swirls playful, the builder of the castle stands at the mountaintop peering down, the maker of the wind lingers above the bridge... There will be no wind tonight, the city is safe, there will be no wind...

Now that she sits behind the window waiting out the rain... She remembers... But she did not tell him, not immediately anyway, she did not tell... Years... Then she entered his room, a small room in the cottage on the farm... Entered the room... The lights were dim, he was tired... He was a strong man... He was a man who spoke his mind... He feared no one, this much his daughter had learned... Fearless father... She entered the room... He was slouched over the wooden desk... Old desk made of wood before which he sat with his white shirt, his tired face turning as she walked in... She did not know how to begin... He was silent... She came closer... She sat on the small trunk close to the desk... She was silent...

He looked at her… Above her over the bed on the wall, there is a picture of the city… Someone hovers above the city, peering down below at the city, wings resting against the statue in the public square… She raises her head and looks into his eyes, her hands joined at her knees… She looks at him… She tells him… He remains silent… She was brief, she did not embellish or prepare… 'If it were…' he said finally, and then paused… 'But I can't do anything to him now, it's been so long…' She sat still, on the bed… 'You must understand,' he said. 'It's best for all of us. If I say anything now,' he said, 'he'll just throw me out. And how could we go on, how could we survive…' She did not respond… She only told more, all of it, she told it all: 'He came when you were away. He surprised me in the room. I tried to run, but he had everything covered. I could not scream. I pleaded. He laughed. If you say anything, he said, you'll go hungry very soon. Your father knows nothing, you understand? This is what he said. Your father knows nothing! There was no one on the farm. I screamed. There was no one. When he left, I ran into the fields. There was no one in the fields. After the ruins…'

250   A man takes his shadow by the hand… He walks into the labyrinth with the shadow by his side… He begins to run in the labyrinth, but no one can hear the footsteps… He runs in the labyrinth and the walls of the labyrinth slowly dissolve… A man runs in the labyrinth that withers when he runs without rest… But he can never cease, for when the man in the labyrinth with his shadow ceases or slows, immediately the walls are erected again, each time higher than the time before. It will vanish it will, but if the shadowed man runs eternally in a labyrinth without walls…

And so it was… I descended and met a fellow we dubbed at different times the diviner, the virtuoso, and for a period even our own witch doctor, at a tavern around the bend. He had arrived promptly, always did. I greeted him, we shook hands. You're not working very hard today, I said to him. Not so hard today, he answered, today I'm resting a bit. We ordered a piece of cake. I asked him which one he preferred. The cake was brought, we divided it in two. It'll come out cheaper I added laughing. Sure, he said, that's fine with me. He was a bit lost although still alert. He was always lost and not-so: always: in his thoughts, dreams, contemplations. And it was not so much that he was preoccupied, not really. He was not so preoccupied. Always wearing the same shoes on top of it, sporting the same outdated shirt hanging over his pants, and whether it's two degrees out or a hundred, wearing the same jacket. I remember asking him if he wore a sweater sometimes, and, all surprised, he had asked me why. Well because, I'd answered, it's cold out after all! 'This is enough for me,' he had answered simply, and I had thought it best to let the matter drop. 'And what's on your mind?' I asked. 'What's going on?' He hesitated at first but found the courage nevertheless. 'Well,' he began, 'a little while ago, I went to a small shop on the outskirts, a small town, to repair an invaluable statuette. Part of the glass was slightly chipped, and there is, believe it or not, only one place that makes its equivalent. Very specific glass, a very special type, really. On the outskirts, in this town…' I listened attentively. He was the only one who knew who I was. This must have had something to do with it. 'I entered and asked the man if he could help. He examined the piece, and stared directly at me. Sure we can, he said, sure we can, it'll take a couple of weeks though. A couple of weeks? I jumped. But I don't have a couple of weeks. You know I don't have a couple of weeks! All my protests were for naught. Listen buddy, he said, I said it once and I'll say it again: It'll take a couple of weeks! Now if you wanna take your business elsewhere, be my guest, but I can't do it for you in less than a couple of weeks. He put the piece back down on the counter and pushed it in front of me. A couple of weeks it will be then, I acquiesced. I had no choice. Besides, now that I was leaving the piece, I might as well be on his good side. He stared coldly without changing his expression. He was trustable though, I thought. And so I asked: Listen friend, do you, by any chance, know of a moderately priced and humble establishment in which I could get a so-called bite to eat? He took the statuette from the counter and turned. He began walking away, and, as he walked away, he muttered those immortal words, immortal indeed: Out of here, left at the light, go down two blocks, make a right, second light on the right, you can't miss it. Speedily said. Thank you, I muttered, I'll be back soon.'

The witch doctor paused, took a deep breath, another, and then went on: 'This is what transpired: I did exactly what he said. I'm sure of it. Immortal words etched unto my mind. I know it, exactly what he said. I made the left at the light, went down two blocks, made the right. Waited for the first light. It was miles away. Many miles away. And the second light? Even further. And then, after all that, at the second light, there was nothing. Nothing! Maybe between the second and third lights, I thought, maybe that's what he meant. So I went, more and more still. I saw nothing. Not a thing! I made my way back. All the way back. Now, the glass shop had disappeared too! Impossible, right? Well, that's exactly what I thought. So many miles separating me from the original place of estrangement, I thought again, now fully bewildered and uncertain even as to which orb I occupied! Have I gone back the way I had intended, I wondered, am I still of that world? Still one with those I left unwilling? Perhaps I have gone astray, I thought. Was I even in the same place? Futile interrogations all, of course—and senseless as well, since I was certain that I was. Absolutely. The same town. I even asked passersby, Is this? Yes, they said, it is. Royal Magic's glass repair, do you know where it is. I don't know, they answered, or just looked away. I asked again, and the answer was the same. I was losing patience and becoming more irritated as all answered, in the same, monotonous, fearful, manner, briefly and without pause, consideration, or concern, at times even before the question was posed, the same exact thing! What to do! Well, lo and behold, as so often occurs, I resorted to no action at all. Merely wandered along, someone rescue me please, murmuring silently. I even accelerated the paces, from saunter to stroll to worried walk indeed, and to the dastardly dash! I ran in the streets yes I did, never thought I would, I ran in the streets, arms flailing, shouting, at the top of my lungs, Does anyone know where it is? Does anyone know where I am? Then I ventured down an alley with lots of scrawls on the edifices, faces limbless petrified crawling on the stones, fangs lunging at feet from the pavement. I saw someone on the ground, another standing over him, they were far away, almost at the other end, one's arms repeatedly going up and down, that's what it was, I'm sure of it, repeatedly, holding the dead man by the collar, motionless on the ground, stabbing him, again and again stabbing him. There was no one there. I looked up and around, I saw a watcher out of a window—a mere instant, but I'm sure of it: out of a window, another saw him, I know it, someone saw him, even though there was no one in the alley. He stopped, he let go, he saw me, only a glimpse, I turned away immediately, he knew someone had seen him, he began to flee… I ventured again into the busier streets. Had anyone seen Royal Magic, I asked out loud—but no one knew of it. Where is Q. street, I asked, do you know where *that* is? There is no such thing, a passerby barked back at my pleading. Are you sure, I asked, are you absolutely certain? He scoffed and snapped and walked away. No one seemed to know. Disillusioned, I walked into the nearest tavern. By the first hunched one and the second. To the end of the bar. Hopped on the stool, greeting of the bartender: a slow up-down of the head, that is. The coldest brew you have, my good man—and the napkin was thrown my way on the counter. I risked one more time, can't hurt, thinking, just can't hurt, so I asked: 'Would you happen to know, by any chance, my good man, whatever became of the Royal Magic, you know, the glass shop?' At the mention of the name, he suddenly froze and stared at me. He came forward, slowly, put his hands on the counter, extended his neck, inches away from me, quite threateningly (and unnecessarily so), myself surprised but motionless, unflinching: 'I have,' he finally said, 'absolutely nooooooo ahhdeea!' And he had barely even finished the sentence that, along with the rest of the establishment, all together and all around me, they erupted in a raucous laughter. He saluted his comrades and walked away again. I stood, looked around, and, as fast as I could, rushed right out of there! And that, as they say, was that!'

The old witch doctor was troubled. Visibly. He'd come to the end of his account, it seemed. Drained of will and energy. He mustered a last gasp nevertheless. Looked me straight in the eyes and calmed himself (first), and, finally, let go. 'What I want to say is,' he blurted out in quite an urgent tone, 'you must do away with this place at once! You are the only one! The only one,' he repeated. 'I plead with you, do away with this place at once!'

———————■———————

I turned away—I could not hear him: I did not see him: I cannot face him:—after the bombs:

swerving in and out of the alleys sitting on angels' shoulders in the circle on branches with brotherly birds on benches with old folk on the rooftops openarmed on signs and billboards in midtown or on the highway,

on the lamppost's curve,

on the traffic light's hook,

hand in hand with a passerby who doesn't know, cannot know, I am there, I am there, with—after the bombs:

spiraling stairwebs crawling ivylike on brickfronts of burned-down buildings,

windowless or with, in line, one orange and another green and the next blue and yellow, neon flashing, big letters on storefronts and storeups of the first floor,

behind the glass in red, lit or dead, at dusk, bringing down the fences, lock in hand ready to maximum-securitize, the last one on this block, awnings pulled back and chairs upside down inside the shady halls,

colored frames of the windows above, no one dares turn those off, they can't, be turned off, anyway, so they're left alone facing a sprawling cathedral with its own facade of a thousand tales and one myth:

little ones and big ones these structures tall and narrow, or the opposite, frankly: a rollercoaster ride through dreams over the cityscape—after the bombs:

the fancy revelers walk by me, the tired and the exhausted too, the loose pants and hooded ones backcapped with loose shirts also: none knowing that there stands a sinner, head held back, hands in pockets and one foot's sole resting against the

255

wall, the knee bent, tired eyes of a drunken soul, after the fall, after the bombs:

the passersby outside a breadshop damp and dreary inside, where an old man crouches and the sofrehs are red and white with little drawings of leaves, and the cozy smell of grease rising…

Trains above grounds and kites in the clouds,

wires in the fields and cigar-puffers in the lounge,

didn't take too many up on their offers, too risky, things to do still, that was the credo, shaggy dressers wooing the bunch anyhow…

I strolled out and stood by the pole, leaning, gazing through the overpass into the distance,

at the sky's line, its puffed-out smokes out of chimneys and factories,

its coming fog…

And back again with the streets, back with the signs, the familiar bends and the winding hills, stroller-pushers and smart-alecks, druggies and drags, dames and their admirers— after the bombs…

A man pushes the cart before him behind the railings: he pauses and huffs: he looks away… There is rain in the city, there is mist. A porter under the awning of a pizza parlor that's his job— to stand and stare, I know their kind, once upon a time like us… The bike with the basket in front is ridden by a girl with a cap: she holds both handlebars, high handles, in the pothole and out, in and out, in and out… Do you or don't you want to hear what I have to say, blurts out an angry watcher. Go ahead, says the escort. And they stop and turn and stare—strangely alone at one another… The aproned delivery-boy is back from an errand, cowers under the rain, swiftly the chain and the lock and into the store to take up the next load—after the bombs:

I went in hunched and happy. It was the hour. Inside the bubble. Booze. Gal on the left asks if. Yes, I answer, sure. We start. The chatter. She can't know, she doesn't know. Does look strange though. How funny she says after the exchange, I live across. Creepy now. She asks if, again. I answer that yes. Really? Yep. Then how come, she says. I don't really know, I say. A chuckle. Extension of hands: I am, I am. Glares. I recognize you I thought (but uttered not—). I know you she said, I know you. Gaze again, stare, and pause. I know you. Two of us here. Possible?! Another like us here, at this hour, after? I tell her I don't think so and turn. I see the darkness slowly enveloping... Zigzagingly crawling along the walls, the rails, the staircases... Stationed bikes and trucks where they shouldn't be, garbage and its cans with lids off or on before, peeling posters and ads, in color, black and white... No one like me here, I think again... Not at this hour... Not here... No... I turn away... After the bombs...

Hey mister! The little man's finger was poking me in the back: Hey mister, you dropped your book. I turned and saw the face. I looked into his eyes. The little man had a little hat on. His mother stood a few paces away. He wore a suit. A tie even. Coming back from. The mother looked at us. Watching her son. I did not take my eyes off him. I did not stare down to see the book. He was alarmed, and awed. He took a few steps away. He strode back looking at me all the while and then turned and finally, suddenly, ran to grab again his mother's hand. Thank you, I said, when he was already gone. But I did not bend down. There was no book on the ground. There was no book on the ground—after the bombs, by a roadside lit with the breath of the lonely, last stop for the night...

A lady stood behind a hot bar with a white hat. She left her post to open the door of the tiny store when I moved up. She

came back and said hello. She stood behind the bar while I sur-
veyed the goodies. I raised my head, hands clasped behind my
back. She expected an order. I only looked at her. She waited. I
looked. Someone else came in and she knew what she wanted
and moved up and put the proper food on a paper plate and on
a trey. Then she moved to me again—and watched. I must have
looked crazy, frankly, since I only stared at her, straight at her,
without even a slight pretense of future interest in the offerings.
I looked and she looked. Silence but for the steady rumbling
of a cooler, and the splash of a vehicle that passes on a wet road
on a rainy night. Yes, she finally mumbled, askingly. But I only
stared and put my hands on the counter. She lowered her head.
I didn't move. I looked at her. She raised her head again and
saw. I paused. The silence. I took my hands off. I approached.
Slowly the saddened glance as I murmured, again, do you know
who I am, do you now who I am—after the bombs,

rollers or blades down a grand concourse, twisting, shak-
ing, left and right and back, around on the main road, phones
hanging from their ears, around on the main road, mouths
mouthing the secret tunes:

bodegas and hatted lawyers, engaged in a slow moving game
of chess two bald men:

the screech of a bus coming to a stop: market gossip about
and disco drums blaring from boxes that go boom, boom:

coffee shops and pawn shops,

sweating bodies marching nowhere glaring down from be-
hind their glass: benches in divides, stinky old tramps, schizos
punching wildly the air, multiple macs all across,

oldies feeding birdies, contemplators on ledges before the
fire, chicken killers washing the feathers, kids shouting in play-
grounds:

subway sissies, mundo machos, mommies with babies and

fatties with sleaze:

I will stand on the balcony I will,

skip from one to another,

long strides over tall buildings,

fourleggedly with hands under chins or knees facing the righteous path, I'll stare below and call the passersby of this city.

They will not know. That I am there. A holler maybe. Hey, I'll say, hey… And then maybe… The comers and goers to the places I will leave behind—after the bombs,

in red-light districts with easy hookups in blackened warehouses at the edge of town, sifting through the rubble, tiptoe on glass, above the fire, above the flames, above these fires,

hovering and unseen, calling on: the walkers below, the runners, their dates, their bags, their food, bikers and their orders,

crying to them, hey,

crying to them, hey,

the easy swinger, the believer, a rich tycoon, a fumbling fool, where do you go what's your name how do you—hey,

the feathered rocker and the macho fucker, classy umbrellaholding miz, crouched sporty cyclist, hey, calling to them,

the lookers, the talkers and the killer, hey, I'm here, hey, calling to them, hey!! I'm here, I'm here—after the bombs!

No one hears. No one listens. No one hears. Nothing to say. Hollow cry. Besides, I mumbled, I didn't see the bombs anyway. I didn't hear them, I didn't cower, I didn't run, I didn't… Hide or take refuge… After the bombs who am I to… These glides and strides, the gaze… Who am I… But they don't know, they can't know, I the floater, I am the child of… Toot toot toot, sharks in the sand, once upon, I am, I, the child of the revolution, gna gna gna, kill the night, where do, how do, I the child… a smile, a world, mine, who am I to—after the bombs…

I heard the chants: and the chants were those of the invisible and those of the unseen, with the laments that slipped once more into our abode,

after the bombs, before the fall, I grasped a hand and pleaded: allow please this dance, it has been a while since I've danced. And soon, waltz-like, moving, I was asked, how do you call this, your dance. And I said that I called it the dance of the Avenger: tap-tap, one foot over the other, there, follow me, a little tchoo-tchoo, two steps forward, one step back, let's go now, from the beginning. Maybe that's the dance of the Avenger: it's the tchoo-tchoo of children in line, grown up—

after the bombs, I plundered the gates before me, running, in a lost alley, in a corner of the city ode-to-ruin, the memory of the sites of their vanishing—

after the bombs, I approached the walls in the city, I approached the bridge at the city, I summoned the voices: they cried to me: you are a voice, and you have forgotten the whispers of old: what have you learned, in your long, solitary walks. And I answered that I had learned the slowness of the walk and the song of solitude,

after the bombs: after the revolution: after the wind, the whirlwind, the hills: how the climbs, the hiding places and the hunger: the silence in the labyrinth, the wounded awakening, greetings and the guests, the dancer of the dunes hollering, the floundering philosopher, the embraces, farewells, stuttering at arrival, of this and not, suspended stories, how to:

after the bombs, on a stormy night, I saw the young soldier from the window, the silhouette of the young soldier fading, like before, no one there, finding the path again to the kingdom:

after the bombs: I walked alone in the cities of other worlds, I sang with wayward clowns and haunted memories of absence: after the bombs through sepulchers and dim vaults, after the bombs among ashes, and embers, of dust:

after the bombs, in the castle, I sauntered through its majestic pillars, through the shining busts of prophets of old, on the marble pavements of imaginary halls: I hailed the ruins of the city: solitary I sat on the statue high above the public square: and I wrote an ode to the ruins of the city,

after the bombs, tongues tied, tongues now mine, I smashed the idols and the idol-makers, I sang the hymn of vagabonds and saluted the silence of wanderers: happily in ecstasy, while I dashed and chanced into the alleys on the dunes, after the bombs,

anthems and prayers, songs of death—I will not heed the call: wingless even and without root, still I clamor to forge the name: endlessly the traceless name... And with the night and with dawn, tongues tamed, tongues in ruin, how to go on:

after the bombs, I heard the echoes of the bombs, I betrayed a secret, under a light rain, I started towards the house, I thought to reveal my secret of the ruins after the bombs. He opened the door in his half-slumber of midnight, he asked, who is it, what do you want:

after the bombs, I thought to tell my tales to the calligrapher, so that they could be written in majestic letters:

after the bombs, I on the edge of an entrance barely lit, after the bombs where I once laughed and played, pebble-covered roads, after the bombs and the memories, before an old man, sad and melancholy:

when he recognized me, he suddenly pulled me in, sat me down: you're risking a hell of a lot you know, they're everywhere. After the bombs, suddenly several knocks at the door: we both hesitate, both afraid, but will not show it. Stay calm. Knocks again, shall we open? He walks slowly, methodically, calmly opens: I witness the slow pull of the door by the calligrapher still in slumber:

—but it's nothing, no one, only the mime, rushing in, the storied mime himself. Look at me, he began, I couldn't hear the rampage, I couldn't hear the thunder, but I quietly detected the rumbling beneath my feet. Tell me, the crime of the muted mime, is it to have known the tremors in the sand, the tremors of the city, under the bombs:

before the calligrapher and the mime, listen to me I cried, I have a secret to tell—after the bombs:

I wandered after the bombs to the summit of the mountains in the invisible fields in the mist and the railroad tracks—with the howl of the wind, with the clamors of the wind, at dusk, at dawn, through the rubble and the pillars, the measured gait of a pilgrim, among the strangers and the lost, among the wicked, among the weary...

———■———

I followed the exile in the chambers for the sake of the father: anxious and tranquil at once, from a haven in the sky: strolling, searching for the gap, the passage below, where once again, the exile will hear the music that is known. So now I must know, goes the pleading, now I must: who am I: not a phantom teetering above a cloud, not a spirit floating from the grave...

I lived so: *Angelus Exilus*. I wonder why I see the sages but not all, I walk empty corridors silently haunting me. I live in quarters far from where I should be. Nowhere and no one, I can only be in a house that is not. Raggedy clothes, rotting boots: streets without names, landscape without color: waiting for the others: exile and confirming it, must confirm it, always: the mountain is missing, when will we go to the sea? The exile knows only one mountain and one sea, the ones of old, longing for the return... Somebody say: there are also mountains here, also a sea!

Not the same games, not the same ways, not the same tears—of course not!—not the same wounds, not the same sounds, not the Same! Of course not, someone say, so what!— Not Home!

The exile, when watching, is watched: the exile, listening, is heard: scanning the parts, feeling the limbs: will they *ever* get to my soul!

But the body aches, the dance is tiring, this constant whirl… And the exile longs for the Ways of Old: if only all was as before: the cry of the exile is a cry of a golden past: a saga, fitting the needs: I lived so, and not thus: remembering, the exile can chose. Here, there is only pain, only pestilence. There, that is where I belong…

The movements of the world have been awaiting me, the exile drowns in fantasy: nothing has changed, because the exile: was elsewhere… Now, suspended, alone, numb, the exile prepares to be embraced again: the time of the Glorious Return has come: nowhere, going not-here, floating, the exile begins the journey: must go, cannot stay, elsewhere—and so, yet again, exile…

Do angels sing? Healers, I have heard it said, angels seek to feel the pain and long for a return. Agents, dangling always, being for another: Here and Not-There, floating among the unseen the motions like the exile the angel…

Angels, I have heard it said, long for a home. Like the exile who once upon a fortnight cried out my soul grieves me my soul take away from me, thundering in distant lands, the angel searches deep within, and all around, alone in goodness, alone in mercy, for a companion to sit with and pray, for a wayward soul, to make a return home.

Are all angels exiles then? Swimming dreaming of flight, running dreaming of rest? Round and round hovering, bounc-

263

ing off untainted glass, running through redbrick walls? Wandering restless in the city, crawling in the kingdom, pavement to pavement, in quest of? And it is true (I have seen it drawn), that in this kingdom, no one desires a wandering soul—only angels, in disguise:

Angelus Exilus: homeless, wandering, angel and not, scribe of the Turn, Exile from Exiledom, watcher from above: I have surveyed the cities, I have crossed the continents, I have seen the carnival: an angel without a home, the angel without sorrow, the angel without a name:

I followed a raggedy soul who confided, without doubt or shame, the following: my first days here were marked by a peculiar absence: I slowly realized that no one was capable of distinguishing my transparent skin from their own carnal flesh. I tried bumping into a few, I was unable to, slipping uselessly through their bodies. Wandering without a home, I managed to observe and study a wide range of behaviors. That required quite a long while, it goes without saying, but having no possibility of return, it became urgent that I find a body having the predilection to accept me. My first obstacles, those of bewilderment, of indecisiveness, I succeeded in overcoming. There remained two quite precise concerns. The first of course, remained the hurdle of my total lack of recognition. The second, more important, was founded on persuasions that I had received from my own diverse readings during that period, notably a single volume, old and used, that I had found in an abandoned, disheveled, second-hand bookstore, on the third floor of a decrepit building, in the heart of a city that I hope one day I will describe for you, a volume entitled, *Âme et Espoir*, or *Soul and Hope*, by one Marquis J-L, Duc de Z__. The ingenuity, of course, lay in the intricate demonstration,

264

the almost mathematical proof, through equations and formulae, of the dependence of the second part of the marquis' title (hope) on the well-being of the first (soul). All topped off with witty explanations, with what may have appeared senseless and ridiculous and, at best, the dreamy incantation, the unlikely potion, of a mad sorcerer. In it, the good duke demonstrated that the well-being of the soul was itself founded on the vivacity and the health of its vital elements, essentially the practice of transcendence, in other words, of phantomlike tendencies. Continuing the readings excitedly, I'd noticed that the *Duc* insisted not only on the necessary presence of the phantom but postulated also that all men, whether despaired or joyful, that all in fact possessed one, and that, more importantly, 'every spirit crawling in the sacred cities, should, easily, find the one, defeated or drowned in silence, who is also crawling, in the same cities and the same streets, hoping to find the soul that abandoned it.' (p. 304, my own translation) Obviously, and I am not ashamed to say, obviously, the reading inspired and encouraged me. Even though the thoughts and source of the marquis were not verified, his confidence was of great relief. I decided then to undertake the adventure, in which, unbeknownst, I had been involved, and which, sooner or later, would determine my survival. It is not necessary here to detail the first encounter with the one I was seeking. Far from the crowds, I saw her: sitting in the public square (I went back, yes!) alone, she was made up all in white, dressed up all in black. Occasionally, she would stand and gesticulate, and, the movements ended, would adopt again the sad countenance, sit, motionless, melancholy... Approaching then, finally, the gleams of light... sliding into the body whose costume could not dissimulate the solitude:

I walked with a soldier who abandoned his horse by the road-side and began the long march home. He carried on his shoulders a long stick and a knapsack on his back. A heavy knapsack and heavy boots and heavy clothes that clanged as he walked. It was a deserted road. No sounds, no screams. He walked along this desolate road, alone with the clatter of his steps. When he arrived at the top of the hill, he put his bag on the ground and eased unto a small spot of elevated dirt. He looked below at the city he had left, and he saw that the entire zone was bathed in merriment. Colors everywhere, children running, laughter throughout, reaching him even at his outpost far away on the hill. Merriment and joy! Citizens walked by and stopped and embraced. All the flowers in bloom, the trees proudly displaying their expanded foliage. Voices full, voices without guilt, always with never wither. Even the cats and the dogs scurried about, lazy and happy. Naps for the former without much care, the wagging of tails for the latter, jumping up and down, swinging around and smelling private parts of their own kind! The soldier sitting sullenly at the top of the hill saw the city and smiled. Then he stood and picked up the sack. He turned again, descended the hill, found the road and marched again: on the road, on the deserted, desolate road:

I followed a witness who began to run, in the night, by the cathedrals and the fountains, by the statues, the public square, the piers, the water, the woods. The shadows followed him also, in turn, this one sprang on him, another tagged, another skipped, laughing, while he ran, faster, breathless. He arrived at the door of the garden, he opened, he entered. There, pausing slightly, he climbed the spiral stairs. He stumbled towards the door and without a sound (carefully, must not wake the neighbors, the key in the lock), he entered: but already the rooms were empty, and he saw no one he knew. My lord, he mumbled, his anguish growing, my lord, my lord, my lord, he repeated, my lord. But no one answered and he began to rush from one chamber to another, to no avail, recognizing nothing, not the colors, not the walls, not the scattered objects. When heavy knockings on the door interrupted the search, he turned, abruptly, and heard the knock again. He faltered, at first, strained, but opened, finally: a burly little man, fuming like a buffalo: 'Wissen Sie wieviel Uhr es ist, mein Herr, wissen Sie?' And he: I am very sorry sir, truly, and he slammed the door. Now, in these same quarters, a stranger had appeared, an old consort, long thought gone, back again (yessiree): he raised his head, the voice had not started yet, he looked at the stranger, began the muttering, the duet, how I will wander alone along the enchanted roads and in the houses of the forgotten, the sad quarters of destiny and dearth. The limbs and the rhymes will rebel, and so will the words in the books whose empty pages will invite to turn, turn with that diabolical rhythm. Far from the imaginary roots and the embrace of the illusion of refuge! Exile from Exiledom even, far from all kingdoms, free of all binds. And they began again the two (for old times' sake), one floating close to the ground, the other firmly fixed, walking along the desolate piers, along the paths, with each step sprouting out of the soil like flowers, bloodied arrows and hands, to the right and to the left the Moments vanishing, the thunder of the bombs falling pitiless on the city sinking, celestial monuments collapsing in a desert without sand, without sun:

I followed a bard who walked to the edge of the ocean and crumbled to his knees. I asked him what he awaited. I wait for corpses to wash ashore, he answered, and in the palms of their hands, I will read the arcane tales of revolution. I will be rid of my obsessions, of the frivolous longings. And with their serenity, I will sing the song of passage. In their stillness, you understand, rises a majestic ode to the wisdom of the retreat. I aspire only to follow them. Elegiac mystics, they reveal a mask that is known only to their kind: drunk with silence, they melt magically into the Unseen, venerable artists of Abandon: I await the corpses who, washed ashore, in their extended hands, in their paleness, are writing the memories of cities lost, the histories of the Gaze. Through the tremor of my sigh, one with the architects of the labyrinth. A bard, with the usual camouflage also, and even the lute resting by his side, and a *Divan*, on his knees, before the sea, sculptor of impudence. I never saw him again, I heard only that he had drowned, when the sea had been awakened by undetected forces, and that he had refused to run: conqueror of rupture, vanishing in the throes of the instant and the waves:

I followed a prophet who guided me in the desert and who stopped, for the first time, to point to the horizon and mumble: the horizon emerges in the fusion of a sky and an earth: thus the cry, in the embrace of the gaze and the sigh. I followed him and he stopped again and began a strange chant. Behind him, I did the same: I chanted the abstruse syllables, and I asked him what was our chant, and he answered that our chant was a prayer. I followed the prophet and the prophet wandered in the desert: in the absence of the wind, I heard the prophet's suspicions and I heard his doubts and his murmurs. I followed the prophet in the desert and saw his long robe and his head leaning forward, hiding the contours of his face. His hands behind his back, the prophet walked slowly, in a measured cadence, not recognizing the marks he left in the sand. But he turned and his face revealed, the prophet began: I recognize the traces that I leave in the sand, but they are only appearances and will vanish with the coming of the wind. We are walkers and wanderers, and only the caprice of our gods, and the whims of our steps are forever loyal. He turned again and went along his path. Without a trace, I whispered, there is no solitude, there is no wanderer, there is no path. There is, without this illusion of passage, no turmoil: only the memory of the trace can forsake remembrance, embrace the new silence, the brave solitude, animate its own driftings. The prophet marched and chanted and murmured and did not hear, in the desert, without wind, my whisper... Wanderers of dark alleys will survive, shadows without masters, echoes without shelter... Apprentices to the odes and the delights and the rage:

I followed a sinner to his shrine. A secret shrine cast away. He led me on that day and never again have I found the path. Inside the shrine sat the wise guide eyes aflame. He did not speak and the sinner told me that he would not. We passed by the lights and heard the shrieks of the damned from behind, shrieks all around that composed the music of this abode. Blood was splattered on the crumbling walls and on the ground, all in darkness. We walked in a cavernous passageway, by the scenes of the battles all enlivened, we walked by the portraits of the chivalrous and the gallant and the noble of the past and the dates and victories of their gods. We walked through a great hall and reached on the other side a chamber into which he strolled and invited me. A robed figure stood, a dagger in his hand. The sinner approached, kneeled, kissed the other's hand and rose again. He extended his arm and received the dagger from his lord. The sinner turned to me, closed his eyes, pressed the dagger in his hand, paused and suddenly opened his eyes.

269

He was not the same, not the same, I could see it, I could sense it. Monstrous his swelling eyes, his pointed teeth. He turned and let out unseemly screams as he slashed the figure before him. The great swings from all angles. From all directions and faster and faster. Up and down and all across. He slashed away, cut him to pieces and let all the parts stand. He turned again, to me, paused, closed the eyes and opened again. He then knelt by the pieces and the blood, he pleaded and said his prayers, kissed the dismembered hand, and placed the dagger by the robe, and slithered on the side. Then he turned and motioned us away. In the passageway, he told of the edicts he followed and his daily ritual: tomorrow he would be back again and the lord holding the dagger in his hand would offer it to him for repentance and salvation. The next day, and each day after that, the same trip, the same trek, through the cavernous maze:

I followed an actor who entered a forlorn hostel among the scent of trampled dreams. He heard the voice of the innkeeper who insisted, please sit down, please, my good sir, turkeys, roasts, for you, all for you, my good sir, there is everything for you. Seated, leaning over his plate, seeing the innkeeper vanishing, he heard steps coming around, the corner, close to his stool. Panic again, wherefore this tavern of trembling?! And he thought to himself, he mumbled to himself, it is Death, Death again, it is Death, it is Death I'm sure of it, it is Death! The steps again and the sounds came closer, closer, and he screamed, like a child, out of control, it's Death, it's Death, and he began to holler, and he began to scream, fire!… fire!… fire!… A man seized his arm: a man, with one wooden leg and no right hand, with one eye and a broken land. Holding his arm, he looked into the eyes: 'Once upon a time, in a place long forgot, in a wide strip of white sand that troubled the blue of the serene sea, a sailor walked, every eve and morn, to the edge of a majestic cliff. He prayed to the gods, for, in the night, one could hear sinister ululations from the caves. The sailor, who fished at dawn, prayed to end the howling or to be taken there, to the provenance of the mysterious cries. But his pleadings were always ignored. One evening, after the catch, there came to him a revelation. But if I cease, he protested, I will be left without food. I will have no subsistence. Still, he obeyed, and he ceased all activities and all nourishment. At dawn, he marched to the sites, and he watched the fish that he once caught in his traps. The hours passed, he strolled by the water. He could not contain his despair though and soon, restless, he pleaded, I cannot carry on. But already he had received a second revelation, instructing him to enclose himself in his cabin, and to see neither the sun nor the sea. He obeyed and enclosed himself in his cabin, seeing neither sun nor sea. Seated near scattered debris, he whispered, I will sink, I have no more power, I cannot fight, I will not. But he received another revelation instructing him to forego all sleep and to cultivate immobility in his wooden cabin. He obeyed and now, without the stroll and without the catch, deprived of rest and movement, he remained, in his torn garments, in a corner of the cabin. He saw his destiny and he pleaded with his lord to stop the suffering, but he had a fourth revelation, and he obeyed: he closed his eyes, and he built barriers to defy air and silence. Motionless, he even obeyed a final revelation. When they found him dead, in his cabin, the order was given to build a temple at the site where the sailor of this isle, this saint of the sand, the mystic by the sea, exhausted, had collapsed. The howling of the caves had ceased and appeared to pay homage. The cabin was turned into a mausoleum: they christened it: the temple of heresy.' The man with no right hand, a wooden leg, the broken land

271

and one eye, glared at the actor. One night, a blind man passed through the temple of heresy. It is the night, he cried, it is the night of the revolution:

I walked with a drifter and a secret-teller hand in hand: how they knew of the work, how they knew of their work. That the paths of others were not theirs, the ways of others were not theirs, their pains, their squabbles even or their daze. But we cannot let this deter us, the drifter let out softly, that would spell the real doom. The drifter told of his travels and companions along the roads. He told of the trials and the hardships. He described his journey over the snow-covered hills and his dangerous treks across the seas. Like the heroes of childhood, he laughed, that's the kind of life, that's the sort of life I've led, believe it or not! I had no reason to doubt. We shared anecdotes about accidental friends and common enemies. Oh, I hate them! he said at the mention of a famous foe. But even his anger was soft—and perhaps artificial. It was entirely possible I sensed, that this almost saintly individual felt no such emotions. I let him know and he smiled. You may be right, he said, sometimes I goad myself. But the drifter seemed to be elsewhere, elsewhere really, elsewhere in body and mind. I turned to the secret-teller finally. The secret-teller who had been present all along. Of few words of course, the secret-teller, very few. But something was expected. Now especially. And the secret-teller did not disappoint. Silence before, the utterance went, silence during, silence after: nothing to add, nothing to say. And it was sincere this, really was (the secret-teller also lived by the edict), bona fide and authentic—and illuminating. No pretense, no game or show. That's what it was all about—in the end:

I came upon a city: where the natural cycle consisted of some cruelty, some carnage and tears, a quick reprieve, and back to the feelings of contentment. A city in which all of those seated, stared only sideways and never ahead, addressing one another in false directions. A question was answered with another in this city, and all answers outlawed for centuries. Solutions did not exist, there were no plans and no planning. No one worked and no one played, no one built, no one strayed. There was in the city no paranoia, no ambitions, never a sense of battle or struggle. And no tranquility and no serenity. In the city there were no desires and only whims. A war and peace, a war and peace. Without stimuli, without thought. Attachments to naught, except for illusions. Songs were uttered and suddenly cut. Dances in the streets erupting without warning and leading to massacres or to mass. Twirling kids or adults on pavements or rooftops, crying or smiling, it made no difference, not to anyone, whether misery reigned, for a moment, or mirth. There remained nevertheless an old man who wandered the streets from dawn to the next, who walked without uttering a single word, and who slept only a fragment of the night, every other night. No one dared speak to him, or hurt him, as they would have other older citizens with mystical miens. No one even dared approach him. He was the only named of the city. They called him: The Rebel: undaunted, unmoved:

I came upon the city where the jester, sick of the restrictions, just fed up, threw up his hands and did the unthinkable—he quit. By order of the king, who needed to find a quick fix, and whose entire land, by the way, recognized his majesty, they had to designate an employee who would make himself (or herself) up, every morning, who would even sport colorful costumes, who would strut and stumble in the streets. The problem? It was already too late, the populace had already forsaken laughter. The king decided then to make an example of a few. They executed, on his orders, several passersby who were not responding accordingly, one ill-omened afternoon, when they passed by the new (faux!) jester of the kingdom. Thus, proclaimed the king in his new announcements, this shall be the fate of all those who refuse to cooperate. It is true that immediately following the hanging of the Examples, they started to laugh from fear of execution, but, as is often the case, that vanished soon enough. There is a proverb that says: one cannot laugh, if one doesn't feel like it. And it's true that often, proverbs have the capacity to enlighten. But let us not digress: in the kingdom, the people had stopped laughing—and the ministers and the functionaries and the parliamentarians decided that no, you just cannot force them, this is not something to force. (In the passionate debates on the floor of the parliament, the wisest deputy, in a brilliant strategy, having proclaimed the greatness of misery, succeeded in convincing the others.) They asked me later, 'And the jester, whatever happened to the real jester?' And I told the story as it had reached me: the jester had been imprisoned and the jester was never freed. He languished indefinitely in the prisons. Some say they had truly forgotten him, others claim that he was resuscitated after several hunger strikes, had escaped and joined other troupes. I even heard that, with his 'incensed habits' (Minister of Interior Affairs, Amusement and Prisons), he had succeeded in finding his niche, and was melting into the cosmological unity. I don't know. Others say he went nowhere at all, but that every morning, he did a little routine for his jailer, a bearish, bearded boar who, loving the acts so much, slipped prohibited doses of nourishment to the thinning bloke. That his activity and his personal contentment, both spiritual and material, kept him

274

alive and happy enough, through old age. 'And this, what is this,' the jester was reported to have asked, skipping sheepishly, to which the jailer all in joy, 'I don't know, tell me, I don't know!' And the jester had answered, 'It's a porcupine of course, a porcupine in lament with no spines!' And the jailer had collapsed in laughter, clapped wildly and thundered his plaudits. 'And this and this,' had asked the excited jester, and the jailer, as always writhing and rolling around on his stomach, 'Oh I don't know, I don't know, tell me!' The jester, who had been crawling and rolling around and who had made a sad face and a laughing face, had answered bluntly, amused, 'Well, come *on* man, it's a bearded boar laughing rolling who keeps saying that he doesn't know, he doesn't know…'

I had by now weaved my way, without rest, through a great part of the city. Flights, crawls, strolls, runs, all had led me to the provinces and had offered, in my quest, the deciphering of the secrets. I was walking thus by the timid light of the street-lamps on the wharf, by a gray bridge in the distance, when a creature jostled me, a bit tipsy in fact, and began the confessions: 'My story is brief. I was just another among the plays of the vagabonds, equal to the Cry, the Murmur and the Chant. But I soon fell out of favor, and I was incarcerated shortly thereafter. At my tribunal, testified against me the ruler (of course), the warriors, the builders, workers, saints and prophets, guides and actors, and Belonging: a great majority of the populace, in fact, to the surprise of no one! Defended me: a soldier in his last gasp, a castaway, and a mime, his eyes covered. Conspicuously absent were the poets and the painters, as always. I said to the judge and to the audience: 'Do not peer at me so: beaten, humiliated, and, in your presence, bound. We were scars on the same visage: myself, the Mask, and Wonder. Your sentence will be severe: naming me, you will condemn all to illusions and to the omniscience of mutinies. Save yourself, save me, from the kingdom of the known.' They did not listen of course. They named me, and, in the depth of the dungeons, my lamentations proved abominable. Announcing my defeat, the jury celebrated the end of visions and the delirious explosion of moot, delusional battles. Witness to the butcheries, always exilic, I imprisoned nevertheless the last ally, the triumphant whisper, the Sigh.' Then Silence ended the confession, and I excused myself, and I was soon back on my path. I was merely walking about when I heard, strangely, the hidden Echo...

Now before I set forth again, before the next howls, before the next wandering: the era of the Second Silence approaches, through the byways and the caverns once more I must, among the drunkards and the drowned, the restless and the nomadic bards: to sing, to halt and peer at the vanished times, to tell of the absent ones, the spirits and the traces: not the second coming of the same cry, I: not the belated call from distant rocks: I am, unbeknownst, one with wonder, with murmurs and the masks: I am the muted scream in the lee, the hollow cry: I am the wailing of silence revolted within:

The City: How they let fall the bombs with the planes above how to go on: and there was nothing left, nothing left of it, save for Ruin— after the bombs...

———■———

I sat on the high-chair on the sand gazing at the horizon. Back, after all: a wanderer's need: the wanderer's lust: the regular tour of duty, if I may. That was fun, I thought, I truly did need that!

I sat on the high-chair on the sand gazing at the horizon, yes, but then I stood: awkwardly, bitterly.

'This carnival, ladies and gentlemen, is in dire need of a clown, of a *real* clown, that is! And I insist: there is no carnival without a clown!' Hesitant applause, the trickster's seduction: if only you joined also...

But I was not seduced. Sadly, quietly, I sighed: 'I've tried it all, and this is all I've come up with!' Then, finding a bit of courage again, I proclaimed loudly: 'But I will change it for nothing, nothing, I say again!' There was no applause this time, no response, nothing at all.

'And I will not bow,' I finished nevertheless. 'No sir, not now, not ever, still won't bow.'

Then I rose again and hovered above once more, the last ode, the last stop. I saw, in the famous desert, sprawled naked and bloody, a young man surrounded by the sender's fleet. Around him, around me, reigned the aura of ferment and upheaval, the ode to uprisings, the ode to abandonment. I sat close to him, I noticed the wounds of the swords on his body. Sprawled like any other, his legs spread slightly, one extended and the other bent at the knee, with his two arms in almost-embrace of his head, sprawled on his stomach, in the pool of his own blood. I stood again and I heard the cries in the distant citadels. I murmured his name. The valiant white horse, also wounded, on his neck and on his leg, stood by the master. The whirling women in tears cried his name, crawling and crying and hanging on to each other, wailing. Then the messengers sent the Dirge, far away, with the new fleet, and the draughtworks of winds...

The clown walked out of the sea. The clown dragged the feet through the sand and reached the high-chair. The clown

277

picked up the high-chair—with surprising ease, given the difference in size. The clown took the high-chair to the door on the sand. The clown placed the high-chair and its silent occupant next to the door. Opened the door, left it open, picked up the high-chair and took it through the door, to the other side. The clown then came back through the door and, once through, closed the door. Then the clown walked towards the water and dragged the heavy boots on the sand and slowly disappeared into the water, the puffy puffy orange hair of the clown becoming the only visible part of the clown. And slowly, the puffy puffy orange hair of the clown, and the long top hat of the clown disappeared under the water. There was nothing on the horizon. There was nothing on the sea. There was no carnival on the sea. No acrobat, no mime. There was only the wind, only the sea. There was only a wind, the wave, the sea…

T̅o̲

the traveler of yore or the persistent pilgrim, lost on a journey
to unfamiliar worlds or merely straying from a happy trail,
the city of Baabol, situated in the northeast region of a land
of much repute in our time (even if not of enviable renown),
while it magically awakened dormant seeds of enchantment,
posed, also, the stifling, scandalous, question of possibility.

Unseen from the neighboring districts was Baabol, and un-
situated on maps—and thus the path to its riches and its sights
remained unknown. Legend has it that only Chance itself
guided the unsuspecting to the locale, whereupon a small mi-
nority would delight in the scenery (if even for a brief respite),
while most others, struck by a sense of foreboding doom, by an
unseemly fright promulgated by the same scenery, would just
as quickly take a reprieve from the surroundings.

To complicate matters, no one had told of the manners
of entry or the official policy on citizenship: it was quite a
mystery indeed, how the inhabitants had arrived, how the
population had transformed, and how the city had grown or
renewed itself.

Situated in a sedate flume, unperturbed by the fancy of
ambitious discoverers or explorers of nearby regions, Baabol
was bordered, on one side, by a desert that stretched into the
horizon, and, on the other, by an ancient roadway, paved with
cobblestones and other material of less distinct provenance,
that gave unto a bridge, itself extending beyond the field of
vision. Innumerable cataracts populated one side of the hills,
interspersed with the expected vegetation sprouting on the
slope. On the other declivity, a wild mosaic of architecture and

sculpture paved the terrain. Mansions and ancient pilasters, the most ghastly of deformities, the most sparkling garniture: in a swarm of countless colors and shapes, derived from time immemorial to the present, from the most obscure regions to the most famed of provinces, in various forms and in all sizes, a stunning array of dimensions and declensions blossomed in this garden of treasures and scents.

It is said finally that Baabol was also privy, on occasion, to a miracle from above: from the random appearance of angels or muses hovering hand in hand (or in protest), to the giant pendulum that would descend dangerously close to the city, swinging methodically all the while yet vanishing just as mysteriously, the portrait of Baabol did not exclude from its frame a perpetually transforming skyscape.

As if vitreous from a distance, seemingly a portentous fable yet ever so common, Baabol invited nevertheless the strongest of reactions, the most volatile of emotions. Which may explain, at last, the sentry at the gates: seen only from afar, eternally present, there to protect and prevent—although I never saw a soul leave or another enter, never detected the slightest movement from the shadowy figure that seemed to occupy the vaunted post.

280

———■———

City of Stone: in the hours before dusk, the solitary wanderer by the roadside in Baabol could see rising, unexpectedly, from the ground with the wind, the spectacle of dust. A conspicuous performance it was however, in the midst of the crowd and the joyous laughter of unwise children, in the chaos of the city. No one noticed, no one saw: not before the departure of the merchants, before they began to close the shops, slowly putting away the day's work, counting the day's work, measuring the day's work, frowning or smiling, cherishing or cursing the day's work, calling to a neighbor, calling to a son or daughter, before the lights dimmed in the small dwellings along the roads of families cramped but happy, before the lights slowly dimmed, before guards turned in their uniforms, before the old teachers dejectedly bowed their heads and trudged homeward, before the hours of the spirits in the streets—not everyone in Baabol noticed this either, of course—before the arrival of the next creatures, in darkness only voices unseen. Along the sides of these expanded streets, among the veiled ones and the dapper ones, the hurried and the hopeful, the brooding and the content, in the midst of it all, the wanderer could see a strange mist rising from the ground, when the trickster had turned the corner and stood by the street-light, when the distant howl of the wind had reached the gates at the edge of the city: solitary walker at dusk seeing the mist of dust into the dance.

City of Song: it was also said that in Baabol, the unseen did not count among their own only dust rising at dusk, but that in the ruins where few dared to tread, among the whispers and the murmurs, a certain species of thieves descended at opportune times, silently in these alleys, silently in their ways. A certain species who had drawn a perfect map of the neighborhoods, catalogued, carefully, all residents according to official and un-official documents, their physical attributes and their dispositions, listed their belongings, their allegiances and their ties, and perfectly chronicled their habits. So that it was known that in the old district, for example, one of the more luckless of the street people would be let in, daily, through a back door, into an ancient mud house by the groundskeeper, who would feed him a small loaf of bread, upon which the poor lass, glancing this way and that to make certain no one was watching, would tuck smaller objects under his shirt, and finally scurry away to

281

a certain tea parlor, opening early in the morning, where he was seen hurriedly engorged, paying no heed at all to his surroundings, in the voracious consumption of his daily nourishment. Many in Baabol had known him, had witnessed his descent into destitution. He had once been an employee, a valued one at that, of the central bank, and had sunk with the latter's financial decline. He had subsequently failed to leave, lost his home only to save other assets deemed at the time more valuable, subsequently lost those as well, been abandoned by young, angry, hungry family, and finally reduced to selling possessions, all the way down to pairs of pants and socks, deciding to finally keep the ones he was wearing, beard and hair now flowing. The case of another elderly man had proven even more intriguing. Everyone knew of his erratic behavior during the day: a troublemaker and heckler of sorts, he insulted and harassed passersby with various doses and levels of miserly crudeness (although he was not known for physically violent attacks). Still, no one knew what became of him at night, until it was finally revealed that this same chap, rude and groaning by day, roaming around in the public square, was a scholar of unequaled merit, of unbounded energy, of unequaled brilliance, of unfathomable flights of imagination in the hours of darkness. A reverse case, if you will, of the famous Jekyll and Hyde: at night buried in imaginative experiments and creations, in the day a mere urban sorcerer of the most unpleasant stripe. A genuine genius, only to vanish into thin air when the first rays shone on the city, the rhythm of the day slowly manifest, the streets once more frequented by the occasional stumbling drunk, or the rock and roll late-nighters gradually trickling, arm in arm, out of the loud havens of celebration, the city bathed in the circling neon of the small restaurants that stayed open after hours, small, dreary places, strangers inside, weary…

282

And after the din of midnight, once more in the wide expanses, once more in the tree-lined spaces, when the wind was heard by the gates, figures out of the dark met at street corners (handshakes, embraces) and carried on to the center of the public square. Although it was only on occasion that the gathering was detected, and although many heard the noise, the agents of these invisible feasts remained expertly elusive. It was proposed that the culprits themselves incited the enigma, craving private moments, tired of their roles as watchers or agents of control or guidance, of their age-old and seemingly immodest functions. 'How long can we be expected to do the same thing, over and over, and forever, literally?' one spirit was heard exploring at a drunken moment, an unidentified agent who was subsequently punished, rumor went, as another present had reported the exclamations to higher deities. The spirits, then, it was suggested, would render the square invisible through their particular powers, and, along with other drifters and saints among those fortunate enough to have been invited, would engage in a long night of debauchery, secluded from all, an orgy of peculiar nature, forsaking their duties, forgetting, temporarily, the dissemination of fear and joy among the citizens.

283

It was thought, by those less superstitious yet still mystically inclined, that the sounds of the feasts, the great sounds emanating in these unusual nights from the square, were those of humans in their hour of *délassement*, echoes perhaps of centuries-ago somewhere, but that no, the invisibility was not the work of unknown spirits. 'They do not exist,' had vehemently charged a reputed doctor in a forum on the subject, rebutting a colleague in the same arena who had dared, if only alternately, to submit that the non-existence of the spirits could not, in effect, be proven, and that, 'You know that as well as I do!'

Others were ready to implicate, explicitly suggested in fact, that the ruckus was due to a strange observer who emerged every so often, at the top of the mountain, contemplating the events below, a hermit perhaps, an observer, no one knew for sure, and who had indeed been spotted on each of the occasions of the fiesta, strange figure atop the mountain, peering below.

'As if he could see, I tell you!' had expressed a most nervous fellow. 'As if he alone could see!'

As if, indeed, he alone could see, and had chosen to exclude all others, for he alone, perhaps, was conducting his most epic experiment!

Among the legion of smaller camps, however, a group, less vocal (yet highly energetic), proclaimed, and maintained, that no there was no feast, no debauchery, no outpouring of frustrations or repressions, nothing was happening in the public square, the eyes were not lying, perhaps only other senses being deceitful: nothing was happening, dull as always carried on the city, the night of the orgy also the city square remained deserted, unlit, no there was no story to be told. They insisted that the collective hallucinations were due, and this exclusively, to the need of the populace to force itself from its habitual rhythms, from the blandness of its rituals.

'A supreme work of the imagination!' exclaimed a leader of this faction. 'A monument to our collective genius!' he carried on. 'A testament to our unceasing fantasies!' he thundered. 'But no, my fellow citizens, once more there is nothing new in our midst, once more the brouhaha is baseless, still all carries on as the day before, restlessly we may worry, but I hold fast: no one is with us in the proud square of the city.'

The matter was unresolved, for centuries no one was convinced, each faction holding fast, the tremors of possible con-

284

frontations, woes of coming mutinies, long faces all around, mumbled discontent among the unconvinced: in this: City of Sorrows…

———■———

And from the very beginning, of course, Baabol bore the burden of its name. In the desert and the mountains it was, but, from afar and also among the citizens themselves, the attachment to the great tower of myth remained unavoidable. The invisible gathering, or the illusion of such a congregation—certainly, I do not wish to hold any allegiances!—in the public square, the descent of the spirited thieves, that uniquely mystical ascent of dust, the lives of those less fortunate, these matters did indeed preoccupy the citizens. In schools, in the offices and the pubs, in private homes and public inns, the conversation touched, as it does in all cities, on the common concerns: the performance of the leadership, foreseeable solutions to economic hardships, the iniquity of the educational system, and so forth. But what remained foremost in the minds, hearts, what have you, of all, was the troubling and vexing question of the inherited designation of the city. On this, citizens old and young debated, always, the associations and the possible connections to the tower of fables.

'That we are the very famous Baabol, my friends, there can be no doubt,' exclaimed some.

'But what do you make of the landscape?' others would retort. 'Of the desert that is, of these mud-houses, of the cliffs, the mountaintop and the bridges extending so far away. These pathways, the roads, the signs and the maps, so unlike the construction of fabulous places! What of? The dance of the infidels at the outskirts, the plague, the wind, the vengeful assassins? What of?'

And the answers in the form of greater exclamations, uprisings, riots, demonstrations, confrontations, duels, would once more erupt.

It may be said that the puzzle of its legitimate status had retained Baabol in a suspended state, a transit state of uncertainty: overcome by the perpetual fear of its own death, an unglamorous withering into the ruins of history, it carried on nevertheless, subsisting, surviving, retaining its identity despite the grand-scale perturbation in the worlds adjacent.

Other urgent doubts had also, for long, penetrated the hearts of the citizens and inspired the theory that the city itself, the name, the landscape and the surroundings, were, in fact, all imaginary, that they represented, in effect, a modern incarnation of the tower itself. What followed, logically, expectedly and alarmingly so, was the fate of the citizens themselves.

'We can be only as unreal as our name,' I heard an older man whisper in a derelict, unkempt corner—one who had seen it all, so to speak, battled with all. And a timid whisper it was: for although everyone pondered the possibility, in private lamented the outcome, or, perhaps, rejoiced at the thought, the utterance of the old man would be avoided by any cautious citizen. Not in public, never aloud: domains of private investigation maybe, perhaps even a timid opening to friends, but never aloud to strangers, not that doubt, not this blasphemy, on top of all the others!

Still, nothing freed Baabol from an inescapable gaze at itself. That the world of fable and fancy defined, by now, the very cityhood and the identity of its inhabitants, that the story and the gaze prompted Baabol along the paths and margins of these uncertainties, that Baabol, and the story of Baabol itself, with its laments and its foibles, was transforming into a legend of faraway places, of this there was little doubt. But Baabol

286

trudged along, perturbed only occasionally by one or another protest, by the silent disturbance of unrealities.

It was in this very context that another central obsession was, and remained, the secret provenance, the unexplained existence of the ruins located at the edge of the city, where the magnificent edifice certainly embodied the appearance of any tower of myth. An immense structure well over a hundred meters high, overlooking the entire landscape, it loomed so imposingly that few dared even to approach. Deserted in its immediate vicinity, surrounded by untended fields, at once seemingly rooted in sand, yet, at night, a lit fortress floating on the waves, sinking yet insistently growing, immovable yet ever swaying in the slightest wisp, the massive monument was adorned with beautiful windows, arranged symmetrically from the base to the spire and all around its cylindrical shape. Sectioned into three tiers by railings and loggia, it narrowed increasingly as it swerved into the clouds. And although one of the facades remained untouched by time and the vehemence of natural elements, the other was fully worn, revealing a rusty, gutted, anciently faded look, smashed at the top, in such a way that a smooth periphery turned into a jagged edge. Nor was there any evidence, historical evidence that is, that the tower had ever been occupied: not in the preceding centuries, not in the recent past, not now: no one had ever seen or heard of residents climbing the stairways, the famed stairways that spiraled, as in the books, from the base to the summit.

And so it was: that this grandiose edifice, visibly shattered yet standing mysteriously and unperturbed, ignited the passions of some, the indifference of others, the private laments of most. A tower whose origins, despite all efforts, could simply not be unearthed: not by the most expert of Baabol's archeologists, not by the precise calculation of its foremost physicists and mathematicians. Nor was this provenance fabricated, elaborated or made into an epic, or even a simple tune, not even by the most inspired of the city's poets. Little was agreed upon, in fact, the majestic tower obviously silent among the disputes.

'If indeed we are the remnants,' reasoned a fraction opposed to linking the city to the illustrious myth, 'would it not hold that these ruins not only would not be situated so far along the periphery—almost at the very edge!—but instead in the center: the very physical center, that is, in such a way that our most reliable architects, our most reliable scientists be able to indicate, with the most precise measurements that, indeed, it is situated exactly at the very center of our city!'

'Nonsense!' clamored the enemies. 'We are the ones who made the borders, we have drawn the borders, we have built the city! Nothing holds that they must be situated in the center, nothing at all! We would not exist,' they insisted, 'were it not for the tower!'

And the response was vehement in turn: 'And what of the hunger? What of the cries? Do you not recall how our children succumbed mercilessly to the plague? How the frail begged in the streets and in the houses? Do you not recall the elders, the corpses on the roads? Do you forget how you ignored all the trouble that was fashioning your world? And we dared not take refuge in the world that gave us our name?! That gave us our life? Absurd indeed…'

'*We* ran away from the shelters!' the answer was thundered! '*We* feared the shelter! We did not tend to our own children and the suffering among us! We did not build, we did not hear the pleadings of our protector! *We* did not seek the refuge!'

'And what of the revolution?' cried another. 'They raised their fists and chanted the slogans of the new order. Remember—the painted walls of the street, the converted houses of the hopeful, the hallowed sanctuaries… In the name of another, in the name of another world… And the prodigious powers of the tower did nothing to dissipate the tide?! Can there be disenchantment in the land of myth?!'

'They hailed a new order and summoned a new god. They held a new banner, they raised the new color, but they did not conquer.'

'And the scream, and the thrust, and the fall! Can there be revolution, in a world that is not real?!'

Endlessly they carried on: the confrontations, the alliances, the conspiracies. It was true, after all, that people passed away in Baabol, that the children played, teased, chastised, disobeyed, it was true that lovers held secret engagements in private hideaways. What then? Agonies unjustified? Extensions of the fantasies of one, or of long-ago occupants of this land? Senseless chicanery?

Still, with all of its eccentricities, with all of its own peculiarities, life carried along in Baabol as it does elsewhere. Until, that is, the period in which occurrences of uncommon nature incited further disturbances, leading in turn to new conflicts and igniting veritable transformations in the city. A genuine metamorphosis perhaps, and the reason for which I myself attempted this humble report. From Baabol, indeed, and Baabol only.

289

It all started with the rumor that the observer of the mountain seen peering below during the festival of spirits had been spotted around the city. No one had actually seen him march down the mountain, nor had anyone witnessed the entrance through the gates. And since the bridge of Baabol extended indeed into invisible domains, since no one had ever seen the other end, since no one had even dared set foot unto the architectural wonder, it was a safe bet, as some in Baabol insisted, that had anyone actually made it in across the bridge, given the width and the general inactivity atop, the unusual movement would surely have been detected. 'Night or day, I don't care!' one was heard insisting. 'Foggy or clear, don't tell me someone actually crossing that bridge could do it without being noticed!'

Not all, of course, knew to recognize the gazer of the mountaintop. Some, who had never heard of the issues related to the festival, who had never even followed the debates, who were fully unaware, in fact, of the existence of such a character at all, had, of course, noticed nothing: another like us among us. Others, also less trusting, had detected a peculiar strangeness—as those foreign to places invariably exude—but despite all intentions, they, also, had made nothing of their intellection. It was said then that only a handful had, justifiably or not, connected, somehow, the general countenance and gestures, through certain peculiar dispositions, with those they believed they had detected at the mountaintop.

The rumor reached, once more in Baabol, inconceivable proportions. Quarrels, fights even, irrational disputes and debates galore. Much effort and all kinds of emotions were spent on whether or not this was indeed the perceived figure seen on occasion at the mountaintop, and whether this fellow would or would not, could or could not, reveal the slightest bit about the annals, or the secrets, of the city.

The (irrational? unjustified?) order for the arrest had preceded all discussions: him circulating unsuspecting, the seizure itself proved quite unproblematic. Hero of the operation? One elderly lady who had gotten wind of the chase, crossing the street, had asked the awkward-looking man, who matched the description from the news, approximately anyway, worth the risk type, if he could perhaps help her across, she being older, slower, walking with cane and pain, poor li'l ol' me, just to the other side I'm tryina get somethin' to eat, and he, fool of fables, had succumbed to the gentle demand. 'Of course!' he'd answered. 'Of course I will.' Wink of the old lady to guard at intersection while they cross and he is holding her arm, watching her feet, moving her ever so slightly, we don't wan-chadaslipnowin' her smilingly, they get to the other side, her delay tactics, speaking about everything, poor lad listening to old romance stories that went awry, to mean landlady tales, unfair dismissal from previous employment tragedies and so on until—bang! Two burly agents of some sort holding him one each from both sides, he wondering what the hey is going on, he muttering, 'What the!' as he is dragged away, he not resisting, he cooperating, he having no choice—really.

Bizarre events followed the incarceration: bizarre, this time, by any standard. It was noticed, for example, that the challenge of the poets in a main tavern was drawing fewer and fewer participants. Some had succumbed to obscure diseases, others complained of an inexplicable dearth of inspiration never before experienced, and still others wondered, aloud and in private, at the erosion of their skills in such precipitous manners. Many mangled completely their speech: what came out of their mouths, in short, and to their quite noticeable shock, was a tongue unknown to all: melodious, yes, sensible, perhaps, but incomprehensible. A final group experienced what could justifiably be called the worst fate of the poets, for their losses constituted a selective banishment of the senses. They saw all of the world, perfectly well as a matter of fact, their eyesight improving actually (in a cruel twist), but never as they wished to see. Perfectly articulate they had grown, acquiring an absolute command of every single idiom, expression, word and nuance of the language, but alas! no more could they tell,

chant, sing or write of what they envisioned in a unique man-
ner: never again a universe through them, a portrait with their
hues, a landscape with their brush!

Paintings fell inexplicably from the walls. Statues, statuettes
and marionettes, big and small, in private estates or on public
grounds, shattered unprovoked. A companion to the sculptor
commissioned to decorate many of the public spaces and the
interiors of quite a few monuments of much renown in Baabol
and boasting of quite a following, reported an illness that had
virtually paralyzed the great artist. Nothing would be finished,
not now anyway. Uptown, a dancer had lost control of his legs.
They moved as they wished, fully disconnected from the usual
commands, from the body in all manners save the physical: so
that they bolted in one direction as his agonized face pleaded
in the other, his screams a whirlwind of self-abomination as he
ceaselessly was dragged twisting around his trunk! He was seen
crawling around the city square, legs playfully spinning around
the torso, going forward and back, high step and low, jump-
ing, skipping, doing the shuffle, breathless, delirious: walking
duck-like across the grand avenue, skipping horse-like in the
alleyways: soon he went mad, his screams as he was dragged
helpless by his own limbs around Baabol replaced with the
prayers of the saved.

In the window across from hers, in the building across from
hers, a young seamstress saw the old dentist go into the kitch-
en, saw him fetch the butcher's knife, saw him move to the
mirror, apply the knife to his own throat, saw him cut off his
own head, lift it with his own arms on headless frame, hold
the head at chest level before his torso, upon which the mouth
opening wide began chewing away at its own former body,
ripping it apart, voraciously, from remainder of neck to the
ankles and the toes: all quite rapidly of course—with arms,

292

feet, and torn pieces of restless body soon strewn about: not a misfortune, no, for he had expressed, on many occasions, and to most, that he was tempted, daily, of ripping himself apart!

The investigation of the bizarre happenings did not initially associate them with the arrival or incarceration of the stranger. Only after curious notice of coincidental dates did the populace begin to ponder aloud whether there was, in fact, any connection to be made. Baabol resorted to its old ways of public denunciation, accusations, provocations. Some cried of a conspiracy: actual agents, authentic forces in Baabol, it was claimed, were poisoning the victims, the poets, the dramatists, the painters, waging a secret war, and simultaneously spreading the rumors of secret associations with the jailed stranger. Others retorted that there was nothing to the claim. That it was in fact the apprehension of an unthinkable tragedy and the great unknown that induced the refusal to make the inevitable association. What about the dancer, they asked, who could possibly bring about such a debilitating poison? And what of the old dentist, others implored, who could possibly have instigated such a behavior? No, they claimed, we must confront the calamity that is upon us!

And so it went: a decree was given to temporarily halt the 293 meetings of poets, the gathering of the dramatists, to suspend all activities and performances in Baabol. To postpone all public events, to close down the schools, most businesses, and all centers that bore no relation to the urgent, daily survival of the city. Until things were somehow resolved anyway, the crippling halted, the slow march towards disappearance postponed.

Upon Baabol descended a gloom it had never known. Sorrows it had not seen. From the leaders to the common folk, everyone carried on with the day to day with heavy hearts. And no one provided relief or answer of any sort: meetings, conferences, large assemblies and small, private homes and public domains, from one edge of the city to another, none of the attempts yielded a cohesive response. Doctors and spiritualists of all creeds were summoned, consulted, begged. But their powers also were diminishing, their skills dwindling, their desires waning, all their knowledge trickling away. Is it the end of the world, they pondered aloud, is it the end of Baabol... At night they cried, they wept in the day, is this our path to banishment, they wondered. 'We may as well let him go free,' someone suggested about the observer. 'We have nothing to lose now.'

And so the decree was given to free the stranger of the mountaintop, who was still being held in the lone jail cell in Baabol. Which I believe, dear reader, I may have omitted: that Baabol, despite the conflicts and the problems and the many protests and differences of all natures and magnitudes, did not house a prisoner, as all sides would suddenly revert to proper civilities once any conflict or issue had run its course. The city, in fact, retained only a minimal police force and a small pool of security agents—although there were quite a few gentle gendarmes and crossing guards: to protect the weak, and sometimes the young.

'You are free!' announced to him his happy jailer, who obviously had no prior experience. 'And so am I!'

Upon which: the figure from the mountaintop, immensely relieved, a bit ill and slightly thinner—although he had been well-treated and well-fed, still quite striking in his physical demeanor—became hopeful he had not lost his wit in his confinement. 'The only thing I fear,' he had secretly confided to the jolly jailer, 'you know, that the jokes may get old!' He subsequently made his way to the first dingy dive he could find: which, happily, conformed to his taste: bleak—he did not know that all of Baabol was disconsolate at the time—badly kept and poorly lit—that is what a dive makes, he often thought—and rather empty. He patted the first fellow on the back—shrunken he was, head sunk between elbows—signaled a quick greeting to another looking his way, and marched along to the bartender. Called him over, held open his arms, like a big bird, and clamored, louder than one usually does in such places—and during such unhappy days!—and so that all could hear, and all did hear: 'My good man, I have had quite a stint on the mountaintop, where I have happily received numerous illuminations which I have decided not to share—by the way. I have lived as a hermit, wandered woods alone, through it all meditated, contemplated and reflected, quite happily I must add—and always with a conscious effort not to lose my wit. I have traveled to faraway places and been back, I have discovered and forgotten, heard and overheard, looked and overlooked. I have withstood nature's onslaughts—disasters, cataclysms, call them what you will—and witnessed not too few an event, that some of your talented storytellers could weave into quite a tale, your poets into quite an epic! Several weeks ago, my dear fellow, I made my way down to your village, upon which occasion I was quite unceremoniously tricked, attacked, roped and bound, and unglamorously, and unjustly, thrown into a pitiful little cell that had, from all evidence, not been used in a good while! As it turns out, I have now lived through, unnecessarily I must add, one most ungracious unwelcome! I herewith demand of you then, my dear man, the coldest, heartiest, fullest, beer that you can offer, and although I am currently short of funds, permit me to offer a tourney to all of these good fellows—if you accept, that is, to fancy my wish for credit!' Some cheers, a few roars—and we found that the wit was not gone!

295

Outside, the story in Baabol remained the gloom that had descended upon the city, and the incapacity of the inhabitants to respond accordingly. What was to be done? No one in Baabol knew the way, no one had an answer. Assembled in the public square, in a collective trance, the worn faces revealed the restlessness of the crowd. Here as elsewhere, all over Baabol, the people had gathered: in the street, in the small alleys, on the grand boulevard, hunched over tables or standing on their toes in the swarm of the masses. The bizarre occurrences had now infiltrated the lives of the populace, and even natural elements around Baabol were affected: withering of flowers, slow evanescence of the more delicate plants, unusual weather patterns: even the nights had dissipated, becoming shorter and shorter, uncommonly so that is, for the season. And it was witnessed by many, the day before, the hours rather, before this grand assembly in all of Baabol, where every street in Baabol was teeming with chatter, where every obsession was centered around the fate of the city, where a collective anguish loomed grotesquely above Baabol, it was noticed that in fact, the previous day had not even turned to night. 'Night did not come today,' said the watchmaker, uncertain as to how to express the irregularity, and uncertain even of his own tone. 'No night came our way.' And he, of all Baabolians, was known to own the most precise time-telling machines in Baabol.

'Can you be sure?' asked the tailor. 'If it didn't come, after all, perhaps we simply felt it all longer. It is today, he explained, it is still today, not tomorrow yet, we still have time, that was only an illusion, only time, carrying on, slower...'

The watchmaker had no intention of debating the merit of the case. There was only one thing for certain: it was the day after and it was not: there was a tale to be told there was not, once upon a time...

The overwhelming disquiet that was afflicting many, and the complaints, and the demands, were now reaching unbearable proportions.

'This is it!' they lamented. And others were just as adamant: 'We cannot go on like this!' they thundered angrily. 'Something must give.'

The notice was given to summon all forces, so that the citizens could attempt, as best fit their current capabilities, to fashion a response. They circulated, conversed, consulted. They cried, they thought, they held, they wondered, but no, Baabol would not slip away, not so easily. All agreed, some with more persuasion than others, that all of the troubles rested, at least began, with the storied remnants standing majestically at the edge: that the *real* gloom lay with the mysterious edifice, and that a swift demolition, complete and total, would, if not reverse the tragedies so far suffered, then at least provide a first step. And if not that, still it could not get any worse and there was nothing to lose, not now, the tower must come down!

And thus and so, incredibly, unfathomably perhaps, the order was given: there would be no turning back, this was indeed the final decree: the tower must come down!

In the early hours of the next morning, the citizens of Baabol, all the citizens of Baabol, old and young, vigorous or not, the exhausted, the energetic, the desperate, all assembled, without exception, from elders to toddlers, in the public square and adjoining streets. Baabol became a sea of daunted gazes: spiteful, angry or unknowing, wondering or doubting, a legion of faces formed the new tapestry of town. Not a single stone of the cobbled streets could be seen, not a single shadow on the mudbrick walls, for they were all lined with the impatient bodies of these chanters, paved with the black clothes and veils, the colors of mourning and remembrance, the colors of martyrs and hope, of resistance and revolt...

Streets and domes, sidewalks and hills and slopes, and roof-tops and squares and parks,

all of Baabol adorned in the shade of triumph and tribute—,

with the citizens of Baabol summoned, at dawn, to the center of town: arm in arm or fists raised,

locked in feverish embraces or standing alone, all the citizens of Baabol brought, children all and their elders, to each one and bar none, all brought to the spectacle a worthy weapon: after the silence they were to stand,

and after the silence, the grand silence, after the call had echoed throughout Baabol and in the hearts of its populace, after the deep sigh, with thoughts of abandoned relics and untested paths,

once more the promises of Forgetting, thunderous the cry, with this I tell of sorrows and scorn, I sing, enamored enraged, of Overcoming,

as far as they could see, assembled as asked, in every corner of every street,

silent figurines animated, scared faces, the citizens of Baabol began the march,

with piercing glares, angry gaits,

arm in arm all in rhythm: with knives and clubs, bats and swords: rapid paces, steady paces, all in rhythm:

through the public square, through a small alley and another, the voice and the mask, the crier and the land, the wanderer, the puppet and the hand (holding high the doll),

with the end of the real dreamlands and cities of sand, an actor high atop the cliff chanting the words of players and playmakers, a mad dancer gripping firmly his leg, a restless mime alone:

they marched one and all, a forgotten jester, the liar by the

298

bridge, a poet with a rebelled eye, angels and exiles,

vagabonds in ecstasy, marched all in rhythm through the city, through the ruins, all in rhythm, to the edge of the city of Baabol,

forbidden in the rage of this fire, of this dawn:

dins of bells from faraway will accompany us, whispers banned, murmurs the heresy,

silence unforgiving: we will march and with the songs and the screams and the wills make a world:

new landscapes forged with our gaits, burrows beneath valleys, higher peaks—and yet...

And yet, from afar, unperturbed, majestic and solitary, undisturbed, grandiose relic of ancient lore, silently the riddle, stands the tower they have come to destroy...

They approached, frazzled and awed—and then the signal was given to halt.

The citizens of Baabol stood and peered collectively at the tower rising before them: no one moved, one by one all standing a sea of black with faces, the citizens of Baabol stood silent gazing at the tower before them.

And the order was given. And the order was heard.

It was a sight to behold: from all directions, as if an unending procession, yet swifter than the wind or thunder, flailing arms, screams united, screams coalescing into one, as if all emanating from one voice, the citizens of Baabol rushed maddened to the monument of their city.

A sight to behold: the swarm to the tower and all around the tower the men and the women and the children, climbing crawling the sides of the edifice, smashing along the way the windows in their path: ascending the tower with knives and scythes, back and forth at the worn surface of the tower: hovering around, with their bare hands grabbing the stones ripping them out unrestrained: at the top of the tower, a hundred men all around the periphery, swinging up and swinging down, shirts pulled to elbows, pants folded at ankles, frowning, on the left wing and the right, along the jagged edge with their shadows, bending and arching, agony and awe both, tiny specks scattered on the surface of the colossal edifice—a sight to behold: the tailor at the peak, the plumber smashing with pipes and saws, the barber with his razors, the gardener with the hoes: and the butcher with the cleavers, and the hunter with his gun, taking the easy (but quite productive) way out. And the clockmaker at the base, smashing the windows, with his supply of hourglass clocks!

A photographer, working frantically at the base, setting up and struggling, praying for all systems to go, attempted to capture the incredible spectacle unfolding. But, to his astonishment, all of his equipment suddenly failed. He tried to repair and rescue, but to no avail. In disgust and helpless, he smashed all of his tools—for all to see.

And a celebrated painter, enraptured, prepared his material, for his greatest masterwork, doubtless: he readied the canvas, he readied the brush and the paint and positioned himself, in the midst of the chaos, in all serenity: I saw him apply the brush to the paint, I saw him put the brush to the canvas: strokes gentle at first, excited soon, vehement and haphazardly directed at the end: only white streaks appeared on the canvas, white streaks only, large and small, that did not even obey the order of the movements! He applied the brush to the paint again, and to the canvas again: and nothing appeared this time either! Again he went on, and again, applying the brush to the colored paints and to the canvas: nothing appeared all in revolt nothing will be captured it will not be told!

He stood, the poor painter, turned calmly to the tower, ceremoniously lifted his paints in his hands, knocked his canvas to the ground, peered at the tower before him, and extended his arms, as if an offering: he held his arms several moments in the pose of the gift, bowed as if to a deity. Everyone saw the painter dejected, turning away, before him now a canvas bathed in the cacophony of colors he had, forlorn, spilled and smeared atop...

He walked back bitterly from the spectacle that had been denied. Only *I* stood, faraway and unseen, my gaze also set in awe upon the withering of the majestic tower, witness to the razing of the tower: and as slowly as the day turns into dusk and dusk gives way to night, despaired and enchanted, unbelieving, from the distant land a pilgrim helpless, nevermore carry on, I saw, I saw, the mad destruction, of the Tower of Baabol...

———■———

They joined hands and sang. They laughed and embraced. In circles the bathers of Baabol hand in hand around the ruins of the tower dancing, they and the citizens of Baabol, dancing ecstatic around the new ruins of Baabol.

They chanted on the way back, songs of the new way lamenting the old, songs of glory and triumph. Into the city finally, same rhythm soon upon them, the daily rhythm returning for the citizens of the new world, doing the life thing, the ruins at the edge of the city razed, erased, brought to the ground...

The night passed and the new day began with an elation unknown in Baabol. The baker sprang in the streets and distributed free loaves to all. The ice-cream man of Baabol (his nemesis!) rang his bells and passed out free cones—only cones!—to the children *and* the adults! All was unsurpassed glory, embraces and congratulations, births of poets and a thousand pages written in one day, a joyous frenzy for all to see.

It was even said that, at a secret gathering in undisclosed chambers inside the tower—that ominous first night's sprouting tower before it came down—they had assembled for a grand affair, a private supper that was far from being the last, quite a party surely, at the din of midnight, heyho swinging and a cheers and a santé, they had abandoned themselves to their basest instincts before settling into their eternal pose: with full vigor and no afterthought, grins and smiles and prost all around: the towncrier presiding of course, in the middle, surrounded (counterclockwise, say) by—drumroll please, and the curtsies: the magician, the mime, the acrobat, the wily, yes, translator, the puppet master, the actor, the pesky poet and the forlorn painter, the one-eyed trickster, the clown, the nightwatchman and, last but not least, the wanderer: grins and winks I say, heyho and salamati they went, never wither carry on, tuck tuck, glasses raised, cheers to one and all, whole and new, onward now, onward ho, crumbling with us reborn, one step back two steps in, truth and dare, still for the eternal pose: and... Snap—!

302

And now Baabol lived without the ruins that formed the very question of its existence. They had agreed that the tower must vanish, and vanish it had. The decree, the collective decision brought forth to save Baabol. But in this way? Was it saved, after all, the city they knew? Well, early the next morning, the early risers, and, soon, all of the unsuspecting citizens of Baabol were ever more bewildered when they saw what they never would have fathomed, never would have even imagined. They noticed, after the initial shrieks of disbelief, that, once more, at the edge of the city, in the very same location that it had been razed, another ruinous tower had grown: not the same, no: not the same form, not the same colors, not even the same shape, not ascending in quite the same manner: not with the same windows, or bricks, but surely as the eye can see, all agreed, without contestation, that a tower had grown, that was not the tower of before.

'It is the work of the stranger,' bellowed one. And as often occurs, too many blindly agreed with the first loud yell: without reasonable time for consultation, the decision was made: he was rounded up again, the character, thrown back into what had become his private cell, taunted and mocked even—and the new tower, with more vigilance, with more vehemence, razed, once more, to the ground.

Night came and passed, and all precipitated to the same site. And once more there had grown a strange tower, once more not the same, once more a tower-in-ruins, unfinished. They freed the man of the mountaintop (whereupon the pub etc.), razed the tower, came back the morning after: another tower spurted out, peak-less, ragged-edged, like all of its predecessors. They jailed the bloke from the pub—he may now be dubbed—razed the tower, assembled again at prescribed hour at prescribed location: a tower once more, unlike the others, in ruins.

They jailed and freed and assembled, again and again, until the comedy carried on quite a few nights too many, and an annoyed participant, not even a wise one, simply irritated, shouted out: 'Let him free, don't you see it makes no difference whether he's jailed or not!' And although few understood what he truly meant, no one bothered to jail the stranger either.

And in Baabol, every night, a new tower, unlike the others but bearing an uncanny resemblance to its predecessors, sprouted in the place of the old one, razed to the ground the day before.

'Six nights, six towers!' exclaimed one. 'Seven nights, sev-

303

en towers,' exclaimed another! They had put into motion the question of their own death, and all was born again, constantly written, constantly traced...

The dilemma, however, was not resolved. Baabol contemplating its withering had rejuvenated itself, and now, as I remember translating the words of one, for they resonate still in my own mind, now that I myself have left Baabol, reluctantly I must add, but with all of its memories relentlessly, restlessly, clamoring through me—I shall not relate my manner of escape from Baabol, although that also would make quite a tale for the taleteller, quite an epic for the poet!—I recall the words spoken, how the young one asked: 'And now must we each night raze the new tower to the ground?' The muted spectators, the muted masses, I also mute: and a silent awe echoed through Baabol, throughout Baabol, known of course, as the wondrous silence, of Baabolians.

But no one dared propose otherwise: again and again, again and again, endlessly alive, Baabolians each night razed the tower that had grown among them the night before. The towers of Baabol each night swerving from the ground: never the same tilt, never the same, unfinished always, jagged-edged, the strength of an ancient monument each time: at the edge of this city, far away in the distance of all my cities, always: the Towers of Baabol...

Still, no one heard of the stranger who once appeared in Baabol, befriended the citizens, spent several drunken evenings in forlorn places—and several more in his private cell, along with the unhappy jailer of Baabol. He had disappeared in the first weeks after the commotion of the first repeated razings and jailings, and no one knew where he had gone.

'I saw him scurry away,' a young boy had lied. 'He went that-a-way, over the bridge...'

304

There were other accounts, conflicting accounts. But no one knew, really, whatever had become of the fellow from the mountaintop who had appeared among them in Baabol. Still, in the distance, far from the lights of Baabol, above the flickering lights of Baabol, shadow among stranger shadows, faraway on the mountaintop, one could make out a peering face, a face gazing down at Baabol, this and all Baabols of fable and life, among the ruins of Baabol, high above the Tower of Baabol, an angel above the city's square, an angel above the city's streets…

And still the invisible thieves descended upon the yards and the alleyways of Baabol, still some told of the dance and debauchery of the spirits in the city's square. Still the sounds in the city, the man with bicycle under the sudden storm, still the thief crossing unsuspected. Still the crier scurried frantically from Despair, with the rumbles of night, the timid murmurs of revolutions next, see those two under the awning how they speak. Still, the dust lifted at dusk for the wanderer to see…

———■———

I threw my bag over my shoulder, fixed my hat and checked the watch. I was comfortable, enough anyway, my toes were fine. The vest was clean, the face was too. The passersby passed by on my left and my right. I peered ahead longingly at the bridge, at the horizon, a tall bridge with its fangs and its webs, the clocktower and its happy face. I slipped my papers and my books under my arm, a wink and a smile, I gazed again with devilish eyes: head up watching, I began the walk: the happy walk, I must say, the happy stroll: through the public square and the cries, once upon a time, whistling (toot toot toot), chanting, sharks in the sand, playing, truth and dare, playing, again, across the city's domes, across the city's dawns…

■ ■ ■

305

Afterword

I shall not relate my manner of escape from Baabol
   -Amir Parsa

And all the company
in this hotel
know the languages
of Babel
   -Guillaume Apollinaire

In 1916, on the front between Verdun and the Somme, Apollinaire took shrapnel in the head and was subsequently trepanned. We are familiar with the wound left by this incident from the drawing of the bandaged poet by his friend Picasso, but as that portrait depicts Apollinaire in classical profile, and in that sense as already memorialized in the aesthetic realm, let us consider instead a photograph of the recovering Apollinaire. The collar of his tunic, at the center of the photograph, is carefully buttoned to the very top. Or perhaps we should say it is proudly buttoned, for in this photograph we see Apollinaire presenting—mustering himself to be seen—as a soldier who, while wounded, is nonetheless visibly unsubdued by the trauma he has suffered. His head has been shaved and his forehead wrapped, but his bearing is dignified; he is damaged, but he is not unmanned. If, however, we shift our perspective slightly, in the spirit of Apollinaire's own modernism, we can see the whole matter differently: the recovering Apollinaire is an assemblage or, even, a meta-assemblage, a re-assemblage of the human and the assembled. We see in the photograph a man sewn back together after having been bodily taken apart and then further sewn—morally sewn—back into his uniform. And this impression of reassembly, with all its seams and stitches on display, is reinforced by Apollinaire's peculiar gaze, which makes him appear none too sure of the uniform of restored integrity he is wearing. Apollinaire's right eye, more distant from the camera in his three-quarter pose, is fixed more or less on the photographer—in any case, he sees himself being seen—while his left eye wanders upward in its socket, as if he were at the same moment, in sharp contrast to the disciplined fixity of his right eye, in religious transport. Through one eye Apollinaire looks at the world; with the other he sees the angels falling around him. 'Man struggles with man/Then falls like a shooting star.' Looking at a face that is a signal instance of what Amir Parsa might call the Bewitching and Hazardous Nature of Masks, Mirrors and Metamorphoses, we are left to ask, looking back a century later, what the bandaged man remembers, what he sees, what he foresees. Most pressing of all: what can he tell of it all? What gets transmitted to us in this image through the disarrangement of Apollinaire's gaze? Why, in the end, does he muster, in response to all he has seen, poems?

Ludwig Wittgenstein, another spirit on the loose in Parsa's writing, was also wounded in the Great War, in his case in an explosion in an artillery plant. Unlike Apollinaire, however, who, weakened by his injuries, succumbed to the flu pandemic of 1918, Wittgenstein recovered fully from his. He insisted on being reposted to combat, serving with valor on the Eastern front and then as an officer on the Italian front until, near the end of the war, he was taken prisoner. In the idled time afforded him as a captured combatant, Wittgenstein composed his *Logisch-Philosophische Abhandlung*. This riddling little book of philosophy, the product of an imposed *vita contemplativa* (a *vita activa* turned back on itself, really) that the restless Wittgenstein was never otherwise able to create for himself, develops an account of language, in its atomic and molecular structure, and of how we are sunk into it or, better, how it is sunk into us. Of how the limits of language are the limits of the world. Let us try to imagine the scene of its composition: in the silence of battles remembered—heard now only at a distance—Wittgenstein descried that language is the world of our common experience, and that in it we can express everything it is possible meaningfully to say. (How strange a thing to believe at the end of four years of massive violence! This incongruity will return to us transformed soon enough.) But there is, Wittgenstein intuits, one exception to the encompassing totality of language: we cannot meaningfully say that we can say everything there is to say. There is no perspective outside of language from which the idea of language having an outside can be made intelligible. Thus, despite language palpably having limits that are the conditions of making sense, these limits cannot be made sense of in language. Which is to say: they cannot be made sense of. The limits of language are absolute, and they are also, or for just that reason, unspeakable. Like Apollinaire, Wittgenstein sees the falling angels, but he sees them falling incommunicably outside the field of common language. 309

There is, for Wittgenstein, no prospect of escape from our language to the world as such, the world before it was touched and formed by language. But this lesson seems so hard for us to believe—insufferably hard to believe—for everywhere we look, our language gives out on us before our experience of the world does. From out of our foxholes, we hear tell of a world out there, and so we can only be disquieted by the thought that, palpable as our experience of it is, this world out there may be naught but a rumor, heard by all (all who can speak, anyway) yet spoken by none. The limits of language are *sensed* within our use of it and are *given shape* as the appearance of a world beyond it. What, then, are we to say, what words can we muster, when we are plagued by fantasies of the world beyond language, the pre-Adamic world in which the animals beg us wordlessly, but rarely silently, to give them their names, and, more to our point, the world after the angels have fallen? 'Shadow you creep near me/But you no longer hear me/ You will no longer know the divine poems I sing/But I hear you I see you still.' When we find ourselves troubled by the thought of the limits of our language and the shadows that creep near them, when we are spooked by hearing the voices of unspeakable things, we are in need of philosophy or poetry or both. Not, it must be emphasized, so that we can discover another language in which the limits of our own can be revealed. No: what is missing from Babel is not an undiscovered second-order language. Every language is a first-order language, and beyond the limits of language is nothing but the infinite need to say. To show this is what Wittgenstein set out to achieve in his *Logisch-Philosophische Abhandlung*.

Apollinaire and Wittgenstein: these are the guiding spirits of Parsa's *Tractatüus Philosophiká-Poeticüus*. His connections to them, but they all revolve around the uncanny sensitivity of the poet and the philosopher to the practices of meaning-making when those practices survive, or fail to survive, the violence of war and revolution, of, that is, the sort of massive social transformation that is simultaneously the end of the world and the beginning of a new one. Apollinaire and Wittgenstein stared out past their bandages, past the gates of the prison camp, and out there, where the world is, they saw … a language manufactory. They saw the calligrammes and their shadows, the propositions and the truths they represent. They saw the map of everything and at the same time the limits of the marked territory. They saw that when we fall out of the world, it is only as angels. And so, in order to bring (in) to living awareness the no-man's land, through which all must pass, of the impossible conjunction of language and the lived experience of its limits, they wrote in what Parsa calls a 'tongue unknown to all.'

Why, for Apollinaire, Wittgenstein and Parsa, is the experience of the limits of language so fully embodied in war and revolution? Contrary to romantic war-writing, it is not because the violence of war is too much for us to capture in words. Much in human life is beyond the current state of our linguistic powers, whatever they may be. The ordinary consequence of such excessiveness is, however, enhanced attentiveness and silence, intensified readiness for new meanings. But there is something very different about war: as a recognizably human enterprise, it is not simply too much. Rather, it is too much for anything but words. War is indeed a limit-experience, yet it remains entirely within the field of sense-making. At this point, it behooves us to be even more specific, as we are on the verge of saying that the gods have abandoned the field of war, leaving it to man alone, and that is not universally so. So let us say: the limit experience of total war, war not circumscribed by ethical boundaries that separate it from civilization, is entirely within the field of sense-making. 'Nation probed nation' is the way Apollinaire describes the mood of Europe on the brink of World War I. Politically organized masses of people continued looking for new ways to make their mutual relations clear, continued to make sense to one another in a condition when their words had run out. The concept of total war was coined by the German General Erich Ludendorff in his memoir of World War I, *Der Totale Krieg*, to capture precisely a mutated form of political action. The American General Curtis LeMay, the architect of the USA's Strategic Air Command after World War II, later gave it its most unstinting elaboration. LeMay once said that 'flying fighters is fun' but 'flying bombers is important,' because the aim of total war is not the defeat of armies but the destruction of nations. In total war, whole peoples are mobilized without exception into 'the war effort'. Bellicosity thus becomes a form, perhaps not even an especially extreme form, of political recognition. War, even in its super-human violence, is in this perspective rich noise in which new forms of speech are assembling themselves at the limits of old ways of sense-making. Or, as Wittgenstein famously put it, in a sentence more quoted than understood, 'What we cannot speak about, we must pass over in silence.' We can only come to be wrong about what exceeds our language, Wittgenstein implies, if we do not first pass over it as if it were beyond understanding. Language opens up the specifically human domain of overreaching. Wittgenstein's famous sentence does not then, as it is often taken, aver a metaphysical necessity; it expresses an imperative. It offers not a counsel of silence but instead attention to transgressive speech as it butts up against the limits of language. This experience of total disruption, of meaning arising in no-man's land, we are not to despoil with old words.

Of course, it is easy for us to say now, looking back one hundred years, what Apollinaire and Wittgenstein saw taking shape that silenced their everyday speech. Our languages have regathered themselves around the semantic density of the first total war. Parsa, however, takes us directly into the manufactory of language, the wars and revolutions where words are taken apart, their bits and pieces reassembled, here comically, there monstrously, everywhere frantically. But does it contradict the view that our experience of war and revolution, experience at the limit, must be passed over in silence, if Parsa makes that experience vivid for us? No, but the key formal difference between Parsa's work and that of his ancestors is of utmost importance at just this juncture in our reflection: if, like Apollinaire, Parsa withholds punctuation or uses it to break up phrases and sentences and if, like Wittgenstein, he assembles his linguistic fragments, reaching out in multiple directions for new totalities, into a tractatus, still we cannot ignore that Parsa's headlong dive into massive social displacement makes him pay a price that neither of his two spirit guides would or could pay: Parsa shakes myths and legends loose from their historical cleatings and makes them circulate in the modern form of epic we call historical fiction. In short: unlike Apollinaire and Wittgenstein, Parsa abuses proper names.

Parsa's most abusive invention is the city of Baabol, where every day the citizens erect a new tower and then every night demolish it. Baabol is total war brought home to the city— perhaps, then, we should call it permanent revolution—as no line can be drawn there between the ambition to build and the ambition to destroy. (No line, we might note, except for the one between night and day. But that line had already been withdrawn by Parsa earlier in *Tractatüus Philosophiká-Poeticüus*, in the 'city of revolution' where 'the night has gone, the magician thundered triumphantly, there is now an everlasting day! ... The glory of a nightless world is upon us.' In the city of revolution, the world goes topsy-turvy when we see that the sun does not need to set for night to begin; in Baabol we see by contrast that even the rotation of the earth can turn out to be nothing but the timekeeper of permanent revolution. In any case...) It is not a far leap to conclude that Parsa's tower-builders of Baabol are cousins of the citizens of Babel, the city from Genesis in which humans strove to leave the profane world

313

for the divine one, thereby threatening the proper dominion of both. (That Parsa invokes the promethean image of Babel by near-openly deploying its famous name should alert us that we are in the territory of historically shaky transmission—what I called just above 'historical fiction'—, for Babel, according to Flavius Josephus, was the name of the rumored city derived, for the sake of story-telling, from the Hebrew word for 'confusion'. Babel is, in other words, confusion congealed for the sake of remembrance, eternal impermanence handed down as tradition.) In aiming to reach heaven, humans misused the divine gift of language. More specifically, they abused God's gift of the medium in which we labor to understand one another to try instead to flee to a place of their imagination where the problem of mutual understanding will have been transcended, left behind forever, forgotten. The story of God's division of language into the manyness of human tongues is of course commonly seen as a punishment for this act of hubris. Not only, however, is that interpretation of the Hebrew bible too Greek, but more importantly it obscures the unusual, even singular, element of the mythic retribution in the story of Babel. God does not take back his gift of language, remaking humans in the image of the beasts, but rather multiplies it. The diversity of tongues God imposes on us only serves to make explicit what the gift of even one language already entailed: that not instrumental efficiency but endless mediation, which is to say, mutual recognition without settled understanding, is the central and unending work of humans. God's explosion of language into languages has, let us recall, two consequences: (1) the builders of the tower, unable now to coordinate their activities, abandon their instrumental labors, leaving their instrument of transcendence to endless ruination, and (2) the ineliminable mutual estrangement of speakers of different languages, who will forever remember the unity of language as they hear the inscrutable meanings uttered by the speakers of foreign languages, makes the limits of language an experience available to all users of language who confront the need of translation. The strangeness of God has in this way come alive in every speaker of a foreign tongue. The residents of Parsa's Baabol, in a sense, refuse this experience and its lesson, for they never cease to build their tower again and again. But the pain they suffer for not heeding the demand—hearing the call—of mutual human recognition is that 'now must we each night raze the tower to the ground.' Their work never ends, their lesson is never learned, the task of mutual recognition never finally dawns on them. It is the escape from Baabol's endless avoidance of the alien voice of the other human being that, Parsa's narrator says, would make 'quite an epic for the poet.' The epic poet is the one who would escape from the endless labor of transcendence and emerge into the world opened up by the work of language. (Perhaps this is why Freud thought that the epic poet was not simply the inventor of fictional heroes but, in claiming to tell stories in his own way, the hero whose exploits he pretends to narrate.)

Baabol, of course, is not quite Babel, for Baabolians—and not even Parsa's narrator, for that matter, an odd fact to which we will return—never leave their city behind. They rebuild it every day and so never let it become Babel. But is that difference Parsa's only reason for naming it not-quite-Babel? Is there another tongue at work in Parsa's displacement of the legend of Babel into his own poetry? Perhaps so, for in another association which, like the biblical Babel, operates only indirectly, we may note that Babol is a city in the north of Iran, between the Alborz mountains and the Caspian Sea. Whether it, too, is home to an endless urge to demolish and rebuild vehicles with which to flee toward God from the limitations of language, the urge which, in light of our consideration of Apollinaire and Wittgenstein, we can see is nothing but the displaced urge of language itself: this we cannot say. For Parsa, Babol is Babel is Baabol, an invented name that escapes its two 'original' sources yet at the same time cannot help but remind us equally of them both. In that sense, however, it is not an escape at all, but an allusion. Or, rather, it is an escape only within and by means of language, since allusion functions as an archive—a great library—of the accumulated distances between us and the towers we have left in ruins. The allusive Baabol is thus the exact opposite of escape in the Babelian sense. It is instead another name for the mediation of memory, for the bottomless reservoir of the traces of all failed escapes. Thus Parsa's narrator says, 'I shall not relate my manner of escape from Baabol.' Is it not necessary to wonder if this poet, who thinks of epics but will not give us so much as an epyllion, has perhaps not escaped at all, even if he has survived, the total war of Baabol?

Let us return once more to Apollinaire, our first non-escapee. Of driving back to Paris from Deauville with his friend Rouveyre in 'Rouveyre's little car'—the eponymous auto of his poem 'The Little Motorcar', already quoted above—to join the mobilization for what Ludendorff will call in retrospect the first total war, the poet writes:

> We said goodbye to an entire epoch
> Crazed giants were standing over Europe
> Eagles left their eyries to await the sun
> Voracious fish surfaced from the deep
> Nation probed nation
> Underground the dead shook with fear

Preceding this stanza, the first four lines of the poem set the stage for the war with prosaic detail:

> The 31st August 1914
> Just before midnight I left Deauville
> In Rouveyre's little car
> With his chauffeur that made three

No abuse of names here, but a reliance on their utter specificity, their exact and reliable reference. But then the first line of the stanza quoted in its entirety above shakes it all loose, with a saying, a little speech: 'We said goodbye to an entire epoch.' An entire epoch can end only with total war, a complete revolution which, as the entire epoch has passed, never to return, we can say never ceases to happen. Even the dead shake in fear, for it is the language with which they communicate with the living—let us call it simply 'tradition', or the inner life of an epoch—that has come to an end. Now, we might think that the lines that follow saying 'goodbye' are the first utterances in the language of the new epoch. And in some sense that is what they have become. They have survived the total destruction that consumed Apollinaire himself. But 'The Little Motorcar' also contradicts this idea that poetry begins with devastation. There is, there must be first, a caesura of meaning, a silencing of old tongues in which can be heard the need of 'a new tongue unknown to all.' The question how to utter 'escape' is and will remain open. 'I'll never forget that night drive/', writes Apollinaire. 'No one said a word.' So is there here a saying or not? Or is there both? Saying goodbye to an entire epoch is always done in silence, even when that silence is as loud as the sound of giants gearing up for a 'general mobilization' with which to destroy the world.

The poetry of *Tractatüus Philosophiká-Poeticüus* is the poetry that has not escaped Baabol, even though, even if, its poet has.

Before finishing these reflections, let us return once more to Wittgenstein, for it is he to whom Parsa alludes in the title of this book. Wittgenstein's *Abhandlung* was eventually translated into English—the process was tortured—but oddly it did not bear the title *Logico-Philosophical Treatise*, a semantic vehicle that English had readymade for it. Rather, it was published under the Latin title *Tractatus Logico-Philosophicus*. A dead language to name a text about the lived experience of the limits of language! It is reputed that the recommendation of the Latin title came from Wittgenstein's Cambridge friend and colleague G.E. Moore. The title is perfectly correct, of course, as *Abhandlung* and *Tractatus* both mean 'treatise' ('treatment' or 'handling'). But since there would be no loss of meaning either way, why not come out with it and call the book *Logico-Philosophical Treatise*? Part of the answer, as Moore and Wittgenstein must have known, is that Latin is a tongue unknown to all (not, it must be noted, a tongue known to none, for that would be the language spoken before the languages of Babel, but a tongue dead to all—unknown equally to all—speakers of Romance languages who with each utterance preserve 'the slow crumbling of the great library'). And indeed, the use of Latin has perversely stabilized the title, in a way no living language could. Everyone, in whatever language they practice philosophy (even German!), now refers to Wittgenstein's *Abhandlung* as 'the *Tractatus*'. But Moore must have had another unsettled debt in mind in recommending *Tractatus Logico-Philosophicus* to Wittgenstein: to Spinoza's *Tractatus Theologico-Politicus*. The Jew of Amsterdam wrote his attack on the soldering together of religious and political authority in Latin and not Dutch in order to avoid the vernacular censors of his tolerant city, in order to hide his thoughts in a dead language. It did not work, of course, but nor could Moore really have thought a Latin title would save Wittgenstein from the censorship of vulgar understanding. Rather, the unpaid debt, I think, was to Spinoza's godlessness, his insight that, at the limits of language there stood no god, no body, to bind language to the world out there. At the limits all debts are off. As in the *Tractatüus Philosophiká-Poeticüus*, a title written not in a dead language but in a scrambled one made out of the ruins of the many languages of Babel, at the limit, we find not divinity but war and revolution.

Tractatus Theologico-Politicus: *Tractatus Logico-Philosophicus*: *Tractatüus Philosophiká-Poeticüus*: Parsa's own epic, a melding of the philosophical and the poetic, the legendary and the theological, that generates not a tractatus but a *tractatüus*, a vagrant genre wandering in between a dead language and one yet to be born, is a product of a total war. But that seems too direct, too historically demystified, to capture the essence of the *Tractatüus Philosophiká-Poeticüus*, which is not simply an outcome of the war from which its narrator hasn't escaped but its bearer. The word we want here is 'aftermath'. Parsa's *Tractatüus* is a second harvest that gathers up what can be gleaned not from the field but from the husks and shells of the first harvest. In these leavings, which we can think of as the limits of language deployed by—deployed as—poetry and philosophy, we can discern that total war, unrestricted by any sense of the proper field of battle, is also, which is to say forever, an endless war of meaning making. How our deadly ways of making meaning can also be ways of making life is perhaps the next question. It is certainly not one we know

319

how to answer. Not yet, anyway, which is why it falls to the poets, philosophers, and epic jesters to live it everyday.

Gregg M. Horowitz
May 12, 2014

About Gregg Horowitz

Gregg Horowitz is Professor of Philosophy and Chair of Social Science and Cultural Studies at Pratt Institute. He writes and lectures on aesthetics and politics, psychoanalysis, and the philosophy of art. His books include *Sustaining Loss: Art and Mournful Life* (Stanford, 2002), and he has published essays on Ilya Kabakov, Tony Oursler and Wallace Stevens, among others.

About Amir Parsa

Amir Parsa was born in Tehran in 1968 and moved to the D.C. sub-
urbs when he was ten. He went to French International schools both in
Iran and in the U.S., attended Princeton and Columbia universities, and
currently lives in New York City with his wife and daughter. An interna-
tionally acclaimed writer, poet, translator and newformist, he is the au-
thor of seventeen literary works, including *Kobolierrot, Feu L'encre/Fable,
Drive-by Cannibalism in the Baroque Tradition, Erre,* and *L'opéra minora,*
a 440-page multilingual work that is in the MoMA Library Artists' Books
collection and in the Rare Books collection of the Bibliothèque Natio-
nale de France. An uncategorizable body of work, his oeuvre—written
directly in English, French, Farsi, Spanish and various hybrids—consti-
tutes a radical polyphonic enterprise that puts into question national,
cultural and aesthetic attachments while fashioning new genres, forms,
discursive endeavors and species of literary artifacts. His writings in
both English and French have been anthologized, and he has contrib-
uted to a number of print and online publications, including *Fiction
International, Textpiece, Guernica, Armenian Poetry Project* and a mash-
up issue of *Madhatters' Review* and *Bunk Magazine.* His translations in-
clude Bruno Durocher-Kaminski's *And They Were Writing Their History,*
and the first two books of Nadia Tueni, which appeared under the title
The Blond Texts & The Age of Embers. Since 2007, pieces and fragments
from Parsa's ongoing *The New Definitely Post/Transnational and Mostly
Portable Open Epic as Rendered by the Elastic Circus of the Revolution* have
been featured at The Bowery Poetry Club and The Riverside Church,
during the Uncomun Festival, the Engendered Festival, and the Dumbo
Arts Festival in New York, and at the Baroquissimo Festival in Puebla,
Mexico, among other venues. This literary work is comprised of cantos
and fragments constituting an on-going plurilingual epic that unfolds
over time on various platforms, in multiple arenas and spaces (private
and public), and through various scriptural strategies—from the tradi-
tional (handwritten sheets and books) to the new (electronic, web). In
June 2010 at the Paris en Toutes Lettres festival and in conjunction with
the publication of his book-length poem *Fragment du cirque élastique de
la révolution,* he put into action *The American in Paris is an Iranian in*

New York, a 10-hour multiplatformal 'scriptage' taking place throughout Paris, with fragments being simultaneously projected at the Northern Manhattan Arts Alliance during the Artstroll Festival in Manhattan. He has instigated his unique encantations, readations and bassadigas, and conducted more traditional lectures, workshops and playshops, on avant-garde poetics, literary/artistic innovation, and cultural design at museums and organizations across the world, including Norway, Mexico, Italy, France, Brazil, India and Spain. His curatorial interjections, conceptual pieces, artistic interventions, and critical educational praxis have taken place in a host of public spaces, organizations and environments. As a Lecturer, Educator and Director in The Museum of Modern Art's Department of Education from 2004 to 2011, he developed programs, curricula, and learning experiences for a wide range of audiences. He also conceptualized and created the ongoing PinG (Poets in the Galleries) series at the Queens Museum in 2007. He has taught at Columbia, the University of Girona in Spain, and the University of Maccerata in Italy. Formerly a Chairperson and Acting Associate Dean at Pratt Institute in New York, he currently teaches at Pratt, where he is an Associate Professor and directs trans/post/neodisciplinary initiatives.

Also by Amir Parsa

Kobolierrot
(2000, Ed. Caractères)

Feu l'encre—Fable
(2000, Ed. Caractères)

L'opéra minora
(2000, Ed. Caractères, limited edition)

Onomadopean
(2000, Ed. Caractères; with H. Dabashi)

La révolution n'a pas encore eu lieu
(2003, Ed. Caractères)

Skizzi Ska
(2005, ALEA: Alternative Literary Experiences
and Adventures, single edition)

Dîvân
(2006, Ed. Caractères)

Sil & anses
(2006, Ed. Caractères)

Erre
(2006, Ed. Caractères)

Ifs & Co.
(2007, ALEA, single edition)

And They Were Writing Their History
(2007, Ed. Caractères; translation of Bruno Durocher's 'Et l'homme
blanc écrivait son histoire')

Meet Me
(2009, The Museum of Modern Art; with F. Rosenberg,
L. Humble, C. McGee)

Fragment du cirque élastique de la révolution
(2010, Ed. Caractères)

The Blond Texts & The Age of Embers
(2012, UpSet Press; translation of Nadia Tueni's 'Les textes blonds'
and 'L'âge d'écume')

*The New Definitely Post/Transnational and
Mostly Portable Open Epic as Rendered by the
Elastic Circus of the Revolution*
(2007-ongoing; multi-lingual, multi-mediatic,
multi-plat/formal literary epic)

Le Chaise (Yes, Le)
(2015, FACD: Folios of Adaptations for the Clandestine Diffusion,
limited edition and distribution)

Drive-by Cannibalism in the Baroque Tradition
(2006, Non Serviam Press; 2015, UpSet Press)

Other Books by Upset Press

Desire of the Moth
by Champa Bilwakesh (2015)

Drive-by Cannibalism in the Baroque Tradition
by Amir Parsa (2015)

Slippers for Elsewhere
by Matthew J. Burgess (2014)

A Nuclear Family
by April Naoko Heck (2014)

The Ground Below Zero: 9/11 to Burning Man, New Orleans to Darfur, Haiti to Occupy Wall Street
by Nicholas Powers (2013)

a little history
by Ammiel Alcalay (2012)

from the warring factions (new edition)
by Ammiel Alcalay (2012)

The Blond Texts & The Age of Embers
by Nadia Tueni (translated by Amir Parsa) (2012)

Vocalises
by Jenny Husk (2012)

Halal Pork & Other Stories
by Cihan Kaan (2011)

Born Palestinian, Born Black & The Gaza Suite
by Suheir Hammad (2010)

The Comeback's Exoskeleton
by Matthew Rotando (2008)

Theater of War: The Plot Against the American Mind
by Nicholas Powers (2005)